LET ME IN

A Japanese American Woman Crashes the Corporate Club

1976-1996

ELAINE KOYAMA

BEAVER'S POND PRESS

MINNEAPOLIS, MN

This is a work of creative nonfiction. The events are portrayed to the best of Elaine Koyama's memory. While all the stories in this book are true, some names and identifying details have been changed to protect the privacy of the people involved.

Edited by Angela Wiechmann
Copyedited by Sara and Chris Ensey with ScriptAcuity Studio
Proofread by Taylor Blumer
Managing editor: Hanna Kjeldbjerg

ISBN: 978-1-64343-976-1
Library of Congress Catalog Number: 2019902923
Printed in the United States of America
First Printing: 2019
23 22 21 20 19   5 4 3 2 1

Book design by Athena Currier

Beaver's Pond Press, Inc.
7108 Ohms Lane
Edina, MN 55439–2129

(952) 829-8818
www.BeaversPondPress.com

To order, visit www.ItascaBooks.com or call (952) 345-4488.
Reseller discounts available.

To schedule interviews, events, and other press opportunities,
contact elaine@elainekoyama.com.

Contents

Praise for *Let Me In*

"In 1976, as the women's movement started to gain traction, Elaine Koyama, a recent Stanford graduate from a Montana farm, entered the work world in what we called a "nontraditional" position. She was an ag (feed) sales person on the fast track into management. *Let Me In* follows Elaine through the funny, absurd, and confusing times for women who were vanguards on this path. With hard work and help from family and friends she succeeded (maybe I should say "endured") where many men and women failed.

This a must-read for those of us who lived it, as well as for those who want to understand what really happened when you were one of the first women in a Fortune 500 company to blaze a path for those who followed."

—Ruth Bokelman Conn, ag sales 1976-2019 at Chevron Chemical, Cargill Seed, DuPont Crop Protection, and Syngenta Crop Protection

"Engaging and insightful, *Let Me In* resonates across culture, ethnicity, and gender. An often-humorous look into managing a career."

—Stephanie Keire, retired executive vice president of Wells Fargo Bank

"Elaine Koyama has lived the quintessential American dream: she built upon the opportunities her parents and grandparents created and made and remade herself as further opportunities presented themselves. Elaine pursued a college education, as expectations for women shifted and a new generation's dreams could be realized. *Let Me In* details Elaine's early life—her growing up in Montana, college years in California, and her break into the business of sales when women were just entering the world of work in larger numbers.

Among the first women to blaze trails through America's boys' club of business, Elaine's story is our American story, as well as the modern history of American business."

—*Ann Swanson, PhD, International Baccalaureate consultant*

"I felt like I was reading my own story. I loved the way Elaine's attitude and perspective shows readers how to face a challenge and figure out how to conquer it. A positive attitude and good humor solve a lot of problems."

—*Ruth Kimmelshue, Cargill corporate senior vice president*
of business operations and supply chain

"Elaine Koyama is a pioneer who moved to Minneapolis from her childhood home in Montana in order to explore the frontier that women faced breaking into leadership in corporate America. Elaine's story is one of navigating the unknown, the inner-strength to tackle insurmountable obstacles, and a triumph of the spirit.

Her perseverance, courage, and humanity will be of interest to both men and women with aspirations for corporate leadership."

—*Dr. Stefanie Lenway, dean at University of St. Thomas and*
Opus Distinguished Chair at Opus College of Business

"An interesting read about the first twenty years of a nontraditional woman in a changing business environment."

—*Jerry Rohlfsen, retired Cargill vice president*

"An artful narrative! A woman born too soon navigating the roadblocks along the path to her goals."

—*Anna Rohlfsen, retired Cargill corporate spouse*

To my husband, Scot, who encouraged and
supported my dream to become a writer.

Introduction

Thirty years ago, I sent a rough draft of this book's first section to several publishers—all but one turned me down. And that one asked me an important question that I couldn't answer at the time: *So what?* That question revealed the gaping hole in my manuscript. It made me realize I had no direction, no story line—that I didn't understand where I fit in the scope of the change that was happening in business and American society. Now, as I enter my third score of life, the *so what* has played itself out.

Women have always worked, but women in corporate America have only recently gained access to management positions. I began my career as one of the first minorities and first women hired as a management trainee at agribusiness giant Cargill, still the largest privately held corporation in the world. In 1976, the opportunities for women were limited; we were schoolteachers, secretaries, nurses, or housewives. So being hired into a management training program was only the first hurdle—success was not a given, and many assumed or hoped I would fail. In fact, we were defining success as we went along.

I was tested early—no cushy office for me. My first job was in the field, literally: the fields of Iowa, starting at the bottom as a Nutrena Feeds salesperson, calling on farmers, knocking on doors. But in fact, even as a feed salesperson, it was not truly "the bottom." Only men were salespeople. The title was *Territory Manager*, so it was more accurately the bottom of the management track. These vignettes are glimpses of the change we were living, of one Japanese American woman's journey on the management track with no road maps or rules.

Women my age who have read this tell me their own stories. They say, "I know exactly how you felt!" or "I'd forgotten how it was" or "The same thing happened to me!"

Young women tell me, "I can't believe it was like that!" or "Why did you let them treat you that way?" or "The same thing happened to me!"

Men have told me, "You were born in the wrong era." Or "I can't believe it was like that!" or "The same thing happened to me!" My own husband couldn't believe some men could behave (in the words of Jane Austen) *in such ungentlemanlike manner*. I have written this memoir as authentically as I could given the lapse of so many years, and to protect the innocent and not so innocent, some of the names have been changed.

My story is about being just another girl in a grown-up world. About being Japanese and how growing up in Montana, on a farm, in a big family shaped my success. About wanting into the exclusive world of corporate management. It's about coming of age in a man's world.

Just let me in.

PART 1

Incubation

An Ending, a Beginning

On May 6, 1976, I sat with my family at the Bullis Mortuary chapel in Hardin, Montana, waiting for my father's memorial service to begin. I had never had a close relative die, let alone a father. I sat next to my mother, still her baby at twenty-one. My birthday was a few weeks away. That day was my brother-in-law's thirty-fourth birthday. My dad was sixty-one when he died, Mom widowed at fifty-four. Also sitting in the family alcove, shielded from the mourners by a screen, were my seven siblings, six in-laws, and a multitude of nieces and nephews ranging from newborn to age thirteen. I had just graduated from Stanford University and had spent most of April with my family in Hardin before moving to Minneapolis. Flowers filled the front of the chapel and lined the aisles. Townsfolk came early to get a seat. Mr. Bullis, whose brother had graduated from Hardin High School with my dad, opened an adjoining room and set up chairs for the overflow. The day my dad died, Monday, May 3, 1976, was intended to be my first day of work at Cargill, an agribusiness conglomerate even in those days.

That week, instead of sitting in the orientation meetings, I sat at the funeral home. Instead of meeting the human resources new-hire team, my sisters, brothers, and I greeted family friends and chatted with guests at the wake following the funeral, shielding my mom, who was too tired and distraught to attend. Ours was a family with a very public face in a small Montana town.

That week in May, I left my childhood behind as I embarked on the great unknown world of corporate America. Growing up Japanese American in Montana on a farm, raising sheep, sugar beets, wheat, hay, and corn, did not hinder but instead catapulted me forward. We had suffered a great loss, but we were raised tough. It was that upbringing that positioned me to succeed at an agricultural company in the heart of the Midwest.

Growing Up Montana-Style

I embarked on my working career in a world of middle-aged white men who seemed positively ancient to my Japanese American eyes. No class at college prepared me for this first job in agribusiness smack in the middle of the American breadbasket. But I actually had a very solid background that prepared me to succeed. I had the luxury of unique and varied experiences that made me the person able to rise to midlevel management in a conservative midwestern corporation.

Hardin High School's graduating class in 1972 was right around 120 kids. As a child, I played alone a lot—the youngest of eight, my nearest siblings were brothers, three and five years older than I. In kid years, that's a lifetime. When I was six, my sisters' ages ranged from thirteen to seventeen, so we had little in common. I remember long summer days, hot and dusty, riding my white Welsh/Shetland pony, Princess, around the family farm, creating adventures in my mind as I roamed the fields and climbed on farm equipment. The galvanized Gleaner combine with front steps to the cab and back steps to the engine and gas tank became my playhouse, reimagined as a parlor, porch, and kitchen. I learned early to catch my horse and saddle up so I'd have transportation. The 160-acre home place was my playground, but our farm was actually a conglomeration of several farms and acreages, at the time around 750–1,000 acres. I'd ride Princess around the outbuildings and equipment of the home place, and then years later, I'd ride one of the saddle horses down to the Bighorn River to dream among the cottonwoods and willows.

The home place was the hub of the farm business. The house was a large-for-its-day two-story, four-bedroom, two-bath home to us eight kids and our parents. Nearly new in the 1940s when my parents first moved in, my dad bought it from Roy Cool, the man who'd helped him get out of the Japanese internment camp and employed him to work for the Holly Sugar Corporation. Our house was a mile from town, but in the summer, we might as well have been twenty miles out. When the last day of school liberated my classmates, it was a prison sentence for me, stuck on the farm—I wouldn't see my schoolmates until the following fall. It wasn't that we didn't get to town, but my summers were busy working or playing on the farm, not doing "town" things. We didn't go to movies, and organized sports like baseball didn't exist for girls. I would write letters to town friends who lived less than a mile away.

The early 1960s was an era when going to college was the exception, not the rule. Most girls had limited options, and most boys I knew had limited options, too—farmer, mechanic, truck driver, insurance sales-man. Only one classmate, Diane, had a dad who was a lawyer, and one boy's dad worked at the bank.

But the tipping point was approaching: as the youngest child, I observed my sisters as they became women. They came of age in the late '50s and early '60s, and they followed the traditional path of mar-riage and family with careers of secretary, beautician, and schoolteacher. I came of age in the turbulence of the late '60s: the hippie generation—a totally different world.

My dad made it clear that the boys would inherit the farm, so col-lege wasn't even on the radar for Tom, my oldest brother. My middle brother, Harry, had a passion and talent for art. It was 1967, and he went to Eastern Montana College for a teaching degree in art, but he never taught. His one option led back to the farm. Robert, who graduated in 1969 and was three years my senior, got wrestling scholarship offers from several schools, ended up going to Montana State University in Bozeman for one wrestling season, then returned to the family farm. He gave me the best advice for college. He said, "Any average guy can pass college courses. You just have to study." Advice he himself didn't take, but I did.

This environment, as limited as it was, allowed me to flourish and dream. I was raised in the comfort of a prospering 1960s economy, within the confines of a traditional family structure, with an emerging women's liberation movement. When I graduated from high school in 1972, I had already experienced how to be independent, how to reach out beyond boundaries, and I learned that it was okay to be different.

Being Japanese

We were like every other farm family during the 1960s. We worked together in the fields, had big farm meals cooked by the women, watched *Bonanza* and *Walt Disney's Wonderful World of Color* clustered around the one TV set after dinner.

Okay, so there was one little difference between our family and most of the other families in Hardin. We were Japanese. My grandfather had worked as a laborer on the railroad at the turn of the twentieth century and likely married my grandmother as a picture bride or arranged marriage. My dad was born around 1915 in Sheridan, Wyoming, and shortly after that, his family moved north to Dunmore, Montana, about fifteen miles from where we grew up. He attended Crow Agency School and Hardin High School. He was a Montanan first and Japanese second.

I always knew I was Japanese, but the first time I realized that meant something different was when I started first grade in public school and my classmates told me I was Japanese. Of course, *I knew* I was Japanese. It was part of my identity. But how did *they* know? Was it my nose? We lived next to the Crow Indian Reservation, and I knew who the Indian kids were. There were a few Mexican families and black families, and I knew who they were. There were even several other Japanese families, and I knew who they were. When I looked at my siblings, or parents, or other Japanese friends, I didn't see an ethnic group; I saw individuals. When I looked in a mirror, I saw myself; I didn't see a yellow kid.

The only Asian on TV was Hop Sing on *Bonanza*, a TV show about rancher Ben Cartwright and his three grown sons working together in the 1800s on a fabulous ranch bordering Lake Tahoe. Hop Sing was the

Chinese cook, but I didn't identify with him. He had an accent and wore funny clothes. My dad didn't work for the boss—he *was* the boss! I had three brothers, just like Ben Cartwright had three sons. My dad was like Ben Cartwright—the hired hands reported to him. We compared our three boys with Adam, Hoss, and Little Joe. Our family was *just like* the Cartwrights. We grew up in cowboy boots, jeans, belt buckles, and cowboy hats. We ran Angus cattle and Suffolk sheep. There were a couple of saddle horses and my Shetland. In Montana, people know the difference between farmers and ranchers. We were farmers. Our livelihood came from the sheep, irrigated sugar beets, hay, and later on, corn, barley, and dryland wheat. I didn't think anything was unusual about being Japanese, because nothing was unusual to me.

Years later, at a Cargill seminar on sensitivity, I learned about *X*s and *O*s. If you have a bunch of *O*s scattered around a sheet of paper and one *X*, a person's eye automatically goes to the *X*, no matter where that *X* is on the paper. It can move around randomly and the eye follows the *X*. That's what it's like being a minority. Many minorities are uncomfortable being the only *X* among *O*s. I got used to it, and it became part of my reality. From my earliest memories, being an *X* among the majority of *O*s was normal.

Getting Along

If someone had told me when I was feeding sheep as a ten-year-old that this would be preparing me for my life's work, I would have thought he or she was crazy. My dad was not a liberated man, and he had some firmly held beliefs: He often said a person's personality was formed by age six; that every person was unique and needed to be treated uniquely. He also believed a little hard work never killed anyone.

I also remember overhearing a conversation my parents were having about my sister Bernice, who graduated in 1965. She was interested in becoming a lawyer. My dad said, "Girls can't be lawyers." I thought he was wrong, but he ruled the roost, and we didn't talk back. He preached that people skills were more important than book learning. He lived his philosophy—congenial, outgoing, a people magnet. I don't remember him ever reading a whole book. *US News & World Report* was his magazine of choice.

Up until I was twelve, I was treated like one of the boys. I always liked farming over housework and labored with my dad, my brothers, and the hired men, side by side. I learned to get along, work along, respect, and appreciate the men who worked for my dad.

Leroy was our mainstay sheepherder. He lived in a sheep wagon that had a camp stove and mattress. No running water, no toilet. He had to have smelled, but smell was never a trigger for me. When it looked like his jeans were so crusty they could stand up on their own, we'd take him to town to buy new clothes. Leroy wasn't the brightest bulb, but he was harmless. He and I watched the ewes together, never certain if I was directing him or vice versa.

These were the days when an average farmer could hire laborers because labor was cheap. Pete and Hill Hernandez and their families worked on our farm in the '50s and '60s. The Chavez family worked around the same time. These families were different from the migrant workers who came up from Mexico; they lived in the community year-round, and all of us kids went to school together.

At about six years old, I went with my dad to meet the Mexican migrant workers who came to town in the summer to work the sugar beets. He and I issued each worker a single bed frame for each member of the family, a stained and dirty mattress (that had been stored, uncovered, in the shed over the winter), and a water can. Near the Holly Sugar factory (which closed in the '70s), there was a row of labor shacks called the Colony Houses. These were a step up from the wooden labor houses, which were often one of the outbuildings on a farmstead. The Colony Houses had stucco siding, and some of the migrants lived there with their families. I thought my dad could speak Spanish because he talked to them with his mishmash of Spanish words. It was only after I had taken Spanish in high school that I realized he really didn't speak textbook

Spanish but just knew enough to communicate. I looked at the migrant workers (who didn't look that different from me, frankly) with their little kids (about my size) and recognized how lucky I was to have a big house with two bathrooms. They had a couple of communal outhouses back behind the Colony Houses.

I knew the black and Mexican families in town, because at one time or other they all seemed to have worked for my dad. Willie Smith was a single black man (though we referred to blacks as Negroes in those days) who worked on the farm in the late '60s—he and I would feed the sheep together every night. I was a preteen girl, he was a late-twenties or early-thirties man who was as strong as an ox. I'd come home from school and change from my good clothes to jeans and a cotton work shirt, and he and I would fill burlap bags with animal feed, carry them to the corrals, and distribute the feed into the sheep feed bunks. We would both carry the bags—I would struggle with one bag, he carried two at a time, one on each shoulder—sharing in the labor. I don't remember talking much with Willie; we just did our jobs. It wasn't a friendship but a peaceful coexistence.

Willie lived for free in a labor shack on one of our farms we called Nine Mile because it was about nine miles north of town. Nine Mile consisted of the main house, which was a run-down white wooden structure with running water, the corrals, and livestock sheds, and then the labor shack was about a quarter mile down the road. Labor shacks dotted the valley. Most were painted white, had no heat, running water, or bathrooms but had roofs, wood floors, four walls, and outhouses. Migrant workers lived in them during the summer.

A few years later, Willie moved to Billings and had his fifteen minutes of fame when he died. The *Billings Gazette* wrote Willie's obituary, detailing his life on Montana Avenue back when the street was for drunks and the homeless. He was murdered on that street, gunned down in his prime. Poor Willie was dead.

There were a few other black workers who came through. Ted was an older man, a general farmhand. Another guy rented the Nine Mile main house and promoted it to people "out east" as a "Montana dude ranch."

Joe and his family lived on a farm we owned, where the barn was converted into a lambing shed. Joe's wife was a dark-haired beauty who worked at the 4 Aces Lounge in town. They had seven kids, all around the same ages as us. Their four boys, Tommy, Jerry, Jigger, and Dennis, would play with Robert and me around the farm. We played War, with Robert leading Jerry, Jigger, and Dennis. Tommy was the kindest to be on my side. Joe was my dad's right-hand man and acted more as a foreman than a farmhand.

I would tag along with my dad when he went to talk to the bulk oil plant manager, his good friend Ken Fox. I'd be there when he bought animal feed from George Staley, or cars from Bud Brown, or cowboy boots from Gayle Lammers' Trading Post. The routine was the same—BS'ing about nothing across a desk from each other, doing some "negotiating" on prices, striking a deal, BS'ing again.

I learned by working with men from all walks of life. I learned by listening to my dad deal with his friends. I learned by watching how my dad treated people, with camaraderie and respect. This was still a white community—all the teachers, cops, and elected city and county officials were white while I was growing up. But on the farm, where hand labor was how the work got done, the Mexicans, African Americans, and mentally challenged hired on because they were the cheap labor we could afford.

Influencers

My dad graduated from Hardin High School in 1933. Twenty-eight years later, the first of us eight kids began graduating from that same school. My dad's family ran a pool hall in Sheridan, Wyoming, and then moved north to Montana to become farmers. The irrigation canals throughout the Little Bighorn and Bighorn River valleys ensured dependable water supplies for the booming farm industry triggered by the construction of the Holly Sugar factory. He was born Yoshikazu Masao Koyama, but on the first day of school, when the bus driver came to pick him up, the driver couldn't say the name, so he called him Tom. The name stuck.

My dad was the oldest of six. There's a picture of him in the high school yearbook as a "yell king" (a male cheerleader), and in later yearbooks, he was a basketball player. He said he was a yell king because he got to participate and go places with the team. He played basketball for the same reasons.

When he and his sisters came of marriageable age, their folks cashed in and returned to Japan, hoping their children could find Japanese mates. The impending war and the threat of being drafted into the Japanese army drove my dad to leave Japan and return to America. He was not going to fight for the Imperial Japanese Army. Shortly after returning, he met my mom in Guadalupe, California, then quickly married her so they could both go to the same internment camp. In 1942, Executive Order 9066 signed by President Roosevelt ordered people of Japanese ancestry living on the West Coast to evacuate their homes. With only the belongings they could carry, these Japanese Americans, most born in the States, ended up in one of ten "relocation centers," and my folks ended up at the Gila River Japanese concentration camp in Arizona.

Many Japanese Americans spent the entire war imprisoned, but my dad knew people in Hardin and knew they needed farmhands in the field. He was able to work a deal with Holly Sugar and the War Relocation Authority to recruit Japanese out of camps to work in the fields of Big Horn County. After a year of incarceration—long enough for my oldest sister to have been born—Tom and Emmy Koyama left the camps for Montana. That's how they started to build their farming operation. When the Holly Sugar factory closed in 1971, Tom Koyama was their largest beet grower.

As an adult, Daddy was an outgoing, poker-playing, whiskey-drinking guy who loved the "deal." He always had sayings that he lived by, and one of them was "You can be a big fish in a small pond or a small fish in a big pond." He chose to be the big fish. Our family, due to its size and longevity in the community, cut a wide swath in a state that, at that time, had a total population of fewer than five hundred thousand. Dad graduated in 1933 and I graduated thirty-nine years later in 1972. There have been numerous grand-, great-grand-, and great-great grandchildren graduating since. We have been cheerleaders, football players, and wrestling champs. We have been Boys and Girls State delegates and FFA and 4-H club members. We have been home demonstration club members, church members, and have held elected office.

As a youth, I identified with my dad. He seemed to have fun. He ran the show. He would bring home business associates on the spur of the moment, and my mom would somehow add another plate at the table. He did interesting things—bought into a gold mine in Wyoming, started a lipstick factory in Billings, and flew to New York City to talk to a celebrity mind reader to promote the lipstick line. In the mid-1970s, after the sugar factory closed, he tried growing peppermint. The steady, dependable farm allowed him to venture into these strange and wonderful areas. Who wouldn't want to identify with a guy like that?

And Mom was always there—cooking for the crews, having babies, raising babies (translate that to changing a million cloth diapers that also needed to be washed out!), sewing clothes, running the household. Yikes! Who would want to do that when you could be swinging deals? What I didn't realize then is that my mom was a Martha Stewart of the '50s and '60s. She was active in Achievement Club and Toastmistress Club. In home demonstration club, she and her lady friends would meet monthly with the county agent and learn about the latest technology available for homemaking. She was an adventurous cook—and a very good one, as her award-winning pies would attest. I grew up eating meat and potatoes like every other Montanan, but also traditional Japanese food, Chinese food, Mexican, Italian. We had *krumkake* at Christmas, Blarney Stones on Saint Patrick's Day, fried chicken on the Fourth of July. We had turkey on holidays, served on the good china and accompanied by real sterling silverware.

And it didn't stop there. One Easter Sunday, I woke up, and my mother had sewn me a little Easter outfit overnight. She taught me how to sew a straight seam—and if it wasn't straight enough, I would have to tear it out and redo it until it was. I hated the housework and would do anything to get outside to do the "real" work. But once a year, I had to sit at the dining room table, where the sewing machine would be set up, and make a 4-H clothing project, then go to the kitchen, where I'd concoct a 4-H cooking project. I confess it now that the prize-winning blue-ribbon cherry pie I made was really a labor of . . . well, I wouldn't say *love*, but I did do the labor: stirring while my mom put in the ingredients, made the lattice crust, and baked the thing. My mom didn't outright tell us kids to compete to be the best, but somehow it was instilled in us. The 4-H judge deemed my mom's cherry pie and Cathy Miller's gooseberry pie the best entrants at the fair.

I did the sewing and cooking because my mom made me do it. I participated with the sheep because it was "real" farmwork. We took our Suffolk sheep to the county and state fairs, where they consistently won championship ribbons. My dad had a passion for competing and winning, just as my mom did in her area of expertise. Without their involvement and support, all the blue ribbons that lined our wall at home would never have happened. Three of us kids were particularly engaged in 4-H and FFA, and we were the ones competing at the fairs. To this day, my name is etched on the Big Horn County Showmanship traveling trophy that also bears the names of my older sister Marion, my brother Robert, and at least one niece since I left home.

My siblings—Carol, Tom, Kathryn, Bernice, Marion, Harry, Robert—were role models. I watched carefully from my baby-of-the-family vantage point. They were all active in school. They paved the way for me through above-average grades and extracurricular activities like class offices, cheerleading, football, basketball, wrestling, and clubs too numerous to list. They plowed the field I played on.

Because of our Japanese ancestry, our family not only assimilated the Western European culture that dominates America but had the Far East influence as well. In my sophomore year of high school, my folks took me (privilege of being the youngest, perhaps?) to visit relatives in Japan, so my worldview changed significantly. It was a great adventure and the first time I was an *O* among *Os*. Suddenly I looked like everyone else. I felt invisible, and that was not a good feeling. It's one thing to read about a culture and eat its food at home; it was a totally different experience being immersed in it for a month.

So it wasn't surprising that the American Field Service (AFS) exchange program impacted me. Every year, the community sponsored an AFS exchange student to come spend a year at our school. For most, it was the only exposure to a kid from a different culture or a different country. I remember Silvia from Switzerland, Pai from Thailand, Bill from Colombia, and Sven from Sweden. Sven was my first real boyfriend—he was in the senior class when I was a sophomore. He asked me to the prom, and we started dating. Prom was in the spring, and he left to go back to Sweden in early summer, so our romance was fast and short. I knew nothing about Sweden, but he was what I'd imagined a classic Swede to be: tall, blond, blue-eyed, with a Swedish accent (go figure!). One night, my mom, the adventurous cook, began reading to us from a Swedish cookbook—words like *krumkake* and *kroppkakor* and *saffransbullar*. Sven would guess what the word was that she was trying to pronounce, correct the pronunciation, and then tell us about the food, his family, his culture. It was entertaining, so interesting, and so funny.

This exposure led me to the next logical step, which was to apply for the exchange program myself. AFS selected me to go on the summer program to Finland and live with a family there. Finnish is a singular language, spoken by a small population, isolated, unrelated to Germanic or Romantic languages. Some say that Finnish may have linguistic connection to Japanese. It didn't really matter, since I didn't speak Japanese, either. I arrived in Finland with a hundred dollars, a Finnish dictionary, and a curious nature. For an outspoken, opinionated American girl raised in the emerging women's movement, not being able to understand a word that was spoken was torturous. Halfway through my stay, I cried quietly in my darkened room shared with my host sister—frustrated, homesick, and lonely. It was this experience that forced me to grow up, learn to be alone, survive homesickness, tough it out.

Winning Ways

I won my first trophy in 1961 as the Best Dressed Junior Cowgirl in the Hardin Rodeo Parade. I was seven years old. My mom sewed me a sage-green western snap-button shirt and jeans. My tooled leather belt sported a rhinestone belt buckle with a bucking horse. I wore new cowboy boots my dad bought from Lammers Trading Post, and my brothers and sisters helped me primp and polish my pony, Princess. It was the Montana equivalent of a child beauty pageant.

In the '60s and '70s when I came of age, competitive girls' sports were almost nonexistent, but I would hang with my brothers Robert and Harry. I was one of the first picked when choosing sides. While I was in the fourth grade, President Kennedy had been promoting fitness. Our school had a fitness day, and I became the regional softball-throw champion. We did have cheerleading. My sister Bernice was a cheerleader throughout high school, and my brothers were all very athletic, excelling at football and wrestling, with a little basketball thrown in. Tom and Robert were state champs in wrestling. Tom was part of a group of football backs dubbed by the local press as the All-American Backfield—Tom (Japanese), Bobby Tate (black), Sargie Old Horn (American Indian), and Mickey Beary (white). For years when I heard people talk about All-American football players, I thought they were talking about diversity.

I was a cheerleader from seventh grade through high school graduation. Girls' track started around seventh grade, too. I had always been pretty fast, but there were a lot of fast girls. I decided I'd go where there wasn't so much competition—I ended up in the field event—shot put and discus. The women who competed at the Olympics were the only role models at the time, and they were lumbering Russian women who looked like men. I was a strong farm girl and the second tallest of my siblings, but I was no Russian powerlifter. Fortunately for me, in those days, to excel in high school girls' sports, showing up was the key criteria. Then competing in a sport as unglamorous as shot put and discus eliminated most competition to speak of. Training was minimal for everyone. There were times I'd go to track practice, put the shot a few times, do a few discus spins, and then spend the rest of the time laughing and joking with George Lammers and John Lundberg, who were the boys' field men. I practiced more than most, but nothing like competitors today.

If the past is any indication of the future, then it wasn't surprising that I did well in track. My senior year, I placed at the state meet in shot put. I held the Hardin school record for over thirty-five years with a put of thirty-six feet, ten and a half inches. Wikipedia defines *flow* as being in the zone. The concept of flow was first identified by Mihaly Csikszentmihalyi. When I put that winning shot, I experienced flow before flow was a concept. What I lacked in size and brute strength, I made up for in effort and technique. I can still feel the power of the push when my legs, torso, arms, and momentum all came together for that placing put.

Hardin's "All-American" backfield. Left to right: Tom Koyama (42), Halfback; Sargie Old Horn (36), Backfield; Mickey Beary (32), Fullback; Bobby Tate (22), Halfback.

I was an outgoing kid. My dad would tell me, "Be a leader, not a follower" or "Get all As" when he dropped me off at grade school. I had seven siblings whom I looked up to, and they all seemed to be leaders, not followers. The American Legion sponsored state programs called Boys State and Girls State, where two delegates from each high school were taught about city, county, and state government by participating in elections at each level. My oldest sister was selected by the high school teachers to be a Girls State delegate. Of the eight kids in the family, six of us were Girls or Boys State delegates, and two were alternates. Those of us who attended won city- and county-elected seats. My sister Bernice was elected lieutenant governor. I was elected governor of Girls State, the highest office, had lunch with Forrest Anderson, the real governor of Montana, and Candy Fox, the outgoing governor of Girls State. She was going to start at Stanford University in the fall. That planted the seed for me. If she could go to Stanford, I could go, too!

Sometimes I think that in a small town, entering the contest is 90 percent of winning, but now I realize that doesn't only apply to small towns. I entered a lot of contests and did my share of winning. I won things that didn't even matter to me. I was like a racetrack dog chasing the mechanical bunny. Vince Lombardi, the famous football coach, once said, "Winning isn't everything, it's the only thing." In high school, our football team was so bad, we changed the slogan to read, "Winning isn't everything, but wanting to is." I feel like I fell someplace in between.

About-Face: Refocus, Redo

Growing up on a farm, driving farm vehicles and cars came second nature. The first time I was put behind a steering wheel was at about age six to drive a hundred yards in a farmyard with several siblings overseeing my progress. The boys began farming (driving tractors) at twelve. I assumed I would also begin farming at twelve. It was my first feeling of discrimination by my father—he wouldn't let me farm at twelve—he only let me drive him around and do the "other work," like feeding livestock, moving trucks, being his right hand. By this time, my dad's health had begun to fail. He had high blood pressure and began having small strokes. At the time, we didn't really understand what was happening to him, except that he lost a lot of motivation and likely struggled with depression. Because of his failing health, I had freedom that came from a lack of supervision but also responsibility that came from a dad who couldn't do much for himself.

At fourteen or fifteen, I got my first ticket—passing on a solid yellow line and driving without a license. I was driving our 1965 Rambler Marlin, a red-and-black fastback, chauffeuring my dad back to Hardin from Billings. Dad let all of us kids drive early, and in my case, I was probably safer than he given his strokes. The ticket didn't deter me; I drove myself to driver's education class, and the instructor, Mr. Hormann, just looked the other way. I had little supervision, so it was easy for me to start hanging with the wild crowd after school and on weekends once I had wheels. And hang I did.

My siblings indulged me, too. The last day of school my freshman year, Bernice let me take her baby-blue '69 Camaro to school. After the last bell, I gathered (or attracted) several friends, and we drove around. In Hardin, there was one stoplight in the middle of town. We would "drag Main." This day, the last day of school, there were parties all over. We ended up at a gravel pit party, and I high-centered her car. That wasn't enough to deter us—we drove about twenty miles to Cathy Miller's place, 'cause we knew she was having a "sleepover." Cathy Miller was one of my best friends—her dad and my dad had gone to school together, and her family was a "real" ranch family on Sarpy Creek. Sarpy was high, dry country, some of it open range. We joined their party and stayed all night. I didn't even think to call home. The next morning, my mom got ahold of Cathy's mom, and I realized I should have let them know where I was and what I was doing. I figured I was going to be in a world of hurt when I got home.

And a world of hurt I was in, except it wasn't because I was in trouble. My parents told me I should have let them know where I had been. They didn't really have to say much else. I knew I had been thoughtless, and I was remorseful and humble. The real problem was *my big toe hurt like hell.* I didn't know what was wrong, but my toe was all swollen and red, and I wanted to cry not because I was in trouble but because my toe hurt!

So my dad got out his castrating knife—the one he used to cut calves and lambs and the sharpest one he had—laid me out on the sofa, and cut out my ingrown toenail. I think to this day it was my punishment for being a naughty girl and not letting everyone know where we were that night.

That summer, I started running with the popular kids. I had a car, I had access to unlimited gas at the farm's gas pump, and I had time. Most nights, I would go to town and drag Main. Many nights, I'd burn a tank of gas driving the three-quarters of a mile south down Center Avenue to the light and the one mile west to the Dairy Queen, where we'd turn around and do the route again. I can't imagine how many circuits it took to burn a tank of gas because I wasn't counting. There may have been some drinking involved. I wanted to fit in; I wanted to be popular. It was an aimless existence, seeing the same cars back and forth on Main, driving, but going nowhere. I felt like I was popular, but not the most popular. I was too good a student to be really popular.

Then one night toward the end of my sophomore year in high school, my parents called me into the office—the back-porch room that my dad's desk was in and where he did paperwork. They sat me down and talked to me about the partying, the dragging Main, the hanging with the kids I was trying to fit in with. They told me it was leading me nowhere. They didn't really have to talk very long or hard, because I think a part of me wanted an excuse not to continue down that path. And the beauty of their talk is that it gave me the perfect excuse to stop—my parents had come down on me.

And I did stop. I started that fall back into school and kept to myself. I was still a cheerleader, involved in 4-H, Rainbow for Girls, and track, but I quit hanging out, quit dragging Main every night, and focused on school. The Swedish boyfriend made me think I could be an intellectual, but while I did a fair amount of reading, I couldn't bury myself in books alone. As in every school, there were the cliques that made up the social circles. I would move from circle to circle, not getting too close to any one group of friends. Some of my girlfriends from elementary school started having steady boyfriends, so I saw less of them. My boyfriend had gone back to Sweden, so I was the odd man out.

The summer between my junior and senior year was transformative. At the beginning of the summer, I was elected governor of Girls State. A few weeks later, I flew to Finland to spend the summer as an exchange student. The next year, my senior year of high school, I was accepted at Stanford University.

When I graduated from high school, I wondered if I could be a big fish in a big pond. I felt compelled to move beyond Hardin and see what else was out there and what I could do without the shelter and support of family. One of my baby steps leaving the nest was going to Stanford.

What made me who I was in 1972 was a culmination of being Japanese on a Montana farm, working alongside men from all walks of life, taking advantage of opportunities as they arose in a tight-knit community, and having a family of supportive overachievers. It helped being a little bit above average in intelligence, halfway attractive, fearless most of the time, and unconsciously self-confident. I was ready to take on the world.

PART 2

Birth

So, Tell Me Again How You Got Here?

I entered Stanford University in the fall of 1972. All I really knew about the school was that they had gone to the Rose Bowl. I had always wanted to go to the Rose Bowl, so I figured this would be my ticket to the game. Like most American families, we would plant ourselves in front of the TV set on New Year's Day and watch the parade and later the game.

My parents drove me from Montana to Palo Alto, California, that fall. I couldn't wait for them to leave so I could start exploring my new world. As a parent today, I know how hard it is to leave the youngest kid in a strange dorm in a strange land, but they had already put me on a plane to Finland the summer before, so they must have put faith in the system that everything would be okay.

I was a Montana girl. I had no idea what California was really like. I thought I was going to a school like Berkeley, on the leading edge of the youth movement—long hair, beads, headbands. Students at Stanford were the antithesis of the radicals at Berkeley. There was actually a student in our freshman class who went to class carrying a briefcase!

Stanford never went to the Rose Bowl the four years I was there. Aside from a student murdering his professor the same fall I started, it was an oasis in the post-hippie era of Patty Hearst, Nixon's Watergate, Deep Throat, *The Joy of Sex*, Title IX, *Roe v. Wade*, Billie Jean King vs. Bobby Riggs.

I never doubted that I could hold my own at Stanford. The beauty of youth is we don't know what we don't know, and we think we know everything. I chose my classes carefully—my goal was to graduate, not to be a rocket scientist. I took an eclectic assortment of classes I could pass,

24

ranging from poetry writing, political systems, and civil engineering to bonehead math. I fell in love multiple times, experimented enough to feel bold, but not so much to do any long-term damage.

Graduating from Stanford in 1976 was a pretty mild event. The sit-ins had ended the year before I had begun school, and *In Search of Excellence* had not yet begun to formulate. I recall walking the campus my senior year the fall of 1975 and noticing that the men and women entering the freshman class were wearing clean jeans and sweaters, more preppy than ever.

Other than the students who were set on getting into med school (and at any given time, it seemed that at least 50 percent of the class had that ambition), the Stanford student body seemed set on going to grad school someplace after graduation. It was either to get a law degree or an MBA. This era predated the tech boom that dominates the Bay Area now. My last quarter, I took an ALGOL programming language class and partnered with a guy to develop a simple arithmetic calculator. We got an A on our project, but I didn't have the foresight to recognize the opportunities in technology on the horizon.

No one I knew in my small circle of college friends was intent on getting a job—except me. I grew up in a family where only 50 percent of us siblings even *went* to college. That was probably a higher percentage than the number of students from my high school class. A graduate degree was otherworldly.

I was burned out on school. Besides, I had no money. In fact, I was in negative money—as in debt. Not that that is unusual for many students nowadays, except that instead of delaying payment, I rather looked forward to zeroing it out as quickly as possible.

Unfortunately, graduating with a liberal arts degree in political science / social science qualified me for nothing save perhaps law school. At the placement office, there were plenty of jobs for engineers, but the choices for liberal arts were limited. A department store, a couple of insurance companies . . . somehow I just couldn't picture myself working in those fields.

Two companies did catch my eye—Cargill and Cook Industries. Both grain companies were in the news due to the massive amounts of grain that were being sold to the Soviet Union and the collusion scandals of the 1970s targeting the grain traders. They had made incredible profits dealing with the Russians, and some of the companies were under investigation for illegal actions. I was attracted to the companies for precisely these reasons.

I interviewed with both companies. Given my ag background, grain trading had a lure to me that insurance companies or department stores couldn't hold a candle to. I had even taken an ag economics class at Stanford. In fact, had Stanford offered a degree in agriculture, I probably would have gravitated toward it. As the saying goes, the apple doesn't fall far from the tree.

I felt that I could fit into agribusiness, even though at the time I had no idea what agribusiness really was.

I interviewed with Cargill first. The interviewer, who still worked for the company ten years later, was a tall, dark, handsome young man. He wore a tailored navy suit with a neutral red tie. I wore my best chest-nut-brown wool pantsuit that my parents had bought me at Christmas. I didn't even own a suit with a skirt! I cannot recall the details of that interview, except that I left the half-hour session knowing that I had a follow-up interview in Minneapolis.

The interview with Cook did not go as well. The interviewer was a nondescript older man (probably thirty-five!) with black horn-rimmed glasses, a white short-sleeved shirt, and a skinny tie. He didn't ask very many questions and didn't seem particularly interested in me, my qualifi-cations, or in being there himself. I tried to dazzle him with my ag back-ground, talking about dryland farming, grain harvests, custom cutters. I interjected that Cargill had already offered me a follow-up interview. Getting no response, I changed my tack and began on my desire to work for his company—still nothing. Then I worked in my decent academic credentials and my ability to get along in and with varied environments and people. He finally looked me in the eye and said in no uncertain terms, "We don't hire women."

He proceeded to explain that if Cargill hired me, I could get good training there and that his company often raided Cargill for good managers, since Cargill training was so good.

He stood up. I stood up.

The interview was over.

If I knew then what I know now, I would have been outraged, indignant, and I would have walked straight out of that interview to the placement director and reported the incident. Heck, I might have even sued! But this was 1976. I knew that discrimination was illegal, but I wasn't so sure how to navigate the real world with this information. As it was, I thought maybe the guy was out of line and that what he'd said was probably illegal, but I accepted his statement and rationalized it away by thinking, *I don't want to work for a company like that, anyway.*

Thank goodness other women and minorities had more moxie than I had and have stood up to incidents like this one, or where would the world be today?

Cook Industries was found guilty of illegal grain trading and soon thereafter went belly-up.

Interviewing at Cargill

My follow-up interview at Cargill in Minneapolis was on a date I shall never forget—Friday the thirteenth. I never really knew much about Minneapolis except that Mary Richards (Mary Tyler Moore's TV show character) lived there, she was a single working woman, and she was one of the only role models for career women of the day. I figured that even if Cargill didn't hire me, I might move to Minneapolis to start my career. Mary seemed to have a pretty exciting life there in her own prudish way.

Cargill flew me to Minneapolis the day before my interviews. I wore my brown wool suit for the flight. Their packet of information contained taxi, hotel, and meal information. They put me up at the Northstar, a four-star hotel adjacent to Nicollet Mall in downtown Minneapolis.

I had time for supper and a quick look at the IDS building's Crystal Court—another MTM landmark. If I had been anyone else interviewing, this would have been impressive already—flight, taxi, hotel, all expenses paid. But I was graduating from Stanford. I thought all second-round interviews were like this.

The next day, I rose early and dressed carefully. I had a new outfit—a navy-blue cotton/polyester print dress that had a flounce at the hem and a little white vest. It was conservative, but definitely not Big Eight accounting firm dress code. I had bought it at the Stanford shopping center with money I had borrowed for books. I imagined I looked serious, businesslike, and smart. I probably looked young, young, young.

I went to the restaurant looking for that expense-paid breakfast. Being a farm girl, I liked big, hearty breakfasts; being a student, I normally never woke in time or had the money for a real restaurant meal. So on this auspicious occasion, I downed a plateful of eggs Benedict, hash browns, toast, and coffee. I felt as though I needed several hours of sleep as soon as I finished.

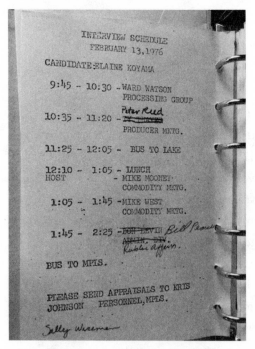

The day consisted of five interviews with managers of four divisions. Three of the five interviewers were older men (no kidding, thirty-five to forty-five years old!), and two were young men who were relatively new to the organization.

I remember feeling keen, alert, and on target throughout the day. Another flow experience. Details were crystal clear; it was like an eagle's vision, and my hearing like a bat's radar. Two of my interviews were at the Cargill offices in downtown Minneapolis. This was a 1940s-looking building, with hospital-beige walls, metal desks, bullpens of traders smoking at their desks, the air a hazy blue. It was a setting I'd expected. My last three interviews were in the Cargill Lake Office, where the upper executives' offices were. The personnel office had warned me that the Lake Office was "unusual." Cargill was known for its low profile. It was the world's largest privately held company, but no one I knew at Stanford had ever heard of it before. The Lake Office reinforced the low-profile image of the company—a large French château on a lakeside, forested setting. I felt like a guest in a home that happened to have people working in it, too.

The last interview was with William Pearce, a tall, distinguished, and intellectual-looking gentleman. His office and demeanor reminded me of the pictures of President Kennedy in the Oval Office with little John John playing in and around his desk. I wondered if this Mr. Pearce had a son and whether his son ever played in this comfortably but elegantly appointed room.

I was feeling positive about the day and positive about the company and my future with them. I had an enjoyable chat with Mr. Pearce, and he told me his daughter had applied to Stanford but had been rejected. *Uh-oh*, I thought. *This could be trouble.*

But instead of being vindictive, Pearce handed me his business card and told me to call him directly if I had any questions or concerns about my interviews or Cargill. I was too young, too inexperienced, and too overwhelmed to realize at the time what an incredible experience I had just gone through. Here I was, a punk kid without a decent suit to wear, absolutely no business experience, flat-out broke, sitting in this executive's office, exuding all the confidence in the world, convinced and convincing him that I would someday be a manager of this multifaceted megacorporation, and the gentleman across from me was telling me to call him directly if I had any concerns. Yep, I could picture myself sitting at his desk in this stately office someday, running a piece of the company.

I was on a roll.

Moving to Minneapolis

So, I got the job at Cargill, and here's the deal: I didn't know what I would be doing, for whom I'd be working, or where I'd be living. It was called the Cargill Management Training Program—sometimes dubbed *college programs*. I was offered a position as a management trainee, and my start date was Monday, May 3, 1976. It was made clear that during the training program we would be based out of Minneapolis, but after that, it was assignment roulette. Many jobs were in unknown parts of America. One trainee requested placement in California. He was placed in California, Missouri. The message was clear: "Be careful what you ask for…"

Minneapolis, with its skyways and the IDS glass-and-steel building downtown, looked cosmopolitan to my Montana/California eyes. I figured if Mary Richards could do it, so could I.

At that time, Stanford was on the quarter system, and I was graduating a quarter early. If I had been smart, I would have taken that spring quarter off and had some *fun*! But money was running low—I had taken a $500 loan out ostensibly to buy books, but I spent part of it on a road trip to Tijuana with my boyfriend, Steve. The rest had to tide me over until I got my first paycheck. My graduation date was April 1—yes, April Fools' Day—and the soonest I could start was the May new-hire class.

I loaded up my little white Opel sedan at 330 Nova Lane in Menlo Park, California, a few days after finals week and drove back to Montana. I didn't have a lot of stuff, and some of it my sister, who lived in Richmond, California, offered to ship to me once I knew where I was going to land. I never thought about leaving Stanford or the boyfriend who still had a quarter to go; I only thought of what lay before me—open road, a short month at home, and a Mary Richards career starting in Minneapolis.

I had a couple of weeks' cushion before I had to start work, so I stopped at home in Montana. My father had been having strokes since I had been in middle school, so I'd grown up with an ailing dad. He was a five-foot-seven, overweight, Montana Japanese farmer. When he was healthy, you could find him at the county fair sitting in the grandstand wearing a Humphrey Bogart fedora, cigar-chew spit all around, usually a couple of buddies hanging around him. In his day, he was a poker-playing, deal-making, extroverted, center-of-attention guy. Knowledge of stroke, high blood pressure, diet, and meds was in its infancy. I was never sure what was wrong with him, just that as he failed, he wasn't able to walk much, and his verbal skills went from easy banter to struggling to find words to just swear words. Sometimes he would just sit with tears rolling down his face.

My folks' anniversary was April 21. Hardin, Montana, didn't (and still doesn't) have a really nice supper club, so I went out to the field where my brother Harry was seeding grain, and we made plans to cook an anniversary dinner for our mom and dad. Harry and I were the only two siblings yet unmarried, so we had a close relationship with each other and our folks. He worked on the farm and often accompanied them when they traveled.

On their anniversary, we made steak and lobster, served with a shrimp cocktail, salad, baked potatoes with butter, sour cream, chives, and dessert. We lived in one of the bigger farmhouses in Hardin, but it still wasn't big compared to houses nowadays. I had set the table for two in the dining room with a lace tablecloth. Mom, like many of the ladies of her generation, had the "good stuff," the china and silver that was only used on special occasions. I used it all. The extra-nice Franciscan Mesa china that was usually seen but not used; the International Prelude sterling silver, sterling butter dish, candelabra, chafing dish. We only had a few water goblets—in a big family, glasses broke frequently—but I used the fancy glasses, too. Harry cooked in the kitchen, and I served, towel over the arm. My parents sat in the darkened dining room, lit by white candles in the silver candelabra, waiting quietly for each course to be served. My dad said virtually nothing at all but ate everything. Mom was fifty-four, and Dad was sixty-one years old. They had been married thirty-four years. It was a special night at home.

I left a few days after that, driving the fourteen hours to Minneapolis into the great unknown.

Unlike the Cargill interview process, where every logistical detail had been outlined in my interview packet, as a new hire, getting myself to Minneapolis, finding a place to live, and setting up a household was on my own. I knew nothing of Minneapolis. I had never been there except for the interview, and I knew no one. I had limited funds and had been told that I would likely be transferred in three months. I had no furniture—even my card table was being stored in California for shipment later.

I got into town and rented a motel room on the outskirts of downtown. I searched for an apartment guide, which were often in the magazine racks at café exits, and then just started driving around. It didn't dawn on me to go to Cargill for advice or referrals. Having just come from a university setting, I zeroed in on an area near Minnehaha and Franklin Avenue, south of I-94 across the interstate from Augsburg College. The apartments I really liked (modern, upscale apartments) were out of my price range, but a square, brick building that faced the I-94 freeway sound barrier had a studio apartment available on a month-to-month basis. I rented a bed, kitchen table, and two chairs from a furniture store, and I was set. It was Friday, April 30, 1976. On Monday, I would start my new job. I called my mom to tell her that I had found a place and that I was settling in.

The Telegram

I spent most of the weekend roaming around my new neighborhood. One of the first Target stores was off Minnehaha Avenue, just south of my new apartment. I didn't know anyone, so I just beat around. Sunday afternoon, back at my apartment, I got a knock on the door. *What? Who could that be?* I thought. I knew no one, no one knew me.

I opened the door, and a lady from the apartment office handed me a telegram. This was the first and last telegram I ever received. This was a time in history with no cell phones, no computers. No internet. I had called my mom from a pay phone, since I didn't even have a phone installed in my apartment yet. Telegrams were the only means of rapid communications, and here I was, standing at my new apartment door, getting a yellow telegram handed to me from a stranger.

I had no clue what this telegram could be about. I opened it slowly and read:

COME HOME IMMEDIATELY STOP DAD IN HOSPITAL STOP

My sister Bernice and her husband, Gayl, were living in Sioux Falls, South Dakota, so I hurried to the pay phone and called them collect. It was a five-hour drive to Sioux Falls—I basically jumped in my car the Sunday before my first day of work and drove to Sioux Falls. I arrived around 8:00 p.m. Sunday night. Their baby, Jeff, was less than six months old. Gayl had a red Grand Torino coupe. We put a box in the back seat, laid little Jeffrey in the makeshift crib, and began our ten-hour drive to Hardin. We drove through the night across the flat and straight I-90. It was a dark night, but the northern lights were streaking across the sky. I had never seen them before, and it was the most awesome, foreboding, chilling phenomenon of my life.

We pulled up to the Hardin community hospital around 8:00 a.m. on Monday, May 3. Weary, scared. The three of us and baby Jeff walked into the hospital and into my dad's room. My sister Marion was there, as was my mom. My dad's breathing was labored—a raspy, snoring kind of gasping.

Mom said brightly, "Look who's here. It's Bernice and Gayl. And Elaine. And baby Jeff!" Daddy looked up at us through bloodshot eyes, and a glimmer of recognition flickered past. He waved his arm in greeting and nodded, specifically to Gayl—almost like his old self greeting a roomful of cronies. Then he faded away again, eyes closed, painful breath following painful breath.

Marion came up to me and said, "Let's go to the house and start getting ready." More family was coming. I'm sure I looked stricken—shocked at how my dad looked and sounded. Scared of the inevitable. She and I left and went home. We began making sandwiches when the phone rang. Marion answered.

Daddy had died.

What would have been my first week of work turned into a week of grieving, planning a funeral, and going through motions mindlessly. I called Cargill and arranged a start date a week later. My sister from California had a flight delay in Salt Lake City, so she didn't make it home in time; she was grief stricken. My two aunts and uncle from San Luis Obispo flew in. Dad's best friend and internment buddy, Yoshikazu Tani—a big vegetable crop farmer from Santa Maria, California—flew his company jet in with his wife, the nose of the jet full of fresh strawberries, lettuce, broccoli, and cauliflower.

The Montana and Wyoming Japanese American community all showed up, many members of whom I had only heard about but never seen. Japanese families from Thermopolis, Wyola, Lodge Grass, Shepherd, Billings, Livingston, Laurel, and as far away as Havre.

And then there were his business buddies from around the state. (My father was a man who cut a wide swath.) Guys he'd played poker with, drank with late into the night; guys he would sit with in their offices—maybe in a grain elevator, a feedstore, a veterinary clinic, bulk oil plant—and shoot the bull.

The flowers were overwhelming. There were too many floral arrangements to put up front, so they lined the aisles and out into the funeral home foyer. Red roses from a chum who, over many drinks, promised he'd send a dozen red roses when his friend Tom Koyama died.

At the end of the week, Bernice, Gayl, Jeff, and I drove back to Sioux Falls. I continued on to Minneapolis. The farther we drove, the further from reality the whole week became. I got back to Minneapolis on Sunday night and prepared to go to my new job only one week late, but a lifetime seemed to have passed.

The Cargill Training Program

I'll never know what transpired in the normal first week of the Cargill training program, but my first week was a cram session of filling out forms, getting schedules, and deciphering the travel board the program administrators had concocted to keep track of new management trainees. The original training program was a six-month rotation through various jobs and locations. By the time I came through, it had been shortened to three months, and even that seemed long.

Each hire class moved through the program together. The initial trips were all the same, but then as our interests diverged, so would our trips. I arrived the second week of May, toting a pleather briefcase my mother had bought for me, a new blouse scratching my neck, a brown silk-like scarf tied in a tight bow under my chin announcing my manager status, and homemade polyester tan slacks with perceptible wrinkles. In 1976, the year I was hired by Cargill, they had two hiring processes: one for regular folk, hired for specific openings up and down the company,

the process for which took a few days to complete; the other, into which I was hired, was the management training program. As a management trainee, I came to work with no specific job except that I was earmarked to be a manager. I was a gilded trainee, one of the first women and minorities hired into this lofty program.

I don't know of many similar programs today, but back then, there were a few. Hughes Aircraft had a program where new hires rotated in and out of jobs until they found a good fit (or not). We were treated like movie stars—every trip was planned out by the training program staff, several of whom had come through the program themselves. They catered to our needs, scheduling a weekend layover if we wanted, working out itineraries, generating NCR paper plane tickets for the following week. NCR, or no-carbon-required, paper tickets were hand written. Our schedulers would be on the phone with either the airline or a travel agent and plan our trips. Once an itinerary was established, they would confirm with the agent and create the plane ticket on this NCR copy tissue-like paper. Our scheduler would keep a copy of the ticket. When we got to the airport, the counter agent would take a copy, and the gate agent would take a copy and then the traveler would have a copy.

We were, after all, the future leaders of the corporation, and our special treatment reinforced the idea that we were destined to become presidents and general managers of the Cargill businesses.

Each month, a new group of management trainees would begin. My class of trainees was unlike anything that had come before—I was one of three Asian women, all three of us recruited from West Coast schools. The other two were Chinese Americans.

Mary was medium height, bookish looking with her naturally wavy hair awry and held down with bobby pins. She had an accounting degree and was destined for the auditing department. The other Asian woman looked like a fashion model: petite, sleek black hair, always dressed smartly in crisp business suits, wearing high heels, and sporting the finest leather handbags. *Expensive* shouted from her clothes. She quit the day the training program trips ended. We speculated she was in it just for the travel, but frankly, she likely wouldn't have lasted in the rough-and-tumble ag business. Charles was the lone black man, light skinned, bright eyed, with a closely cropped Afro, also destined for audit. Rick, a Kansas boy with the twangy accent, was the son of a Cargill feed plant district manager. He knew more about Cargill than any of us. George was a hefty, barrel-chested reddish-brown-haired giant of a man who filled a room. While we all started the first of May, we traveled in small groups together or with hires that had started before or after us, whatever worked out. Many trips were solo.

On Fridays, we'd stride to work, fresh off a trip, into the training program area of HR. The staff assigned to us would give us the next week's marching orders, and we would lounge around the conference table, squinting at the oversized whiteboard with our names and trips scheduled on a big matrix:

ELAINE KOYAMA

WK 1: ORIENTATION IN MPLS

WK 2: TRADING DESK, LAKE OFFICE

WK 3: POLYMERS, LOS ANGELES

WK 4: MINNEAPOLIS GRAIN EXCHANGE, PORT CARGILL

WK 5: GRAIN TRADING, MAUMEE, OHIO

WK 6: EGGS, JACKSONVILLE, FLORIDA

WK 7: GRAIN TERMINAL / SALT MINE, NEW ORLEANS

WK 8: RESEARCH FARM, ELK RIVER

WK 9: TERRITORY SALES, OKLAHOMA CITY

WK 10: TERRITORY SALES, ROWAN, IA

WK 11:

WK 12:

The blanks were the weeks that were yet unscheduled. The theory was that as time went on, we would have a better idea where in the company we wanted to work, as well as managers who would be able to raise their hand and say, "I want you." The trips would align with our interests and the recruiting divisions, allowing both to take a look at each other.

My itinerary played like a travelogue: Los Angeles to see the polymer business; Florida to egg-production facilities; Oklahoma City to ride with a salesman; a week at the Elk River research farm, where we stuck our hands into a fistulated dairy cow (a cow with a hole cut into its side to study the ruminant digestive process). We killed chickens by wringing their necks (a test of our intestinal fortitude), inoculated baby pigs, and fed animals Nutrena feeds. We spent a week in New Orleans at the grain terminals. We toured the grain elevators, riding up the elevator lifts to the top of the grain legs, where a person could see for miles and miles from the top of the facility, walking catwalks of grated steel that you could see ten stories down between bins.

We went underground to one of the most fascinating production facilities on earth—rock salt mines built in the salt domes of Louisiana out on the Mississippi Delta, where the only way to get there was on a ferry that the workers rode morning and night. We took another elevator—this one hundreds of feet down into the ground where salt is mined by the room and pillar method.

At each location visit, the daylight hours were spent on "work" and the evenings were ours to tour about or more likely have a business dinner with the guys we had just spent the day with.

We traveled so much that one time I boarded a flight and the flight attendant said, "Hi! You again?" Several times, the gate agent just upgraded me to first class because they had room. There were no frequent-flier programs, just people recognizing people. I wasn't a highheels kind of woman—and still am not. The only shoes out of college I owned were a pair of the original Earth Shoes, with the negative heel, and a pair of Vibram-soled hiking boots, not because I hiked but because I wanted to look like a hiker. I had to buy work shoes that were practical for hiking in airport terminals—platform shoes were popular in the '70s and could be pretty comfortable. Euro clogs, wedge soles, and shoes with heels like big square chunks were stylish and practical. Wearing bell-bottoms, polyester, silky, shiny shirts with wide, floppy collars paired with a suit jacket or vest, I attacked the business world. Add the carry-on shoulder bag and hair like Farrah Fawcett, and it shouted *working woman*. Or so I thought. We were finding our way. We hadn't started to dress exactly like men just yet—that would come in a few years. I still wore my cotton peasant dress with the short white vest, but as I added new pieces to my wardrobe, I got less peasant and more professional.

But that was all good—the men didn't look all that much better. We'd be sitting side by side with grain merchants who spent their days in smoky, open bullpens, desks upon row of desks, shirtsleeves rolled up, cigarette hanging from a lip, calling farmers to originate grain or elevators to sell grain. There were no computers—this was long before desktop computers were available—but pencils, pens, papers, and calculators were strewn around, with pads of paper, buy sheets and sell sheets lying around in haphazard disarray. The guys were chained to their desks via the telephone cord (mobile phones were still fifteen years away), and activity would ebb and flow, depending on whether a railcar or unit train was in need of a few more bushels to fill, or if the market was fluctuating.

They'd gesticulate with a free hand, write deals on notepads, and hand the deal sheets to a secretary (always a woman), who would enter the information into the ticker tape machine. The ticker tape machine didn't do dots and dashes, but printed words. Every office had the ticker tape machine that was constantly spewing tape out. Every trading office looked the same—grubby men in sweat-stained short-sleeved button-down shirts, shouting into their phones, swinging deals with unseen voices on the other end of the line. The glamour of the Minneapolis Grain Exchange or Chicago Board of Trade—where traders waved and shouted trades in the pit, bought and sold by some mystical telepathic communication—didn't happen in the field offices. The field offices were smaller, with beat-up wooden or steel desks lined up, traders sitting for hours on the phone, talking to their sources, buying and selling corn, by-products, and soybeans.

My fellow trainee Charles and I traveled together to Maumee, Ohio. We had three days to spend at the Maumee trading office and the nearby grain elevators. We flew into Detroit on a Sunday afternoon and rented a car to drive south to Maumee. I had never been to Detroit before, but I knew a kid at Stanford whose dad was a big executive with GM. He was actually Canadian. When I realized how close we were to Canada, I told Charles we had to go across the border to have dinner. He was easygoing and agreed. He had distant relatives in Detroit, too, so we were going to call them first, visit if they would have us, then go to dinner in Canada.

We drove northeast from the airport into Detroit. We were on a lookout for a phone booth to call his relatives. We pulled up to the first one, and Charles jumped out to call. He came back quickly. "There's no phone. It's been ripped off," he said. We laughed and drove a bit farther into downtown Detroit. We spotted another phone booth. We stopped. This area was a little seedier; the phone booth was on a street corner, and graffiti covered the nearby building. Again, Charles jumped out. He jumped back in the car. "No phone," he said again. The phones had been stripped from both booths.

This time, he didn't laugh. Instead, he said, "Let's go to Canada."

Charles asked me if we needed a passport. I breezily waved my hand. "Of course not! We have an open boarder with Canada. You can just go back and forth!" In 1973, I had gone from Montana to Lethbridge, Alberta, with my parents, and it was as easy as my breezy wave. The border patrol had just waved us through.

So we drove to the border control booth. It looked not unlike the entrance to a national park. The Canadian officer peered into the car, looking first at Charles, who was driving, a black man, then at me, an Asian woman. He asked for our passports. Obviously, we had none. We showed him our driver's licenses. I could see the sweat popping out over Charles's forehead. The officer took our licenses into the little building. I turned to Charles and said, "They didn't do this when I went with my parents! Really!"

The border patrol officer came back, handed us our licenses, and said, "I can let you in, but there's no guarantee they'll let you back."

We drove forward. Both of us were shaken. What if they didn't let us back in? We'd miss work! We'd get into trouble! We might never get home again! Charles pulled over to the side of the road and stopped. We looked at each other. "Let's go back," one of us said. We turned around directly, and the US Border Patrol waved us through, just like I'd remembered it was like in 1973 when I had driven to Canada with my parents.

Like good new employees, Charles and I were at work bright and early the next day. For Charles, it was learning the business, as he was already slated for audit. For me, it was a job interview. We obediently observed and asked questions. I tried displaying enough interest to get a job offer, studying enough to figure out if I would like this kind of work. The traders took us out for lunch. Three or four white guys, a black man, and an Asian woman—I'm sure the residents of Maumee had never seen anything like it. It was no mistake that they took us to a strip joint for lunch. It was the first time in a strip club for me, but not the last. White men taking me out to strip joints seemed to be the "fun" test that they liked to give me. I put on my poker face and kept my back to the stage. Not the optimal seating arrangement, now that I think of it. I looked directly into the eyes of the men who were talking, joining in when I needed to. No furtive glances at the stage for me. When I went to the restroom, some of the girls were primping for their show. They were chatting it up when I entered, and then one of the girls asked me if I was a new girl. I looked at her in her flimsy, gauzy outfit. I looked down at my navy-blue slacks, long-sleeved oxford dress shirt, and blazer. Practical wedge tie shoes. "Uh, I don't think so. I'm here having lunch."

Oh, well, we were all just making a living, after all.

Grain trading. Not the life for me. I tried to picture myself sitting at one of those desks, shouting into the phone, *sitting* all day long! Argh! Not me! I was a people person! I was an in-your-face type! Sit all day? *No way!*

So if that wasn't the life for me, joining a grain-trading merchant company seemed like a misstep on a very short career.

Except that Cargill had recently begun selling products—in particular, Nutrena Feeds and Cargill Salt. These were products that weren't traditionally traded on the exchange but sold to businesses and farmers. So my final trips on the training program were to divisions that had sales organizations.

I went to Oklahoma City to travel with a top Cargill Salt salesman. He met me wearing aviator sunglasses and a crisp white shirt with a dark tie. He had a jawline like John Travolta and a body like he'd just left the gym. He had a new Chevy four-door company car, lots of chrome, vinyl top. He was an ex-jock—college football, if I recall. We drove around Oklahoma City making sales calls. That night, he took me to the Holiday Inn, where I was staying for the night.

He was so looking forward to dropping me off, but not for the reasons you may imagine. In Oklahoma in 1976, the drinking laws were strict. You couldn't just go to a bar, and you couldn't go to a hotel lounge *unless* you had a guest vouch for you. This guy wanted a drink in the worst way. So, since I was the guest, I vouched for the guy so he could have a couple of drinks. The next night, he invited me to his home to meet his wife. She was a gorgeous stay-at-home blonde. I felt like the proverbial country bumpkin next to her sleek hairdo, fit body, and perfectly made-up face.

I tried to picture myself working on a team that had a guy like this in it. It would be hard.

My next trip was to deepest, darkest Iowa to work with a Nutrena Feeds salesman. Picture Purina dog food except for pigs. It was Iowa. Uneventful, nondescript farm after farm. The contrast between the swinging salt salesman and the Farmer Jones feed man was extreme. I chose to sell feed. Maybe it was because I imagined a hundred years (give or take fifty) in the future, when I had little grandkids on my knee, I could tell them I sold animal feed door to door, farm to farm, in a land called Iowa in the 1970s.

I chose Nutrena Feeds, and they chose me. It was a marriage made in heaven. I spent the next month at the Elk River research farm with another young man who was entering the feed business. He was ex-Vietnam helicopter pilot. Good looking in a pilot sort of way. Think Val Kilmer in *Top Gun*. He came with a wife and baby. I think he was from Texas. We kicked off our business careers together. We were starting at the bottom, but the ladder only went up.

PART 3

Crawling

Belmond, Iowa

The day came when I got my job location assignment in Nutrena Feeds. I would be the first woman and first nonwhite person in their sales organization. The company had, by this time, invested over four months of time and money into me. They placed me into the Rowan, Iowa, district—one of the top-producing smaller areas about two and a half hours from Minneapolis. Rowan, a town of about 200 people, was home to the feed production plant. The facility consisted of a small office where my district manager and boss, Carl Benjamin, worked. His staff consisted of his secretary, Jim the order taker, and Jerry, who was the office administration manager. Five to seven salesmen reported to Carl. There must have been a plant manager and his employees, but they weren't on my radar screen. Several grain bins, ingredient mixers, bulk storage bins, a bagging line, and a finished bag product warehouse rounded out the plant. I opted to live in Belmond, population 2,300, about fifteen miles north. Belmond was about the same-sized town as Hardin, so I figured life would be similar, too.

I rented a little white house on a side street. Trees didn't line the streets as they had in Minneapolis, but I learned later that it was because a tornado had screamed through Belmond in the '60s and destroyed the main street and most of the town. Instead of historic brick buildings, Belmond had a midcentury blue-metal-trimmed main street with street lights stuck out of the metal awnings. There were hardware, grocery, clothing, five-and-dime, and jewelry stores, along with an optometrist and the obligatory tavern. The Laundromat was at the end of the street near the movie theater. The buildings were glass and metal, maybe some cinder block thrown in. It was characterless and utilitarian. The house I rented had been blown to the middle of the street like Dorothy's in *The Wizard of Oz*. They had moved it back onto its foundation, but everything was a little cockeyed.

I reported to Carl, but my first assignment was to work with Roger Roan, the star salesman in the district. Roger called on larger producers and feed dealerships. I was the apprentice. I shadowed Roger for a month or two, all the while going to Minneapolis periodically for product and sales training. When they figured I couldn't shadow anymore, they cut me a slice of his territory to call my own.

Roger Roan

Roger was an amiable, self-deprecating, appealing class-clown guy maybe in his mid-thirties. He was on his second wife, Roberta, who hailed from the Sioux Falls, South Dakota, area. Her CB radio handle was *Dakota*. Roberta was one tough cookie, and I didn't mess with her. She had lured Roger from wife number one, and she damn well wasn't going to let anyone do the same to her. She was the perfect salesman's wife—fielding calls, taking messages, keeping Roger on track.

My job was simple. Shadow Roger and learn everything I could about selling feed. I would go to product training classes in Minneapolis at least monthly to get the product knowledge—hog, beef cattle, dairy, chicken—each session put on by the product line managers and the research feed scientists. I was also sent through professional selling skills training (think features, benefits, minimizing objections, asking for the sale), but at that point, I knew nothing about making the actual sales call in the real world.

Roger had built Roberta a dream home just outside of Rowan. Each morning, I'd drive to their home by 8:00 a.m., and Roger would be on the phone, talking to customers. I'd pull up a chair to their kitchen table, and Roberta and I would have a cup of coffee. Roger would join us, and around 9:00, we would hit the road to make sales calls. This was rich black-dirt farmland, thousands of acres of some of the richest, most fertile ground in the country. In the '70s, farm prices were skyrocketing, and family farms were beginning to consolidate, but almost every farmstead had a hog operation, and the owner made the buying decisions. We called on farmers, but most of Roger's sales went through farm stores and feedstores. These businesses would keep bag and possibly bulk inventory of feed, mostly MCM 40, which was a 40 percent protein hog concentrate that would be blended with the farmer's corn. The baby pig feed looked good enough to eat—it smelled like granola mixed with molasses (which, now that I think of it, it probably was).

For me, having grown up doing farmwork, I would look at what was the same as our farm and what was different and then study the differences—it sped up my learning curve. I mostly had to figure out what a salesperson's job was, since the technical part of the job wasn't telling the farmer how to do his job but what our product specifications were and how it would affect his bottom line.

And I learned quickly that *trust* was the most important ingredient, both for the feed products and the relationships. Roger established trust between himself and the farmer/dealer. Once he had that trust, the farmer could buy. I had to establish trust with the farmer/dealer and the *wives*, because no man was going to buy from me without his wife's okay. Another adage I lived by: "Don't mix business with pleasure." It was always clear to me a person had more to lose than to gain mixing sex with business. This proved to be key in gaining the trust of the wives.

I learned the hog business by calling on pig farmers. There were lots of hogs in Iowa, so I got lots of practice talking to hog farmers. Dairy, on the other hand, was different. Those farms were few and far between. We had run beef cattle in Montana, so on my first visit to a dairy farmer, I asked him how many cows he ran.

He quickly called me on the carpet. "We don't *run* dairy cows," he said, looking down his nose at me. "You run dairy cows and you injure their udders. We *milk* cows."

I didn't have many dairy farmers to call on, so I asked to work with a dairy farmer outside of Hampton, Iowa. The family took me in for a week—had me help in the barn milking, feeding the cows morning and night. I even watched them artificially inseminate one of the cows with semen purchased from a high-producing bull herd. It was an impressive education from a generous Iowa farm family.

Before taking this sales job with Cargill, I had met only one door-to-door salesman in my life. When I was in high school, there was a knock on our door. A man was on the step and asked if my dad was home. I said, "No."

I asked him who he was. He said, "I'm the Moorman salesman."

The Mormon salesman? I thought. *What difference does it make what religion he is? Or is he selling religion?* I was puzzled.

He handed me a brochure. The front of the brochure said, "Buy MoorMan Feed for your Livestock."

Oh, I get it.

Moorman, which was a large feed concentrate company out of Quincy, Illinois. Not Mormon.

And about Roberta. I understand that a few years after I left, there was a number three, the administrator manager's wife.

How's the Weather?

The first sales call alone for any salesperson is like falling in love the first time. There may be more important accounts, there may be more significant sales, but there is never again a first sales call. And like that first-time love, we never forget, however many years pass.

To drive around Iowa for a Montana farm girl was an epiphany— here was farmland so rich it looked like a bag of topsoil purchased at the garden store. Irrigation? Who needed to irrigate when nature would miraculously drop plentiful rain on the seeded fields at just the right time? It reminded me of the song from the musical *Camelot*, about the weather being perfect, rain on demand.

Iowa was the farmer's Camelot. Weather, soil, and geography were perfect for raising acres and acres of corn, soybeans, the occasional oats, grass, or alfalfa hay. Farms were well kept, lawns mowed literally to the edge of the highway—vibrant, lush, and green. Hardwood trees populated the groves, and barns and trademark dark blue Harvestore silos signaled another farmstead. I had grown up in semiarid Montana, where if you didn't irrigate the gumbo, claylike ground, nothing but weeds and sagebrush would grow. Montana farming was a constant struggle, fighting the lack of rain by gravity irrigation that needed to be managed daily, hourly, and required lugging irrigation tubes from row to row. Land had to be leveled so water would run directionally or else you'd end up with a flooded field. Farming in Iowa was *easy* by comparison.

My first solo sales call was just north of Ventura, Iowa. Ventura was little more than a wide spot in the road, located on the west end of Clear Lake in Cerro Gordo County. My job was to develop the Nutrena Feeds business in the northwest corner of the county. This meant stopping farm to farm, introducing myself and my company. I had to somehow get these guys to switch from doing business with the local co-op elevator to buying my feed delivered from Rowan, Iowa, which was a thirty-five-mile trip one way. The co-op was right in Clear Lake, smack-dab in the center of my territory. This was fringe country for Nutrena. I was fighting for market share in an area that was being well served locally. But from the company's perspective, a rookie like me could do no harm.

I drove into that first farmyard on the west side of S14, north of Highway 18, in my '75 Chevrolet company car that I had inherited from the former sales rep. I was wearing nice corduroy pants with sensible brown shoes and a conservative button-down shirt. My normally long black hair was cut shorter and pulled back in a ponytail. My weapon was a green three-ring binder with a printed form for each farm where I could write down the farmer's name, address, acreage, head of livestock (by species—beef, sheep, pigs, chickens, etc.), and an area with space for a date and comments. I also had in the back seat my Nutrena Feeds manuals (beef, dairy, hogs, chickens) that were product books I might need to make recommendations on best formulas for the guy's livestock. I was guided by the county plat book—a map of every county, township, section; it identified every farm and most of the time listed the owner's name. It was the salesman's bible.

The first farm I stopped at was a small ninety-acre plot with an aging man running the place. I drove past the driveway several times, building up the courage to turn in. Rehearsing the first lines I would say, silently, my lips imperceptibly moving as I shaped the words in my mind. Finally, I slowed to a crawl and pulled into the drive. The point of no return. The white wooden farmhouse was on the left, the red barn on the right. The farmer was working near his corncrib, west of the barn, grinding cobs to mix with his hog concentrate for finished feed. I walked up to him and introduced myself. We picked up the conversation, and as the joke goes in Iowa, the topic turned to the weather.

Now, I understand farmers—or so I thought—and how important the weather is to them. Their livelihood depends on it. But my task was to sell feed for their animals. I figured I would be asked questions about my product. I had studied the feed concentrates, the mineral mixes, the baby pig feeds. I never felt like I knew enough about the products. Little did I figure what an impression I would make in deepest, darkest Iowa by being a twenty-two-year-old Japanese American female selling feed. So, in the middle of my spiel on the benefits of the Nutrena feed products I represented, the farmer looked me square in the eye and asked, "How's the weather in Japan?"

Japan?! I thought. *What in the world does Japan have to do with the price of hog concentrate?!* My brain was reeling. We had covered a lot of topics in my sales training classes: how to handle objections, features, benefits. But Japan just wasn't one of them.

I had been to Japan once with my parents when I was in high school. It had been in February, and it had been cold. But I certainly did not consider myself an expert or even familiar with Japan's meteorological phenomena. I tried to maintain a poker face, and I am sure all these thoughts raced through my mind in less than a second.

"Weather's good, real good in Japan. Things are really green there," I fumbled my way through and somehow brought the conversation back to *feed*.

I left that farm not knowing whether to laugh, cry, or kick the car bumpers. I look back and laugh at not only the farmer's naïveté but at my own. I had forgotten the first thing this guy was going to see was *not* a Montana farm girl but a Japanese.

It took me most of my life to realize people see Japanese first, me second. It was a lesson constantly forgotten and yet constantly reinforced.

The Bokelmans

My first real task as a Nutrena Feeds salesperson in 1977 was to develop the hog feed business in a county where the farmers' co-op had a stranglehold. We had one major account, a husband and wife couple in the area. Hank and Irma Bokelman lived outside of Ventura, Iowa. Hank had continued faithfully with Nutrena Feeds for his hogs, cattle, and sheep. He, his two sons, and his wife had a large operation that had been homesteaded by his great-grandfather. His dad and uncle, Henry and Lyle, each lived on a farmstead and still helped out. Lyle had never married and lived the bachelor life alone on his farm about a quarter mile from Hank's. Around the corner and up the road about half a mile was Henry's home and pasture, where draft horses from a bygone era still grazed. They had a piece of virgin prairie—ground that had never been plowed or seeded. In Iowa, that's less than 0.1 percent of the land. These were salt of the earth midwestern farm folks.

Hank's son, Hank Jr., lived on another farm with his wife and two kids. The second son, John, was a very eligible bachelor and had a home on another farm but for all intents and purposes lived at home. Hank and Irma also had two other kids, Jane and Ruth. Jane married a boy from Clear Lake, who later became a pharmacist in Okoboji. Ruth became my best friend.

The first time I met the Bokelmans, I felt I had come home. Hank and Irma were ten years younger than my parents but felt like surrogate parents all the same. Their kids were in the same age range as my siblings and I. They were farmers, they loved to go hunting in Montana, and they raised hogs, sheep, and cattle—these were my kind of people. They welcomed me with wonder and curiosity and a frankness that I appreciated. And they ate like farmers.

Irma was a wonder woman. She worked side by side with her men but always had home-baked bread, steaming tasty food, and dessert. Her husband was the extrovert—inquiring, warm, with smiling, laughing, weathered eyes. Irma was quieter but just as accepting and willing to go for any ride that came along.

We knew this was going to be a special relationship when, after our first dinner (lunch), we sat around the table, talking, laughing, getting to know one another. The eating ended, the conversation lulled, and the next thing we realized was that every one of us had a toothpick in our mouths. Chewing, picking, twiddling. It made for a great laugh, and we realized that we were more the same than different.

Hank and Irma were a fun couple, had a great relationship, and took me under their wings. They treated me as one of their own and never made me feel like an outsider. They were a very private family, and while well-known and respected in the community, they kept to themselves. I visited them regularly because they were my key—and for a while, only—customers. I thought of them not only as clients but as surrogate parents and mentors.

They wanted me to meet their daughter Ruth, who lived in Charles City and sold ag chemicals for Chevron. Ruth had graduated from Iowa State in Ames and had a job very similar to mine. Hank asked me to drive with them to Charles City after work; I was anxious to make friends and readily agreed.

This was one of my first after-hours, personal interactions with a customer. I was less than a year into my working career. During the day, I understood the rules of business etiquette. After hours was a totally different deal.

I drove to Hank and Irma's farm, where I was going to leave my car and ride with them to Charles City, about an hour away. Hank was running a bit late, as he had to clean up after working all day. I waited with Irma, visiting like I would have with my mom. We gathered up the stuff Irma wanted to take to Ruth and walked down to the car.

They had a big Buick sedan with bench seats front and back. We threw the stuff for Ruth in the back seat. Hank took to the steering wheel, and I jumped in the front seat. Irma moved in beside me.

Then I realized I should have let Irma in the car first so that she would have been sitting next to her husband. Instead, I had jumped in as I had all my life with my parents—so I was sitting in the middle seat, with Mom and Dad on either side. It was a split second of not thinking, just acting, but it caused an hour of discomfort—for me probably more than for Hank and Irma.

That night was the start of a lifelong friendship with Ruth and her family. And I never again knowingly came between a husband and wife at work.

Carl Benjamin

Carl Benjamin was my first boss. He seemed like an old guy, but with kids in middle and high school, he couldn't have been much older than late thirties. I thought he was a big dang deal, and he was to me, but in reality, he was a middle manager at one of the company's smaller plants.

Carl was entrusted to train me up and likely didn't get much more direction than that. I was the first woman in sales in the entire company, so there were no neat little handbooks to follow. We were winging it. Most of the sales territory managers had come from within the district, and none started as green as I.

His first mission was to teach me about how a feed business ran. I was exposed to every person who worked at the plants, from his personal secretary, to the inside sales desk, to each field representative whose job was to work for the territory managers to boost sales. As a management trainee, I was skipping ahead of the field reps to a territory manager position, but that didn't mean I didn't have to do the same work.

The tough thing about sales is that gratification is often delayed. I worked with each salesperson and gleaned as much as I could from them, but ultimately, I had to make my own sales calls on my own prospects. And no one buys the first time you meet them; if they do, they probably have bad credit. So I began calling on accounts up and down the road in the territory I had been assigned. And nothing happened. I imitated the methods that had worked for Roger Roan. Still nothing. I wondered how long I'd be employed without selling. I lost weight. I caught a cold that wouldn't go away. I popped cold meds like they were jelly beans just to function. I feared missing work.

Seated in front of Carl Benjamin at one of our monthly update meetings, he grinned his Cheshire cat grin at me and asked, "How are things going?"

I couldn't say, "Great!" because they weren't. I couldn't say, "Horrible!" for fear of failure. I looked at him, his body leaning forward, waiting for a response. I had one of those out-of-body experiences where I saw the two of us in the room—Carl bigger than life, towering over his desk, dwarfing me as I huddled in the chair. I felt as little as a mouse. I started to cry.

It wasn't the loud, sobbing crying, but more of the kind where you are still trying to maintain dignity even though tears are running down your face and all attempts at holding them back only make your face more screwed up. I was trying to stop and at the same time assure Carl that I was okay. It was just a crack in the armor.

I composed myself. I was more than a little mortified. I knew it was fatigue, stress, likely some homesickness, and of course fear of failure all converging at once. I was full of adrenaline with no means to burn it off.

Carl never once said anything condescending. As a matter of fact, he said hardly anything. He never moved from his chair on the other side of the desk. He waited patiently for me to recover and kindly handed me a Kleenex. He told me to hang in there, that things would turn around, that I was doing fine.

He was right. I did hang in there, things did turn around, and I was fine. I'd like to brush the episode under the carpet, never have to be reminded that in spite of my brave face, I was scared and lonely. Later, Carl teased me a few times about it. I found it irritating and a bit embarrassing, but it was a small price to pay in the process of growing up.

The First Sale

My territory was on the edge of our feed plant's market reach, so I was always fighting against competitors' feed plants that were located closer to the customers. It is much harder to break new ground than to take over sales from an established territory, but I didn't know that at the time.

In spite of the enormity of the task, I thrived on the challenge. There was nowhere to go but up in sales volume, since virtually any sale would be a new sale. On the other hand, being a rookie, it was difficult to face the rejection day in and day out. My job was to take a plat book and stop at each farm and try to sell them feed. It was the coldest type of cold-call selling you can get.

Years later, after I had sold salt for a period of time, I learned that not all products are equally difficult to sell. In business terms, this is referred to as *switching costs*. Feed sales are particularly challenging because it is a primary ingredient in the farmer's recipe for raising livestock; salt sales in comparison are easier, because though it is a necessary ingredient, it is not the main ingredient. Consequently, the barriers to changing are considerably lower, and the switching costs are negligible.

I am almost embarrassed to admit that the first sale I ever made by myself took six months from the day I started with Nutrena Feeds. A normal person may have quit or have been fired for such a long wait for success, but I had no gauge for what "normal" was and nowhere else to go. I also imagine that I would have stayed for however long it would take to make that first sale, since not making a sale would have been failure and I was too scared of failure to quit! Now, granted, I was in training for three months, working in the feed plant, and working with other salesmen, but I did not contribute a dime to the bottom line for six months! And then the contribution was miniscule—one ton of Shoat 40 MCM, a hog concentrate feed.

One of the Broadchurch brothers bought from me. There were three or four Broadchurches that farmed near Clear Lake, all descendants of early settlers in the area. All of them lived and farmed separately, and all were feed prospects of mine. This particular Broadchurch brother had a farm on the south end of town. The road out of Clear Lake passed by his new residence and then continued to his farm with its red barn, old farmhouse, and a few outbuildings.

The day he placed his order with me, he was standing at his hog barn door, with a fence between us. I had driven back to where he was working with his hogs. I stood outside his open barn doors (in the feed business, it is taboo for a salesperson to enter the actual feedlot, for fear of transmitting disease from farm to farm). I had been calling on him regularly, and we had gotten used to the salesperson/prospect relationship. Our conversation began the usual way, chitchat about the weather, what some of the other farmers were up to that I had just visited, what the current sales promotions were. I asked him if I could ship him anything, expecting the "No, thanks" that I had been getting used to. He said, "I'll take a ton of Shoat 40." I am sure I looked thrilled. No one had ordered from me before!

Before I could speak, he leaned over and kissed me on the cheek!

I jumped back. He had a Cheshire cat grin on his face. He leered at me, cocking his head to the side. I said a hasty "Thanks!" then turned away and jumped in my car to drive to the nearest phone booth.

I placed my first order with the feed plant, excited and triumphant. I also felt angry and confused. Why did the guy have to ruin my first sale with a kiss on the cheek? I knew it wasn't a brotherly kind of kiss. And he was an old married man.

I thought back on that day and for many years had it marked on my calendar, for it signified my coming of age in salesmanship. But it was tainted. He gave me an order but took from me a kiss.

I put the farmer's kiss in a box in my memory as another lesson about being a woman selling into a male-dominated industry. There were many other sales after that first one, but never another stolen kiss.

Love Long Distance

When I left Stanford and moved to the Midwest, I left behind a college romance. Steve and I, not unlike most optimistic young people, believed that our relationship, if it were really meant to be, would last the time, turmoil, and distance that the separation forced. We thought we were stronger, smarter, more able to beat the odds of a long-distance romance than the average couple because . . . well, because we were in love.

Steve, like me, was a profuse letter writer. I would receive letters almost daily. They were newsy letters about college activities (I'd graduated a quarter early) and spring at Stanford. I would respond in kind, telling him all about the wonders of the outside world.

But, of course, letters were not enough. We would have marathon phone conversations nightly that reinforced the written word.

I was making $11,000 per year. When I first started working, I thought that was so much money I'd have trouble spending it all. Gloria Steinem was quoted as saying, "Most women are one man away from welfare," meaning most women relied on their husbands for their livelihood. I had no husband, so the first thing I did was open a checking and savings account at the Belmond State Bank, and I began to establish credit by getting a Mastercard, an American Express, and gas cards. I had begun paying off my school loan, which seemed larger than life. What I had not anticipated were *taxes* (which, along with FICA, insurance, and other miscellany, seemed to eat up almost 30 percent of the check) and the cost of living in a small town in Iowa, where rental properties were few and relatively expensive. Indeed, the rent did not sound too bad for a one-bedroom house—$125 per month—but this was a house that had ended up in the middle of a street after the Big Tornado of 1966.

I remember sitting alone in my little Belmond, Iowa, house furnished with an old upright piano bought at a church sale, an oak library table (no chair) from a secondhand store (a.k.a. *antique store*), a molded plastic love seat, and sheets that I had sewn into curtains. I remember seeing, in the dead of winter with the wind howling and the temperatures down in the minus twenties, the sheets covering the windows moving from the draft coming through the cracks in the window frames. I also remember paying those first horrendous heating bills! Over $150 per month—more than the rent itself!

And then I had clothing bills. I came out of college with blue jeans and bell bottoms . . . not exactly business dress, even for Iowa.

So picture on top of these expenses a monthly phone bill of over $250! It was mind-boggling to me. I hadn't factored in how lonely it was going to be, pursuing this dream to be a senior manager (maybe president!) at this megacompany. Phone calls were my only connection to the world outside of work. On one of our Saturday afternoon dialogues, I mentioned this to my recently graduated, applying-to-med-schools, living-at-home, no-serious-job-in-sight boyfriend. I wasn't complaining, mind you; I was just trying to get some sympathy out of a most sympathetic friend. To prove my point, I compared the cost of our phone conversations to the fact that we could have paid for a round-trip plane ticket for him rather than these frustrating long-distance phone calls.

Well, that sounded like a good idea to him (and to be honest, it sounded delightful to me, too). The next thing I remember is driving to the Des Moines airport—an hour-and-a-half drive for me—to pick him up. The bill went on my credit card, of course!

We had plenty of time to talk on the drive back to Belmond. And most of that night and the next day. It was wonderful to have someone with a shared background around to say, "Isn't Iowa different?" "Isn't the farmland refreshing?" "Isn't life strange?" "Isn't work nothing like you'd thought?"

Of course, when we got to the work question, our grounds for commonality were weakened dramatically, since *I* was working and *he* was not.

That fact didn't bother me. I *needed* to work. Steve was planning to get into medical school. (He was a part of that 50 percent of the Stanford student body who intended to be doctors.) So while I drove off to work each morning, Steve's plan was to "discover Iowa" and somehow get some med school to invite him to attend.

Perhaps if I had been in New York City or Chicago or even Minneapolis, Steve could have really "discovered" something. As it was, for a city kid stuck in the farmlands of Iowa, he couldn't relate to the land, the people, or the passion I had for my work.

And I realized that my occupation was no longer a job, but had become WORK—in capitals, with a meaning and impact that would go further and last longer than the relationship with Steve.

It wasn't that I didn't love him any longer. It wasn't that I loved him any less.

It was that I had discovered a dimension in life that I had always thought was there but had never experienced before. It was a feeling of independence, of proving myself, of winning at life. I couldn't turn away from the path on which I'd found myself. And as much as we tried to ignore the fact, as much as we tried to steer toward each other, Steve and I were on different paths, and neither one of us was willing to get out of our vehicle to join the other.

Steve eventually returned home—Seattle, then Stanford, then Seattle. I stayed on the "frontier," alone.

Photography and Iowa's Dr. Rietz

My first winter in Iowa was severe not only from a climatological perspective but also from a personal one. I suffered from heat-bill shock, adjusting to a new job, new home, new community, a past-tense boyfriend, and few friends my age. I did have a steady income, which was consumed quickly, and nothing but time to kill after work.

Several in my family are artistic, and I admire that trait. Unfortunately, I lacked the artistic gene, and I hoped that a camera could mechanically capture what I could not seem to do physically.

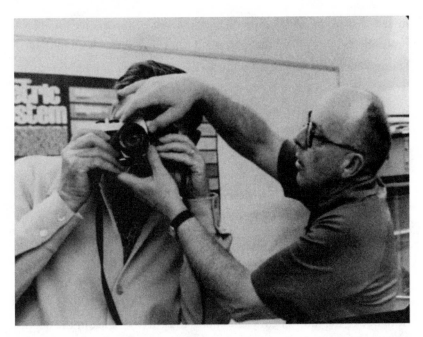

I purchased a single-lens reflex camera that first winter of 1976/77, long before 35 mm cameras became the rage. It was a mail-order purchase, chosen by painstakingly analyzing choices from a print catalog. The day it arrived, the wind chills were sixty below, and visibility was zero due to blowing snow. I knew I couldn't be driving out in that weather making farm sales calls, and the frustration of sitting at home when my new purchase waited at the post office was more than I could bear.

I prayed that my Chevrolet company car would start in the cold weather and keep running. I braved the inclement weather to capture my treasure at the post office. While the one man working that day looked at me quizzically, I didn't care—he had obviously made it into work, and I had obviously made it to the post office. The fact that the radio and TV warned everyone to stay home unless it was an emergency only reinforced the fact that retrieving my package was my personal emergency.

All day, I played with my new possession—all the more precious because it was the first expensive item that was totally mine. I chose not to purchase a Nikon, the top-of-the-line, name-brand camera, but a Pentax. My research had driven me to the Pentax, and while I convinced myself that it was of a higher quality, the fact of the matter was that I probably couldn't afford the additional price that a Nikon commanded. So my Pentax was purchased with funds I had earned, saved, and spent. It was precious because I had gone without for years before being able to acquire the precise model with the just-so features and the out-of-the-box crispness of *new*.

Unfortunately, I had no film yet. These cameras worked only with light-sensitive film. I had only the camera, the manuals, and time on my hands.

I have always been a believer of taking classes to gain skills. There is nothing like a good coach, counselor, or instructor to accelerate the learning curve. Belmond had a community education night program that offered a photography class. I jumped at the chance.

The first class stands out in my mind not because of the content of the lesson but the caliber of the attendees. Here I was, newly graduated from one of the most talent-rich schools in America, stuck in the depths of the Midwest, where the untrained eye sees nothing but cornfields next to bean fields broken by the occasional silo and farmhouse. I enrolled in a small-town night-school class and discovered that those farmhouses were occupied by intelligent, educated, creative humans, not unlike the ones I had recently left at Stanford.

They were attending the class for many of the same reasons I was attending—interest in photography and a way to get out of the house and into the community during the depths of winter. Virtually all had graduated from college, most from Iowa State. I felt we could have become good friends but for an insurmountable barrier. I was single; the other women and the men were not. While I just wanted to make some friends, the other women, all probably farmwives, didn't trust me. They all knew I was the "Feed Lady," not a very glamorous moniker, and they saw a young, attractive, unattached Japanese woman. It screamed, "Danger!" to them. They were put off by me, and they certainly didn't want their men talking to me in class.

Dr. Rietz, who taught the class, was the town optometrist. He was a small, careful man with a true enthusiasm for photography. We quickly formed a teacher-student bond, cemented by our mutual love of photography. His wife tolerated his passion for photography and therefore tolerated me.

The photography class taught the basics of black-and-white photography and soon ended.

My friendship with Dr. Rietz continued for years.

We spent much of that summer comparing photographs, talking about techniques and new cameras. I ended up buying his darkroom equipment when he upgraded. We both entered the Fort Dodge, Iowa, photography show, where one of my prints won an honorable mention.

One cool summer evening, after we had spent some time visiting about photography, we stood in his front yard, chatting as I prepared to leave. Our conversation lulled, as it often does before one says good-bye, when Dr. Rietz brought up the topic of World War II.

I had never talked to him about World War II. I really never had a reason to. He never asked me how the weather was in Japan. He knew better. Dr. Rietz must have been my dad's age, since he had children that were my contemporaries, but that never seemed like an issue. Our common bond was photography, and that was a large and always-changing topic of entertainment. I often forgot that my face was Japanese. But clearly when he looked at me, he saw more than just me. He saw Japan. He heard the roar of the plane engines, the clouds engulfing and releasing him. Forty years fell away.

So on that cool evening, with the glow from the porchlight illuminating the driveway of his home in Belmond, Dr. Rietz spoke to me about his duty as a United States Air Force pilot, flying over Japan, dropping bombs on unknown Japanese families in their homes. He told me of the pain he felt then, as he did now, looking at my Japanese face, for the untold lives extinguished by the bombs he dropped.

He said softly, "I'm so sorry."

"War is terrible."

"Yes, it is."

Wess

Clarion, Iowa, in addition to being the county seat, was the home of one of Nutrena Feeds' largest dealers, Clarion Trading Post. The trading post was run by a father and son by the name of Beaumont. I got to know these folks not only through the feed business but also through a common interest—tennis. Jonathon Beaumont, the dad, was an exceptional tennis player. Pete, Jonathon's son, though slight of build and not that tall, was also skilled, and with his wife, Ellen, they made a fierce doubles team.

I liked Ellen immediately. She was younger than I was by a few years and had a warm charm and crinkly, smiling eyes that made an outsider like me feel at home. Although I was a novice at tennis, Ellen encouraged me to play in some of the local summer tournaments.

One day about four months after I had moved to Iowa, Ellen and Pete came to the feed plant in Rowan to pick up feed. I stopped to greet them. Ellen casually mentioned that I might like to get to know her brother, Wess. They knew that I was also an avid downhill skier, and Ellen said her brother was also a skier, though I don't remember why, since Iowa is as flat as a hardwood floor. I remember thinking *Wess* seemed like a strange name, but I was the lone stranger in a strange town in a strange state, doing a strange job. Any new acquaintance was not only warmly welcomed but gratefully received.

Fall is an appropriate name for autumn in Iowa, because of the rapid, helpless, headlong plunge into winter. I had never lived through such torturous, long, hideously cold months as I did in Iowa (until I moved to Minnesota!). And unlike other parts of the world where winter brings a wonderland, Iowa winters create frozen, barren landscapes of corn stubble and clumps of shivering trees huddled around farmsteads.

Maybe it was the weather, the short days wrapped in long nights, or the dimming glow of my college romance that made that first phone call from the unknown Wess seem like a blast of warm air. All I know is that the call lasted hours and did not seem long at all. And we had plans to go skiing the next morning at seven.

And where, one might ask, does one go skiing in Iowa?

Minnesota.

At least that was where we were going. There were rumored to be ski areas in Iowa, but I never had the opportunity to ski at any of them. Minnesota was only slightly better on the grand scale, but on a relative scale, Minnesota was the Tahoe basin, the Summit County, the Little Cottonwood Canyon for Iowa.

My excitement was uncontained. I got my skis out, cleaned up my boots, spruced up my jacket and mitts. I washed my hair, scrubbed my face, laid out my best warm clothes. Powder pants? I didn't own a pair, nor did I have a sleek ski jacket with matching hat. I was a rough-and-tumble, self-taught skier with roots in Montana, not Aspen. I had more desire to ski than I had skill or money.

At six in the morning, my phone rang. It was Wess. He asked if we should cancel our ski trip. In typical Iowa/Minnesota fashion, the temperature high for the day was predicted to be minus twenty degrees.

Not go? Out of the question! Unspeakable! This was an opportunity I did not want to pass. A chance to meet the mysterious Wess and ski, too. I craved a friendship relationship.

It wasn't that I had no friends. I had met many people in the course of my sales job. But those relationships were all business-related, and I had a deep-rooted conviction not to mix business and pleasure. Since so many hours were spent at my work, it left little time for developing friendships away from work. I also found another disconcerting fact: an unmarried, professional, working woman living in a small town in Iowa in 1977 was not a hot commodity but rather a threat to other single women and "their men." My outgoing personality, which allowed me to break into the business world, was interpreted in small-town social settings as threatening.

So here was Wess, suggesting that we cancel our trip, right when I thought I was on the brink of a social breakthrough! Little did he know with whom he was dealing—a socially starved ski fanatic who was not about to be held back.

Needless to say, we went skiing that day. And indeed, the temperatures did not rise above minus twenty.

I should have listened more carefully to the *other* atmospheric readings: my unsettled college romance, my raging hormones, the long winter. They would have been an excellent predictor of the outcome of the ski trip.

Wess was a tall, gentle man with smiling eyes like his sister's. He had graduated from Clarion High School but had never gone on to college. He worked for a hog processing plant, "rolling hogs."

And what, exactly, is *rolling hogs*? It is the backbreaking job of taking a 250-pound hog immediately after it is killed and rolling it into position to be hooked by the overhead conveyor that then mechanically moves the hog along the processing line. Wess would handle hundreds of hogs in the course of the day and do nothing else for eight hours. It is one of the most physical jobs on the line and paid on the high end of the union scale. Needless to say, Wess was in *very* good shape. Some people spend thousands to have a toned and muscled body like he had.

The type of work that Wess did made no difference to me. I had come from a farm family, and physical work was no stranger. Not having a college education was no big deal, either, since several of my brothers and sisters never had the opportunity to go to school. So what that I had graduated from Stanford? That was then. I was a simple feed salesperson now. And this wasn't marriage; this was fun.

Wess solved my problem of not fitting in. I now had a plus-one for parties, for social events. I was no longer a threat—as I was accounted for.

We had a torrid relationship. We would ski, play tennis, bask in each other. We were passionate. I was controlling, driven, and obsessive— much the same in the relationship as I was about work.

I looked to Wess to fill the entire social and sexual portion of my life that was being eclipsed by my work. I mistook that need for love, when in fact it was more like an additional meal (breakfast, lunch, and dinner satisfied nutritional needs) for the libido.

It took actually quite a long time for Wess to begin to recognize what a destructive relationship he had gotten into. I continued to take energy from him to fuel myself. I thought I was returning "love," but in retrospect, I was like a fisherman reeling in a catch, cranking the reel, cutting some slack just enough to keep him on the line.

We talked of marriage. Iowa for the rest of my life was a scary thought. I was not ready, nor did I think he was the "right" man. Yet a part of me wanted to be married, traditional, stable. I had decided marriage to Wess was not an option, but relinquishing Wess was like giving up chocolate. Every morning, I would vow never to indulge again, and every evening, my resolve would melt.

Likewise, Wess knew the relationship was not good for him and several times said it should end. We often discussed a parting of the ways.

Obviously, we didn't. We were codependents. It was sexual addiction. It was a debilitating spiral that, as strong as we thought we were, we were not strong enough to stop and do the "right" thing.

No Good Deed Goes Unpunished

About six months into my tour of duty in Iowa, another management trainee was assigned to the Rowan office for his sales training. Steven Silverman was a short, fiery redhead and graduate of Georgetown University in DC. Our paths had crossed prior to Rowan, as most of the management trainees from the summer hiring knew one another. Steven had no background in agriculture, but he was a smart-as-a-whip guy and plenty assertive.

His training had mirrored mine—we rode with feed salesmen, were supposed to pick up tips and tricks of the trade, and then apply them to the little slice of territory we would be given.

I was following the rules and was finding success along the way. I liked the ag world and felt comfortable there. With my background, even though I didn't look the part, I was able to fit in, make others feel comfortable with me, and sell feed.

Steven, on the other hand, was a square peg in a round hole. He was a city kid from a very prestigious college back east. His intensity put mild-mannered midwesterners off. And he hated living in the country.

One night, after about nine months into my assignment, I got a call from Steven. He said he hated the assignment and never was going to sell, so what was the point of this death sentence in Iowa? It caught me by surprise—not that he hated the assignment but that he would call me. We weren't that close, but maybe our kinship as trainees made him think there was a bond. I listened and then asked him what he wanted me to do about it.

He didn't know. I said, "Do you want me to call Carl and let him know?" He said, "Yes."

Today, I would have told him, "Call him yourself." But at the time, I didn't understand the dynamics. I was a take-charge kind of person. He had a problem. I wanted to solve it.

I called Carl and told him the situation. He asked me why Steven didn't call himself. I really didn't know. He said, "I'll take care of it."

Shortly thereafter, Steven was moved to a sweet position in Kansas City, Missouri, as the merchandising manager. It was the choice job for the fast-trackers in the Feed Division. Not a bad way to land for a guy failing in his first job.

He had reached out to me for help. I helped. He landed well—very well, as it turned out.

The Other Japanese Ladies

In all my time in Iowa—about two years or so—I ran into only three other Asian people. I don't even remember a Chinese restaurant.

I had heard stories about Japanese men who traveled farm to farm in the *Grapes of Wrath* years—migrant workers of a sort—who were "chicken sexers." I had no idea what a chicken sexer was, but here's how it was explained to me.

Chickens are good for only two things—meat and eggs. And just like any other farm animal, they are bred and cultivated to maximize their production of either meat or eggs. Chickens that are grown for meat are not the same ones that are grown for eggs, just like most dairy cows are bred to produce the most milk, not the most muscle.

Likewise, the chickens grown to lay eggs (layers) are bred to produce the best and most eggs possible. Obviously, the chickens you need for layers are the girl chickens.

Sorry, boys, you are worthless since you can't lay eggs, and you aren't built for meat production.

Thus, the need for chicken sexers. As the story goes, in the 1930s, '40s, and '50s (maybe earlier and/or later; it was never clear), crews of Japanese men would go farm to farm to determine the sex of the baby chicks. The girl chicks would be put in little grower units, and the boys—well, it was bad luck to be a boy chick, because the boys would be tossed in a barrel to be disposed of. The girl chicks would then be raised to the point they were able to lay eggs and then put in cages to do their laying.

Why the chicken sexers were Japanese is still somewhat of a mystery to me. I asked my mom about it, and she really didn't know, being the Southern California girl that she was. The farmers in Iowa told me that the Japanese men who came in could quickly and accurately determine the sex of the chicken by flipping them over, checking their anus area, and—presto!—the determination was made. But they kept their method and process a trade secret, and so they were in high demand.

Knowing the sex of the baby chicks early saved the farmers thousands of dollars on wasted feed. By destroying the boy chicks as babies, they didn't have to feed the useless birds any longer than they had to. Boy chicks went into the kill barrel; girl chicks went into the comfortable grower pens, with warm lights and clean sawdust.

The Japanese chicken sexers built a clientele and began to do repeat business. Hank Bokelman, my key customer farmer, remembered the Nayematsu name—a Japanese family I had grown up with—because of the chicken sexing. It was one of those weird and interesting coincidences a person comes across in life.

But things change, and they did for the Japanese chicken sexers. Chicken breeders developed layers whose sex was not determined only by the mysterious something or other that the Japanese knew about but no one else did; they developed layers whose sex could be determined by the configuration of feathers on the chicks' wings. And just like eight-track cassettes, demand for Japanese chicken sexers evaporated, and so did the presence of the Japanese men in Iowa.

By the time I came to Iowa, the chicken sexers were nearly a forgotten part of agricultural history, and there were no Japanese—or any other people of color—that I could see.

I lived in Iowa from 1976 to 1978. My neighbor across the street in Belmond, Iowa, was a World War II vet whose wife was an Italian war bride. They invited me for Thanksgiving dinner—the first time I had pasta served up with turkey. They had three daughters, one of whom looked like Sophia Loren. And then I met two Japanese war brides—one from World War II, who had lived in Belmond for thirty years, and one from the Vietnam War, who had only been there for a few years. And while they looked like me, our lives were so totally different, I couldn't relate.

The war brides were a generation in age apart. The World War II bride had raised her family in Iowa and seemed happy enough. Though she still spoke with a heavy Japanese accent, she had become American. Her children, "hapas" as we called half Japanese / half Caucasians, were all adults and on their own, launched and successful. Her husband was a good man, and they had found their peace. It was like looking at what could have been my own parents, had circumstances been different.

The Vietnam war bride was my age—her English was still rough, and the acculturation to America's breadbasket was in the throes of evolution. Her husband was a young man who seemed to have been attracted to the Asian woman mystique. He ruled the roost. She was subservient. And pregnant. She cooked me mochi (a rice flour treat), and we tried to communicate. I would have befriended her, but her husband, probably tired of struggling with the cultural divide, took a liking to me. I was all the things his wife looked like, but totally American. No language barrier, no cultural barrier, no "being different." But still exotic looking. He gave me the creeps. So no friendship developed, and our meeting was fleeting.

The third Asian person I ran into during my stay in Iowa was my greatest surprise and a precursor of the future. It was 1978, and I was making a sales call on a farmer in the Clear Lake area, and the young man came out carrying his little girl. She looked normal enough from the back in her winter snowsuit—but when she turned around, she had the little round head, round black eyes, and unmistakable Asian face. She was a three-year-old Korean adoptee—as cute as cute could be. And I saw how the landscape in Iowa would change over the course of the next few years as these overseas babies came to become part of the Midwest.

I was always searching for Japanese like me—sometimes called "bananas" because we are yellow on the outside and white on the inside. Complicate that with growing up Montanan. A banana tree in Montana. It could be a book.

And just to finish the story of the chicks, what I said earlier isn't totally true—egg-laying chickens do eventually get eaten for meat. At the end of their egg-laying careers, what's left of their bodies ends up in those savory cans of chicken noodle soup found in grocery stores everywhere.

The Dead-End Road

My first job was calling farm to farm directly, selling feed to the end users, the farmers. As I got more proficient, my responsibilities expanded to include managing a dealer network—small businesses who would buy from me and then resell to the farmers. I would make the rounds to my dealers, and once at the dealership, I was the "expert" on feed. Often, this meant that I would go out to farms with my dealers to make sales, troubleshoot, or introduce new products to established feeders.

In one particular area, there was no established dealer, and so the Bokelman family financially backed me in an effort to start a new dealership. Hank was the banker, and my job was to find someone interested in establishing a small business. As it turned out, my mentor, Roger Roan, had a brother who was in the feed business and was interested in going off on his own. So Robert, Roger's brother, became the Clear Lake Feed and Supply manager.

Robert was a rotund little man—middle-aged, with a wife and four or so children ranging in age from sixteen to twenty-five. He was the perfect gentleman at our first meeting, but as we got to know each other, he liked to play the lecherous old man.

Robert and I worked together a lot. We were building a business from scratch, so there was considerable missionary work that we had to do. In addition, he had to learn the Nutrena Feeds line, since he had been selling a competing brand.

We rented a small building and brought in inventory. We worked at fixing the place up and running ads in the local papers. I would sit him down to study the product lines. We drove from farm to farm making calls together.

During this whole time, Robert would tease me about taking our relationship beyond the "business" into the "personal." We would banter back and forth—my stand was always that I didn't mix business with pleasure, and his stand was on the order of "there's always a first time." We kept it in a light, joking manner, and I never felt threatened or unsafe.

Because we were almost always alone together, the opportunity was certainly present. Driving through the country, at any given time, a quick interlude could have taken place. Robert often pointed this fact out to me.

One afternoon, while we were making farm calls together, I was driving in an unfamiliar area. Robert was trying to figure out how to get to the next farm based on the open plat book on his lap. I was clipping down the section road and turned down a drive that seemed to be headed where we wanted to go. I drove for only a few seconds before it became clear that this was an abandoned farmstead, and it was obvious that it was not the road we wanted.

Before I could say anything, Robert looked up from his map, realized that it was the wrong road, and exclaimed, "Oh, *no, no, no*! This is wrong! We don't want to go here!"

I stopped the car, and Robert and I turned and looked at each other. We both burst into laughter, and Robert weakly regrouped and said, "Oh, *yes, yes, yes*! This *is* the right road! This is my golden opportunity!"

We must have sat in that car on that abandoned road for five minutes, laughing and laughing at Robert's missed opportunity and the irony that in spite of all the teasing and innuendo, he knew this was business and nothing more. It was two friends laughing at a private joke. It was realizing that our goals were the same—making the feedstore succeed—and that the goal superseded sexual, racial, and age barriers. For us to arrive at this point in our working relationship was new in the business world in 1978. Back in those days, the only time a man and a woman were in a car on a lonely country road was to neck in the back seat.

Clear Lake Feed and Supply survived for a while longer but finally closed its doors. The momentum we had generated together gradually dissipated. Robert operated some of the business out of his home for a while and then went into buying and selling silver and gold out of a storefront in Mason City.

But I can still see the narrow dirt road, smell the clean, fresh fall air, and feel the merriment rise in my heart as I think back on that day in the car with Robert and his missed "opportunity" with me!

Renwick

It's funny how our memory fades. I can remember the feedstore owner's name, Tiny. Of course, he wasn't tiny; he was, as is so often the case with a name like *Tiny*, just the opposite—a giant of a man, broad shoulders in a plaid shirt, on the downhill side of fifty. Maybe I remember his name because in addition to the feedstore, he owned Tiny's Tavern—the local watering hole that also served grilled and fried food during tavern hours.

But for the life of me, I can't remember the name of the man who managed the Renwick feedstore for Tiny—the guy I worked with one day a week for ten months. I can see him in my mind's eye—midforties looking sixty, teeth that begged for an orthodontist and a whitening session, taller rather than shorter, and trim from throwing fifty-pound feed sacks all day. John (not his real name, or maybe it was, since I can't remember) had an eighth-grade education, a heart of gold, and an outgoing, friendly, coarse kind of humor that endeared him to me and to the community. If he wasn't a volunteer fireman, he might as well have been; he was just that kind of guy.

John's wife was a local lady, with sandy-brown hair cut in a bob. Short, soft, kind. I can't remember her name, either, so maybe it was Sandy. She was one of the town beauticians.

My job with the Renwick feedstore and with John was to be the Nutrena Feeds expert. He and I would go from farm to farm, talking to the hog farmers about baby pigs, feeders, sows, and finishers and the best nutritional recommendations for them. John carried the relationships, since he lived and had grown up in the area with most of these landowners. I carried the feed nutritional knowledge. We would spend at least six hours together when I was in town, working the territory to build his business and in turn make Tiny more money.

At the end of the day making farm calls, I would often take John to the local café or to Tiny's and buy him dinner. It was part of my job, and I had an expense account for it. More times than not, Sandy would join us, and we three would sit at the Formica table for four, visiting about life, kids, and community while eating the evening special of roast beef, mashed potatoes and gravy, and green beans or corn. There'd be a square piece of cake, complimentary. Then I would drive the twenty-two miles back home to Belmond.

One day working with John, Tiny took me aside and told me Sandy had cancer, that she'd had it for quite some time, and it was bad.

I continued to make my visits. John and I didn't talk much about her diagnosis, but I knew she was going through treatments and had begun wearing a wig. I continued to invite them to dinner at the end of the day, but as her condition worsened, we quit going out, as it became too hard for Sandy to leave the house, and John went home to take care of her.

Her funeral was attended by everyone John and I had called on, most of the townspeople, and me. Renwick has a population of about 235 people today; back then, it was around 400. I'd say at least half of them were there to say good-bye to Sandy.

John wore a dark suit, shiny with wear, and a white shirt and patterned tie. I'd never seen him in a suit before, and it looked old enough to be the one he'd worn when he'd married Sandy. The funeral was sad as only funerals for people who have died too young are. John bantered with the guests as only a man in shock can do at his wife's memorial.

Our work routine continued for several more weeks. I would arrive around 8:30, we'd make farm calls most of the day, and then I'd offer to buy him dinner. The first few weeks after Sandy died, John wasn't up for dinner, which I understood. Then one night, he accepted my offer.

We walked into Tiny's Tavern and went to the same Formica table where we had always sat with Sandy. I saw the eyes turn to look at us as we walked in. I was pretty used to attracting attention walking into Iowa restaurants in the 1970s—a young, single Japanese woman was an unusual occurrence.

But this night was different. I felt the surreptitious glances, the low murmuring between couples, the knowing stare.

John, in his friendly, outgoing manner, seemed oblivious to the tension our appearance made, or maybe he just ignored it, but I couldn't shake the skin-crawling, blushing, emotional response I had to the room. They thought I was taking Sandy's place! I must have looked like a whore to them, even wearing the conservative tan slacks, long-sleeved button-down shirt, and Nutrena company jacket. And even though I didn't look the part, I felt the insinuation from every eye in the room.

John and I continued to work together, but our dinners were curtailed. He would ask if I was staying to eat, but I got busier—too busy to stay. He was grieving, lonely, scared.

I was just scared.

Scared of what people were saying or thinking. Scared to get involved. Not that I was afraid of getting involved romantically with John—he wasn't my type, he was too old, and he was, well, a feed salesman. I had my own prejudices to deal with. I was afraid of getting involved with his loneliness.

Shortly thereafter, I was transferred to a job that didn't include Renwick, Iowa, Tiny's Tavern, the feedstore, or John. Or whatever his name was.

Buying My First House on Sunset View

The influence friends have is incredible. I had always been pretty independent, going my own way, marching to my own drummer. I was usually the first, except when it came to buying a house. Enter Ruth Bokelman.

My friend Ruth owned a house in Charles City when I met her. She was an ag chemical salesperson—a job very similar to my own. It hadn't even dawned on me that maybe I could buy a house.

I had always admired Ruth for her sensible, solid ways—and a single woman, not yet twenty-five, buying a house in the 1970s was another sensible, solid investment, albeit a rare event.

Her home in Charles City, a growing and relatively prosperous town, was impressive. It could easily shelter a family of five. She gave up glitz for a sound buy of a very nice, three-bedroom, hardwood-floor home on the outskirts of town.

Using Ruth as my role model, I thought, *Okay, what should I be doing with my money?* Prior to meeting Ruth, I had been living a very single life—lots of trips, lots of buying stuff, and lots of rent. Buying a house wasn't even a consideration.

Suddenly, I was confronted with thinking about making a responsible investment.

I had read that buying a house was the largest investment the average person ever made. I was twenty-four and searching for ways to creatively finance a house I really didn't want.

My aunt in California was into real estate, and so I called her for advice. Unfortunately, my aunt was an expert in California real estate, not Iowa real estate. In short, she said she could have advised me if I had been buying in California, but she had no clue as to the real estate market in Iowa.

It wasn't her fault that she didn't give me advice. I had hoped someone would help me make a decision. That wasn't going to happen.

Many times, I have envied friends and peers because they had fathers that they could talk to about major life decisions. Their dads were sounding boards. And so many times it *was* the *dad* to whom they turned. I didn't have a dad, and the one person I had reached out to wasn't willing or able to lend me advice. I was on my own.

I had always envisioned myself living in a stylish, modern, up-to-date home. My choice for a first house was nothing like my vision; it was a small, three-bedroom (you see, Ruth had three bedrooms) house with a very bad addition hooked to the back end. It was all my creative financing would allow me to buy.

The most striking feature of the house was its color.

It was red.

And not just red—not that gentle giant red barn red but fire-engine, screaming, glowing, enamel red.

I mean *red*.

I often think that my father's poor health and early death have been fundamental to my success. I have had to make life decisions; I have had the monkey on my back; I have had to be my own counsel. And each time I had to make decisions by myself, things have been basically okay. I have had a high percentage of "right" answers.

And so was my house in Iowa, on Sunset View Lane. After six months, that fire-engine-red house netted me $10,000 cash—with a zero down payment.

Ah, creative financing.

Ah, inflationary times.

Ah, good decisions.

Thank you, Ruth.

Last Call Before Lunch

Days blended into each other—my goal was a minimum of eight face-to-face calls a day. That didn't seem very daunting until I was on my own and I had to pull in to at least sixteen driveways, walk to sixteen homes, knock on sixteen doors, and maybe bat .500 at catching a farmer at home. But the goal helped me pace my days and measure my success, and at the end of the day, I could say, "Good job," or not. There were many days that were *not*, but on average, I hit my mark. Early on, not only were those knocks on doors the first hurdle in my race to success, but even if the farmer were home, the next wall I'd hit would be the *no* at the end of the conversation.

I'd be a liar if I said it was easy or if it didn't cut to the core when the *no* came. It was a time when self-examination could have cut the legs out from under me. I was so afraid of failing—of not making enough sales calls, and in turn not making enough sales—and filled with the worry and stress of not knowing if success loomed on the horizon. I had to keep forging forward, or the reality I had created would have crumbled.

Sales was a numbers game. Make enough sales calls, and sooner or later someone would buy.

There weren't many memorable calls when a person makes so many. Each one blended into another, and every farmer started to look alike. I have a condition called *face blindness*; I have trouble recognizing people. The saying "They all look alike" is my reality. Faces all looked alike, or at least very similar, but my compensating strategy was to use clothes, hats, hair, and voices to identify people.

Farmers tended to have a way of dressing that I could distinguish, and of course, they would be on their farm places, which I could describe in detail. The Bokelmans' home was set back from the road on a rise. It had a longer drive with the lawn on the left and the livestock pasture and pens on the right. Big trees, probably oaks or maples, lined the drive; a machine shed sat directly in front of the parking area, the barn on the right, the white farmhouse on the left. A drive between the shed and the barn led to other outbuildings.

One day, I was making my calls and had been having an uneventful morning. It was about noon, but I had time for one more call. I decided to stop at a small operation run by a farmer and his wife.

I drove into the yard, which was hidden from the gravel road by lilac bushes and trees. Their white clapboard house was on the left and was reminiscent of the painting *American Gothic*. Put a Pioneer Seed cap and bib overalls on the guy in the painting, and you have a good idea of what the farmer looked like. I didn't know his wife and had only met her at the house door once when I was looking for her husband, but it would be safe to describe her like the woman from the painting. As I pulled in, I could see that the farmer was just beyond the house, grinding feed between his corncrib and barn. If I hadn't seen him, I would have stopped at the house and knocked, but since my target was right in front of me, I just drove on up.

This wasn't my first visit, so he knew who I was. We talked of the weather, the price of corn, the latest feed promotion. He was in the middle of finishing some hogs (meaning, putting on the last pounds before market) and wasn't going to be switching feed in the midst of it. After they were sold, he would "consider" buying from me. These were all facts I already knew. Farmers rarely, if ever, switched feed on their animals during a growing season—they wanted no blips to hamper the fastest weight gains possible. Change could put animals off feed for days, just because it looked or tasted different. But I wanted to be there after he sold this batch off and before he started the next bunch of pigs.

We said our good-byes, and I headed out the drive. I imagined that his wife was holding lunch for him, maybe irritated that he was being detained. I turned left and went into Clear Lake for lunch. It was only a two- or three-mile drive, and I went to a local café on Highway 18, run by a Clear Lake family. I had gone there frequently, and they knew me by sight. The restaurant was on the north side of 18, with a row of windows facing the highway running east-west. I sat and did paperwork, watched the cars driving by, and ate my lunch special. I finished the day with four more calls.

The next day began like the day before. I started my sales route where I had left off and continued my routine going door to door. On the second call, at the Holdens', we started in on the usual weather-and-corn conversations outside his barn, when Dave said, "Hey, did you hear about the guy down the road?"

I said, "No. What happened?"

"He went in to lunch and found his wife hanging."

I felt myself grow still, my ears buzzing and goose bumps rising from an unseen air-conditioning draft. All in a heartbeat. I verified that it was my *American Gothic* farmer.

Depression? I've heard depression can drive a person to suicide. Visions of the lady, peering out from behind the curtains, watching her husband talking to the lady feed salesperson. Did she have self-doubt? Did I look too confident, too threatening? Did I make her feel insignificant? Or was I egotistical to think I had any impact at all? She may have been swinging before I got there, before she began the noon meal.

Either way, I never went back. I couldn't face the farmer, couldn't imagine being a trigger to take him back to what must have been a horrific find. Not every fear has to be faced.

I drove past his place and never again turned in to his yard. It was the sale I wasn't going to get, now or ever.

Moving On

Two and a half years after being hired as a management trainee and living and working in Iowa, my number came up. At the time, career tracks were upwardly mobile, transfers every two years whether you needed them or not. There were lots of middle-management jobs to rise to, lots of lower senior-management jobs, senior management, and ultimately the C-suite. There were actually fewer C-level positions back in the day; there was the CEO (executive) and maybe a CFO (financial), but COO (operating), CMO (marketing), and CIO (information) didn't even exist in the same way. It was the true pyramid organizational model. And unlike today's business world, where the organization is touted as very flat, moving up was the plan. Being happy as a middle manager wasn't an option for me. I had my eyes set wherever up was. And that was pretty high in the org.

So the opportunity for me was the fast-track job in Kansas City. I would be following the footsteps of Steven Silverman, whom I had helped escape from Iowa. I would be moving from sales—trying to convince people to buy my goods and services—to buying ingredients for the feed plant. I didn't know what that meant exactly, but I didn't care. I was ready for the next step.

The winter before my transfer, I won a sales contest to Monte Carlo in Europe. The contest was for employees and their spouses and customers (large farmers and dealers) who met or exceeded buying targets. Nowadays, it would be nothing for a winner to take a significant other, but in those days, unmarried partners were not recognized. My boyfriend, whom I didn't really want to take anyway, stayed back. I took my mother. As I look back on that trip, I can't recall another woman who won, only women as spouses. I never thought of it as special at the time, although it was. There was only one other single person, a guy who came as a representative of his feed dealership in southern Minnesota. We ended up together primarily because we were the only single people but also because he was a dapper dude and very attentive. But most of my time was spent bonding with my mother, who had only a couple of years earlier become a widow.

It was a fabulous trip—the first trip to Europe for my mother, the second for me. Company-incentive trips were hot commodities back in the '70s and '80s. We traveled in fine, air-conditioned buses, stayed at the Loews Monte Carlo hotel, and had lavish dinners in the casino and neighboring villages. Incentive promotions were big business and an integral part of a salesperson's compensation; earlier, I had also won a microwave oven in a sales contest. Today, a microwave is something that anyone can buy, but back then, they were like magic.

The Bokelmans won the trip as my customer, and they were so gracious to my mother. Hank and Irma took her in like a sister. My mom had a curious interest in Europe—perhaps as a Japanese American trying to fit into the mainstream, her interests were driven by an attempt to internalize all things Western.

Thinking back on this trip, I also realize we were the only minorities. In my mind's eye, I don't see another person of color—black, yellow, brown. There were only a handful of youngish people—the aforementioned single man, a couple from a feedstore in Minnesota, and me.

Woman. Single. Young. Japanese. That described me on the trip to Monte Carlo, and it described who I was in Iowa.

It described me but did not define me.

I moved on from Iowa not in spite of who I was but because of who I was and what I had done. I didn't dwell on the differences but used them to propel me forward, up out of the sales job in Iowa to the merchandising manager job in Kansas City.

It was the perfect way out of the relationship I couldn't seem to quit. It placed the blame on the company and not on me. And it physically took us out of each other's comforting arms.

My sister Kathryn once told me the best way to recover from a boyfriend was to get a new boyfriend. That and the adage, "Out of sight, out of mind." I was cured.

PART 4

Stumbling

Tennis, Anyone?

I didn't know a soul in Kansas City when I was transferred there, and the other managers at work were okay, but they had their own lives away from work. Besides, the men were married, and the one man that wasn't married tried to sell me a watch one Saturday night from a display inside his jacket. The credit manager was a woman, but she was married and had no time for me. She was the queen bee and I the interloper. I really didn't have a life after work when I first arrived, but being the creative, take-charge-of-my-life person that I was, I got out and about.

One way I began meeting people was through tennis. I lived near Westport Plaza, a very trendy, upscale part of Kansas City. The plaza area had beautiful tennis courts at one end that were lighted for night play. These courts also had an enclosed area with a backboard so that if you didn't have a partner, you could hit against the wall, scope out the other lone players, and strike up a tennis game with someone.

I had pretty good luck finding tennis partners at the backboard—one time, it was a woman who could hit well against the backboard but could not hit well against a moving target; another was an average-level tennis player. I was no Chris Evert myself, so I couldn't complain.

One night after work, I was hitting against the backboard, not really intending to stay long enough to start up a game with anyone, when a man approached me and asked me to play a game. He was medium in height, his hair blond, bordering on white, and probably thirty years old. I had seen him hitting, but nothing special jumped out at me.

He was an excellent tennis player. It was apparent immediately that I was out of my league as his opponent. I love playing tennis against skilled players, and while I was enjoying the match, I wondered why such a good player would have asked me to play.

The man had an easygoing style, and after the match, we sat together on a bench and began to talk. We chatted about the usual tennis topics—where we learned to play, tips for improvement, equipment—and then we chatted about broader topics: where we were from, what we did for a living, where we worked.

Well, when we came to what I did for a living, my explanation was easy; I merchandised feed ingredients for a feed mill. When I posed the question to him, he said he was in the escort business.

Now, mind you, I was only three years out of college. I had grown up in a small town in Montana, attended a prestigious private college, and spent four months in Minneapolis (the Midwest's answer to cosmopolitan) before transferring to sell feed in Iowa. Here I was in Kansas City, chatting with a man who said he provided "companionship" for businessmen.

Honest to God, I did not know what an escort service was.

He proceeded to tell me that he thought I would be a good escort because I was friendly, attractive, and had a nice conversational way. He asked me if I would be interested in being a companion to see if I would like it. I could do it on the weekends and evenings, too.

Well, I had been a traveling salesperson. I knew that a person could get lonely on the road, and many times in my career, I had thought how nice it would be to share a meal with someone in a strange town rather than sit in a restaurant alone.

While I understood and sympathized with the premise that it gets lonely on the road, I wasn't looking for a second job, and I had a queer feeling inside that this wasn't a normal offer. I told him that I had a full-time job, and whereas I could see the demand for his service would be great, I could not see myself fulfilling that demand. We parted cheerfully and sincerely. I never saw him at the courts again, and shortly thereafter, I moved from Kansas City.

I trusted my gut.

Then a couple of years later in 1980, I saw the movie *American Gigolo*. It dawned on me what his escort service provided.

Two Girlfriends

I lived in Kansas City less than six months, yet two girlfriends that I met there will always have a place in my life. Neither knew each other, and frankly, I knew neither well.

THE PURCHASING CLERK

Deb Knutsen was the purchasing clerk who was supposed to work for me, the merchandising manager. Deb was slightly younger than I was. She had married and divorced quickly. College had not been an option right out of high school, so she was attending night school while she worked for us.

It was obvious that Deb was one smart cookie. I remember working with her on some inventories where a column of numbers in a ledger needed to add up and match the physical inventories. Her fingers flew over the keypad. She *never*, in the few months that I was there, made a mistake. I felt overwhelmed. Here I was, a Stanford graduate who had never taken the time or initiative to reconcile a checkbook, "managing" a clerk who could outmaneuver me on a calculator seven ways to Sunday.

But it was not only on a calculator that Deb excelled. She had a good grasp of the business and how it worked. She was street tough and had the moxie of a person who had taken a few hard knocks. Because of that, she was driven and knew that she wanted more out of life than her current position would allow. She also knew that she had to clear a few hurdles before she would be allowed to achieve her goals—thus the night school and the day job.

I quickly understood how secretaries and clerks through history could become frustrated and angry at the system that allowed young, inexperienced people like me to come in at management positions. The big difference was that the inexperienced new managers that preceded me were all men. I was the first new female manager.

Yet Deb was neither angry nor did she undermine my already-faltering efforts on the job. She instead recognized my strengths, and we enjoyed each other's company on a social level.

I did feel conflicted at times. Deb was a *clerk.* I, on the other hand, was a *manager.* Having never worked in an office before, I really didn't know if it was "acceptable" to go out on the town with nonexempt, hourly workers. But Deb was a leader, and I was, in this instance, a willing follower.

Well, paint the town we did. Deb was a lively, fun-loving, high-energy person. She was tall and attractive—barhopping was fun because we were both eye-catching, although for different reasons. We left work behind us and seldom talked about our jobs. We talked more about life, the future, where we were going from here.

When I transferred from the Kansas City feed plant, I lost touch with Deb. I heard about her through the Cargill grapevine.

Deb did finish night school and earned her degree. Cargill, good to its word, promoted Deb to be manager of a feed terminal outside of town. I am sure she was great at the job. She was so incredibly competent and smart. I had great faith that she would have a stellar career.

Her first Christmas after becoming a manager, Deb was driving home to Kansas City for the holidays and was killed in a car accident. I didn't know her family, but I called her mom. I wanted her to know that Deb had extended her hand in friendship at a time when I had no friends and that it touched me to the core. High potential, cut down in the prime of youth. I still feel the loss.

THE RAILROAD WOMAN

There have been times in my life when I felt I have made an impact, only to find that I had been a mere blip on the screen. Once in a great while, usually when I am looking the other way, I find that indeed, I have made a difference.

To this day, I do not know what it was about my daily work contact that made an impact on Susie Chambers, but I must have. Though we had never met face-to-face, we became buds for several years after I left Kansas City.

Susie worked for the Missouri Pacific Railroad. Every day, I would call her on the phone to get a listing of the railcars we had on track in the local yards, and if there were lost cars, she would help trace them for me. I pictured her as a washed-out blonde with a thin cigarette in one hand, a phone wedged between her shoulder and her ear, and a pencil and clipboard teetering on the corner of a messy oak desk. She talked tough like I imagined a railroad worker should talk. She had to be tough to be able to take care of herself and her customers. She would also have to be tough enough to fend off the lewd and suggestive comments of her all-male coworkers.

She took my calls and read back a list of boxcar numbers that were destined to our siding. If there were lost cars and we were in dire need for the ingredients in those cars, our conversations would become stressful and intense.

Susie was my contact to make things happen at the railroad. If I had cars on track, she could get them to us faster if we needed or slower if we didn't need them. Even though I was the customer, I was also at the mercy of Susie.

I never seemed to have a problem working with her, and normally when there were lost cars or delays, there were reasonable explanations. We tracked the cars daily so that we could pick up on delays or unusual positioning of cars before they became major problems.

It seemed to me that Susie was sincerely sorry to hear that I was leaving my job when she found out. She called me and inquired into my decision. Like so many other people had done when I had transferred or left school, she asked for my address and said she would keep in touch. I didn't really think much about her call, except to note that she really didn't need to do it and she did anyway.

I learned more about Susie after I left Kansas City. Much like Deb, Susie was working hard toward a goal in life—to become an engineer with the railroad. After I left Kansas City, Susie was accepted to the engineer's training program and moved to Omaha.

Many of her letters spoke to the issues of sexism and bias that she faced within such a totally male-dominated business as the railroads. She told me about her loves and disappointments. She dabbled in drugs to escape reality, when reality was too real. It seemed like even though our lifestyles and our approaches to life were radically different, we had much in common, since we were both striving to achieve leadership positions in our male-dominated organizations.

Susie, like Deb, was trying to infiltrate the organization from the bottom up. They were the fish swimming upstream. I entered the organization on a management training program, also trying to get upstream but starting considerably ahead—the advantage of four years of college.

We were women with the same goals, different entry points, similar struggles, parallel paths. We had sisters out there. They were just hard to find.

Another Blind Date

I loved Westport Plaza. There was plenty of action, lots of young people, and a comfortable apartment in a safe neighborhood. My friendly landlady and landlord kept an eye out for me to make sure I was okay.

On one of the first nights at the apartment, I heard the most unusual banging and tapping and shuffling coming from the apartment above me. I was intrigued by the noise. It wasn't a fight. It wasn't sex. But it was a rhythmic, loud, solid sound. It wasn't drums, but it was like drumming. I couldn't figure it out.

And there were many Japanese at the apartment! These turned out to be real Japanese, from Japan. I knew a handful of Japanese words and phrases. (I had barely passed my basic Japanese language class at Stanford. The instructor told me some people just didn't get the hang of it.) So it was with humor and delight that I found out that the drumming and beating I was hearing came from my Japanese neighbors who worked at the local teppanyaki Japanese restaurant, the Gojo!

That explained a lot—teppanyaki restaurants are the ones where the chef cooks on a large hot grill, and cuts, chops, flips and pounds the knives, forks, pepper shakers and ingredients before the captive audience. The guys were practicing on the floors above me! My nice landlady introduced me to one of my upstairs neighbors—and set me up on a blind date!

So we went to—where else?—the Gojo Restaurant on the young man's night off. And ate Japanese food. So picture this: a trim little Japanese chef who speaks no English; a big-boned, Montana farm girl who looks Japanese but knows only a handful of Japanese words (mostly bad ones and food items), feeling awkward and fat.

No, the date went nowhere fast, but I did get a good meal out of the deal and a Gojo sake set.

The Lunch Ritual

Coming out of field sales into an office was like a Soviet coming to America. There was something new and unfamiliar around every corner. I was learning as I was doing. The only desk job I had ever had was as an intern at the local Hardin, Montana, weekly newspaper, where I wrote the society column for one week and part of the time I straightened up shelves of paper due to a lack of "real" work. The Kansas City job was a handful by itself, reorienting myself from being a seller to being a buyer, but the social mores in the office were all new. I understood how a person worked from home and traveled farm to farm in an automobile, but I had never had the daily grind of office work.

I came into the office setting not as the low man on the totem pole (well, I was from a management perspective), but there was the support staff (all women, of course) who were lower in the pecking order. The credit manager had her own office and was the only other woman manager. The rest of the staff consisted of two older women and three younger women in clerical support roles. It felt so strange, as they had so much experience and they clearly knew the office side of business better than I.

One secretary was a lovely-looking young woman who, according to the other ladies, was meeting a trucker for lunch and "exercise" in his tractor cab sleeper. The other was my friend Deb Knutsen. Then there was the temporary part-timer who wore skintight sweaters and not much underneath, which set off her ample bust and areolas in a most unsavory way. I wasn't sure what she did in the office.

The two older ladies were matronly and seasoned—they had been in the office since time began. They knew where all the bodies were buried, and they didn't take crap from anyone. Looking back, they were the ones who kept the place running smoothly.

And everyone seemed to know a lot about everyone else and *talked* about it!

Then there was the coffee ritual. Certain people made the coffee and cleaned out the pots. Others (me included) drank the coffee but never had to make it or clean up afterward.

There was some magic surrounding office work. I had an in-box and an out-box. Things appeared and disappeared from these boxes. I had no clue what happened to the stuff I put into my out-box. Like, where did it go? Who touched it after it left my box? And what was okay to put into the out-box, and what was taboo? Or was there anything taboo? It may seem odd that something as simple as an out-box would stymie a person, but that was just how naïve and new I was to business and also how new it was for a woman to be served within an office. What the men took for granted was all foreign turf to me. In the past, I had taken my cues from the men I worked with—it had been their jobs to show me the ropes. In this group, it was every man (and woman) for himself.

The lunch ritual was for managers only. Every day at noon, the managers (those with offices) gathered and went to a restaurant not far from the office. We would sit at the same table, pass the breadsticks, and order off the menu. Every day, we would then discuss baseball, football, other miscellaneous sports and business.

The traffic manager was a woman, but as I said before, she was no ally. She and I never became close, and our chance for interaction was limited to lunch.

Why the lunch ritual stands out in my mind, I'll never know. Perhaps it was the one venue where I felt equal to everyone else. Perhaps it was the artificial social group—none of us would have elected to go to lunch with each other, given a choice.

Perhaps it was the lack of a choice—*all managers eat lunch together*—that made the lunch ritual so absurd.

As a salesperson, I did not enjoy eating alone all the time, but it was part of the job. Since that time, I have come to recognize that lunch rituals have origins in the reluctance of individuals to dine solo. Most people hate eating alone. And the lunch ritual is different in every group I have ever been in.

I didn't last very long in this first office job. Where the sales job felt at least familiar and suited my personality, from the very first day at this merchandising job, I was like a fish out of water. I went from selling to buying. I went from warm-and-fuzzy sales, to a screw-or-be-screwed mentality to get the rock-bottom price.

But I learned a lot from that job. One weekend, I went into work while everyone was gone, and I wandered around. I ventured away from my office to the basement, the bowels of the building. I was too timid to ask the ladies to show me around during the day, but I was fine wandering around on my own. It was there that I found the mail room, where the stuff in my out-box went. The place was cold, institutional—it looked like a movie set from the 1930s. Oversized walnut desks, managers' offices on the outside walls, each with a window to the outside world and half-glass interior wall, to see the pool of secretaries' and clerks' desks, bullpen-style.

The building itself was in the stockyard area of Kansas City, Missouri, with the feed plant set behind it. One of the oddest things to me was that we never ventured out to the production area. We managers never got our hands dirty. We stayed in our offices, phone to our ears, dealing with our suppliers over the phone.

No wonder this job was never going to work for me. And now, looking back, I realize that the part-time woman in the tight sweater served a dual purpose: her nebulous job and the vicarious pleasure of the men in the office—which totally went over my head at the time.

Derailing

In every organization, there are jobs or locations that are considered the "plums." The plums are highly visible, fast-track, brass-ring jobs. My Kansas City assignment was considered a plum. I got there by being very successful on my sales territories.

In Kansas City, I went from selling to purchasing virtually overnight. Cargill's philosophy at the time was to give their management trainees extensive exposure to the feed business, usually starting in sales, moving to merchandising, then to administrative management, and then up to district management. The career path was pretty clear-cut, and I assumed success at each step was required even though that didn't seem to be the case for Steve Silverman.

But Kansas City just wasn't meant to be my career stepping-stone.

One of the first days in Kansas City, I was cruising around the suburbs, getting myself acclimated, and I got a moving violation—I ran a stoplight. To add insult to injury, I couldn't just pay the ticket; I had to show up in court, midweek, in downtown Kansas City. That meant time away from my job—never a problem when I was in sales. Then I could just plan my work around a midweek, midday appointment. In this first office job, I had to ask for permission to take time off to appear in court. I felt like my absence from work was a gaping hole in the day.

Then I got called on the carpet for expensing a meal for my mother. She had come to town to help me move in to my new apartment, and since I did not yet have my household goods, we ate out. My new boss informed me that this was not acceptable, and even though married people could expense family dinners, I could not expense a meal for my mother. I tried to explain that she was helping me so that I could be at work while my furniture arrived, but to no avail. The rules were clearly not in my favor, and no one was willing to cut me slack.

And then Steve Silverman, who was assigned to train me, was the young man whom I had helped out of a jam in Iowa a few months earlier. Instead of creating a bond, this former association seemed to be a source of embarrassment to the man and the first of many sore points between us. He confided in me again—that his first-choice college was Stanford and he had been rejected. Ouch!

The objective of the merchandising manager's job was to buy ingredients for the feed plant at the cheapest price in a timely manner, so that the plant did not shut down for want of ingredients. This group didn't consider there might be other reasons to buy besides the cheapest price. From the first day on the job, I felt out of sync, out of step, otherworldly. There was no *flow* for me.

There was a sign hanging in the office that said, "Screw or Be Screwed," with a graphic visual (let your imagination go wild) to illustrate it. The Stanford reject who was training me, nicknamed Little Napoleon by ingredient suppliers, was indeed a tyrant who relished making a supplier squirm. The district manager, our boss, was a man in his early thirties who smoked a cigar, spoke seldom, and reminded me of a heftier Humphrey Bogart in a gangster movie.

I was young, inexperienced, and new at facing a situation where people seemed to want me to fail. In the past, I had supportive bosses, and I ultimately won over those few individuals who were initially jealous of the success I enjoyed.

I found the purchasing job difficult to do within the framework of the office atmosphere. I had always done business on a personal level. Here I was being asked to take the personality out of the job and focus on price, price, price. Past favors meant nothing—that was then, and this was now. Each buy/sell transaction with a supplier was to stand alone, out of context of the day, month, or year.

A good buy was expected, and *good* meant *cheap*. There was no praise, no recognition. A poor buy was berated and held up for all to see. And in those glass-walled offices, *all* could see.

I lost weight in Kansas City. Like most young women, I felt like I was overweight, and the stress and pressure I was under in this merchandising job made me lose my appetite. In addition, I never enjoyed cooking, so the sales job fit me just fine—I could eat out every day. In this office job, I had to fend for myself for breakfast and supper—instant weight control.

I wasn't only losing weight. I was losing self-esteem. Little Napoleon took delight in berating me after a trade. He would stand over me and shout! The clerks, secretaries, and other managers would look furtively at us and then quickly look away.

I never felt any trade was good enough. Every buy could have been at a better price, a different volume, timed better, done another way. I never quite knew what I was doing well, what I was doing wrong. Everything felt wrong, and Little Napoleon reinforced that feeling.

Every morning, the merchants and suppliers played a market information sharing game. They would give me their best guess what the market would be doing that day, based on activities planned or that had happened the previous day. I would do the same, although my relatively short time on the job limited the amount I could contribute.

One morning, after I had been royally chastised by Little Napoleon, I got on the phone and talked to a grain supplier. Through innuendo and mock innocence, I got him to believe the market had taken a dive and he would be lucky to unload his ten railcars of product at sixty-four dollars per ton. The actual market was more on the order of seventy-five dollars per ton. We struck a deal and set up a delivery schedule for the ten cars.

After hanging up the phone, I reported my success to Little Napoleon. He was actually excited! He was pumped! He praised my buy! It was one of the best buys ever made. I had misled the supplier and bought product far under the market price! I had been the screwer, not the screwee.

It brought me no joy.

Two days later, I was sitting in my glass-walled office. Little Napoleon was yelling at me for some infraction. I told him I had had enough yelling, and I walked out of my office, into the district manager's office, and resigned. I picked up my briefcase and purse, then walked resolutely out of the Nutrena Feeds Kansas City office. I never returned.

I called my mother and told her I had quit. She was shocked and worried. What would I do? Where would I go?

But I wasn't worried at all. I was relieved. I didn't realize what a strain that merchandising job had been on me emotionally and physically. I had enough money in the bank to tide me over for a couple of months. I was confident I would find another job—sooner or later. The critical issue was not getting a job at this point; it was that I had made the decision to get out of a job situation that was intolerable.

I did not feel pumped up or good about screwing suppliers. I had just come from a sales job—I would have hated to have had customers treating me the way I was supposed to treat my suppliers. There had to be a win-win kind of relationship, and that seemed to be unacceptable at the Kansas City office.

If I knew then what I know now, I could have stayed in that job. I would have outlined the terms I would work under. I would have been more assertive. And upon reflection, maybe yelling and berating me was Little Napoleon's way of validating his own self-worth by undermining mine.

Would have, could have, should have. The beauty of maturing and gaining life experiences is that we reduce the number of would haves, could haves, and should haves.

The beauty of books like this is that one does not need to live through the experience to learn from it.

PART 5

Reverting to a Crawl

How I Got to Denver

When I told my mom over the phone I had quit, there was this incredible silence on the other end of the line, and I realized she must have been afraid for me.

I was not afraid.

I was incredibly relieved, and I felt better than I had felt in months.

I contacted an employment firm and told them I was looking for a position, and when I told them my qualifications, they were most anxious to work with me.

There was money in the bank and plenty of promise—no regrets, no second guesses. People from Cargill called me to find out what had happened. Senior managers asked about the conditions I worked under at Kansas City. I told the truth (partly) that the job did not work out. I did not disclose that Little Napoleon shouting at me was the straw that broke my resolve. It was not in my nature to lay blame anywhere; I just took the responsibility on. I had a good track record with Nutrena, and they quickly tried to find something else for me. They suggested a feed sales job in North Carolina—*ha*! Why would I want that? I knew I could sell feed, and that was not what I wanted to do for the rest of my life. Thanks, but no, thanks.

I went to Minneapolis to interview with the public relations department, thinking that it might be a career path I might like to pursue. They did not want to pursue me.

Coincidentally, my "little sister," Tiina from the AFS exchange program, came from Finland the following week. My mother arrived in Kansas City shortly after that.

We all drove back to Montana together, and I began a one-month vacation the likes of which I had not had ever in my life.

Because of my guest from Finland, we had the perfect excuse to travel around the state of Montana. Tiina, my mother, and I hopped in the car and toured Yellowstone National Park, Virginia City, and points in between. It was a wonderfully relaxing few weeks.

I knew that I would have to eventually find a job. I still had the apartment in Kansas City. But I didn't worry. I needed the break, and it was welcomed.

One day, while I was in Montana, I received a phone call from Bob Hauser, one of the executives with Nutrena Feeds who had always taken an interest in my career. Bob was sincerely concerned about my rapid departure from the Kansas City office and Nutrena. He wanted to know if I would be interested in talking to a gentleman in the Salt Division about a sales job that they had in Denver. Cargill Salt had recently acquired Leslie Salt based out of the San Francisco Bay Area, and I would be the first Cargill salesperson in the newly acquired company.

I was lukewarm on another sales job, since it would be a lateral or downward move for me, but I was *hot* for Denver. I had even thought about Denver as a possibility after Kansas City in my many what-if scenarios.

I called the man in Salt and set up interviews in Minneapolis.

My interview with the Salt Division took place the day after one of the worst salt mine disasters in their Louisiana mine. The miners had hit a pocket of methane gas, which is highly flammable, and there was an explosion. The president of the company, who was on my list of interviewers, waved at me on his way out the door to catch the company jet to go to Breaux Bridge, Louisiana, the disaster site. Several men had been killed in the explosion.

Still, I was able to talk to four or five managers, one of whom was a woman, Coco Summers, the personnel manager. Bob Lee, whose dad had been the president of Nutrena Feeds before it had been sold to Cargill, had heard about me through Bob Hauser and was also on the list. When

I had been a trainee with the company, I had worked with a salt salesman in Oklahoma City. The playboy type, ex-football player was one of the reasons that I had not chosen the Salt Division back then. Now, with the prospect of living in Denver in front of me, the Salt Division looked much, much better. Cargill Salt was going to pay to move me to the city I wanted to go to anyway—how propitious was that?

Coco Summers stands out in my mind because she was the first woman I had ever interviewed with. The only female manager in Nutrena Feeds corporate was also the HR manager, but she was never on an interview schedule.

I left Minneapolis knowing I had the job in Denver. More firsts: First woman. First Japanese American. My hiatus was coming to an end. I was ready for a new chapter. I felt strong. I was back on the rise.

Two Bobs stand out in my mind from this episode—Bob Hauser, the Nutrena executive whose informal networking kept me with the company; and Bob Lee, who became my mentor and whose influence still affects me.

Sunset in Kansas

My worldly possessions were packed in a moving van, and my car was loaded down. All signs were pointed west. I said a fond farewell to my landlord and landlady in Kansas City and headed to my new home in Colorado. My stay in Kansas City had been too short to reinvest the financial gain I had realized on the sale of my Iowa house, so I bought a town house in Westminster, Colorado. I planned on staying awhile. It was a stylish split-level—two bedrooms up, one bedroom down, with room for my office, a living room, and a kitchen.

I left Kansas City at midday. By evening, I was on the plains of Kansas. I kept driving steadily, anxious to start fresh. As the sun began setting and the shadows grew long, I looked out on the hayfields to my right and to my left. The sun was setting straight ahead of me, the globe blinding. The huge round hay bales cast long, mountainous shadows in the golden hue. My car sped along, not willing to stop long enough to capture the awesome landscape in a photograph. The cool evening air was pungent with the smell of alfalfa. This was nothing like I had imagined the flatlands of Kansas to be. The fresh field smell, the warm copper glow, the hum of the highway—it all filled me with promise.

It was a wonderful prelude to Colorado and the Rockies and the life flowing before me.

Trust, Luck, Love

Transferring to a new city is a cleansing and invigorating experience. Naturally, it is sad to leave old friends and coworkers, but the anticipation of new friends and coworkers is offsetting.

I looked forward to moving to Denver for several reasons, first and foremost because Denver was a skier's paradise. Second, it was a business and cultural center for the West, and my family in Montana frequently visited Denver. And Denver was the first place I had ever moved to where I actually *knew* people. They were mostly extended family connections, all older, but at least familiar.

But I still went out seeking new and interesting people my age. My luck at venturing out before had been good, and I had no reason to believe this transfer would be any different.

I have always enjoyed sports, but many sports require partners of some sort. I joined a tennis club and met a woman originally from Kansas City, and we began to hang out. I had a college buddy who drew me into a circle of skiers. Aerobics had not yet become a national pastime, so there were no classes to join. I ended up going to the Westminster Health and Fitness Center, in the community where I lived. This facility had a weight room, which was perfect—no partner needed to lift weights.

As chance would have it, a young man began talking to me. He was nice enough looking, and he was really physically fit. He said he worked out at the center quite regularly, and he looked it. One thing led to another, and we ended up making a date for the following Saturday night.

Fred was a fun guy. He was outgoing, personable, and intelligent. He could be an excellent listener. I was quite taken by him, and we began seeing each other regularly. Fred said he was in graduate school at Boulder and worked a backhoe to earn money. He was studying to be a psychologist. His family all lived close and seemed like humble, hardworking folks. Though his parents were divorced, it did not seem to affect Fred at all. He was basically a stable kind of guy. Or so I thought.

Our dating continued. We became serious. I was on the road most of the week, so it was nice to have a social life on the weekends. We would do inexpensive things, since he was a poor student, like cruising through the mountains seeing the sights.

One day, Fred said he wanted to share something with me. He got out his bankbook and showed me the balance brought forward in the check register. A balance of over $100,000.

Wow. He didn't seem like a person with money in the bank. He led an austere lifestyle, drove a beater of a car, and never went out extravagantly. He explained that he had begun a small business delivering liquid calcium chloride to farmers for weight in their tractor tires in Ogallala, Nebraska. One thing led to another, and he bought in to the backhoe business and had several crews working in the Denver metro area. He said he hesitated to tell people about his hidden wealth, because too often he was pursued because of the money and not his inner self.

That was all okay with me. I could believe how some people were attracted to money. I never looked for money, because I have always felt I could live the lifestyle I wanted by my own earnings. Besides, if I had been one who dated for money, I wouldn't have dated Fred, since he, for all intents and purposes up to that point, was a poor student. And his story didn't seem so far-fetched. I was familiar with using calcium chloride for weight in tires. I just didn't know a person could rack up that much money delivering it.

Suddenly, after his revelation, our casual conversations on marriage took on a new light. I was no longer wonderful but had faults that were examined and critiqued. One of those faults turned out to be religion.

I had never considered myself to be a religious person, nor had religion ever been a barrier in my life. When I was a child, I'd gone to the First Congregational Church in Hardin. I quit going on my sixth birthday, when I refused to go to Sunday school. I was too shy to get up in front of the class to put six pennies into a cup in honor of my birthday.

My mother had been raised in the Shinto religion. She and her mother had decided to raise us kids as Christians because there was no Shinto church available. They felt some religion was better than nothing. As a result, I never thought much about religion or the impact it may have had on my life.

Until now. Suddenly, Fred—the fun-loving, witty guy that I had met months before—turned into a judgmental, critical, unforgiving man.

Fred belonged to the Church of Christ. I figured, no problem; the Congregational Church had merged with the United Church of Christ, right?

I was right on the merger part, but it turned out that the Church of Christ and the United Church of Christ were significantly different in their philosophies. The Church of Christ that Fred attended was a fundamentalist group that had some extremely conservative outlooks. Fred gave me some books to read on religion as he espoused and told me that he would expect his wife and children to follow the doctrines in the books.

Fred fled to Montana, but not before entangling my family in his web. He stayed with my sister and sister-in-law. He met up with family friends in Bozeman. He stayed at the Baxter Hotel. I realized later that he had picked a lock on a room and stayed without paying.

Fred was the worst. I trusted him, and my family trusted him. I loved him and gave my heart away. I read the books he gave me and realized that I could compromise on many issues, but I had some deep-rooted spiritual beliefs that I never knew I possessed. They were issues that I could not compromise on.

Fred was also one of the best experiences in my life. He forced me to assess my beliefs, and the experience made me realize that I am a very spiritual person, although not a religious one. He lied to me about his money. (Really? I was so stupid.) It turned out that he was caught stealing from a grocery store—one of probably many similar transgressions. I learned how trusting, naïve, and blind I had been in falling in love.

Fred gave my sister a couple of paintings—they might have been stolen. My sister-in-law said after he stayed with them, she saw footprints in the attic dust and wondered what he had been looking at or for.

Luck was on my side, perhaps. No one in my family or close to me was physically or financially hurt. I never married Fred, and I was able to terminate the relationship, albeit after many tears and sleepless nights.

One Thursday night, I returned from a multiday sales trip on the road. The sliding door to my town house was ajar. I walked in hesitantly and saw a few drawers in the kitchen open. The upstairs bathroom light was on, so I moved quietly toward the light. I could smell a hint of perfume—strange because I seldom wore perfume, being sensitive to fragrances. I turned to the right and entered my bedroom and then saw my jewelry box open, my closet doors ajar. Inside the closet, I had a black locked trunk pushed back under the clothes. The lock had been jimmied open. I had nothing of value in it, but the contents of old clothes and blankets had been gone through and left in a jumble.

My jewelry box, meager though it was, held four items of value—an 18-carat pearl ring and an 18-carat watch—both given to me by relatives in Japan—a 14-carat solid-gold moose necklace, and a real emerald ring that my jeweler uncle Tom Kubo had given me. Only those four items were missing. None of the 10-carat rings or necklaces were gone, and of course none of the costume jewelry. The thieves knew what they were doing.

I called the police, and they came straight away. They filled up my small town house with their dark blue uniforms and wide black belts with guns and radios attached. One guy dusted the place for fingerprints, probably more for my peace of mind than actually thinking they would find the culprit. The dusting left black smudges on knobs and door handles. Nothing ever came of it.

I considered hitting some of the pawn shops in the area, but I didn't even know where they were, let alone how to start notifying them. I just let it drop.

I will always wonder if Fred broke in, his final attack. I will never know. The damage could have been much, much worse.

Harassment in Wyoming

Part of my Salt territory covered eastern Wyoming. I loved driving through Wyoming. What some people might see as barren and useless, I found barren (yes) and beautiful. I loved the wide-open spaces and the rancher mentality. It reminded me of Montana.

I was comfortable calling on ranch supply stores. They would buy salt blocks and range mineral for livestock. But I really enjoyed supplying salt to the booming oil industry that was sprouting around the state.

I put on thousands of miles working Colorado and Wyoming. I drove the previous Salt salesman's car—a flashy baby-blue Ford Thunderbird with a white vinyl landau top. Put a young, long-haired Japanese chick in it, and it shouted, "Hot!"

One of my routes took me from Cheyenne to Laramie and then up to Wheatland, on the way to Casper. The route between Laramie and Wheatland was a paved two-lane road that cut across some rugged terrain. Along that road were several uranium mines.

If a person has never driven through desolate areas of the West, it is hard to imagine the isolation and the distance between points of civilization. Unlike driving through metropolitan areas, where drivers ignore each other, drivers in the West wave at each other because passing another vehicle is so rare.

So it was a welcome sight to see a pickup gaining on me on that cut-across road up to Wheatland. In the back of my mind, I saw it as insurance in case I had car trouble.

I thought nothing of it when the pickup truck passed me. I waved without thinking.

I knew immediately something was amiss when the pickup slowed and forced me to pass. I took note that there were three young men in the vehicle.

When the pickup passed me again, I kept my eyes straight ahead. I certainly didn't wave! I began thinking of escape plans and what-if scenarios. Suddenly, the isolation and desolation of the region struck me. I had no escape. It was me, the pickup, and the road.

Looking back, I should have tried to get a license plate number. It should have been easy enough to do, since we passed each other several times. I remember, though, that it took considerable power of concentration to stay steady and calm.

The uranium mines were approaching. There were several along the road. The pickup had quit passing me, although it stayed on my tail. I said to myself I would turn in to the next mine if they began to pass again.

To my relief, the pickup turned in to the first mine and kicked up dust as it sped up the dirt road. I continued up to Wheatland.

When I got to town, I was shaken. First thing, I called my boss. I needed to talk to someone and vent my anxiety. Brian listened sympathetically. He then suggested something that made my heart speed up. He suggested that I carry a gun.

I shouldn't have been surprised at the idea, but I was. I remember when my sisters first moved away from home, my dad gave them a gun for their trailer home. In fact, they once had an intruder in their trailer, and though they never used the gun, it was there in case they needed to use it.

The gun rack in the pickup window in Montana was commonplace. We had one in our farm pickup, too. My parents slept with a gun under the mattress. Hunting shotguns and rifles were in the gun rack at home.

But *I* did not own a gun, nor had I ever felt like I should have one . . . until this episode.

At the next sales meeting, I asked several of the other salesmen whether they carried guns while they were on the road. Quite a few did.

I would like to think that the three young men in the pickup were outsiders. That they were in Wyoming for the fast buck that the mining industry could give them. I would like to think that they weren't home-grown boys, who would have been raised with more respect for the isolation and desolation of the West, and that harassing and scaring a solo woman on a solitary road was in bad form.

I will never know.

I never began carrying a gun. I didn't feel it was the right answer for me.

This era preceded the abductions, kidnappings, and rapes that have happened in this area since then. I dodged many bullets during this time of life, figuratively. Terrible things could have happened, but they didn't. And it's not to say the next solitary woman driving a back road of America won't be victimized. It just didn't happen to me.

And that's not to say a gun wouldn't be a solution to the problem. It just wasn't the right solution for me.

Scottsbluff Blind Date

In Torrington, Wyoming, my customer was a state senator whose job in "real" life was running a feed mill. Between Torrington and Scottsbluff is a small town called Morrill, Nebraska, which was dominated by a grain-and-feed business named Galt Feeds.

Naturally, I called on Galt as I called on all the feed businesses in my territory.

The senator/buyer at Galt was a born-and-bred border man (he lived on the border of Wyoming and Nebraska) who had worked at the company for twenty years. We got along well; he was curious about my background but was too polite to ask much until my third or fourth call on him.

At that time, he cautiously asked me about my marital status. He explained that he had grown up in the valley (the North Platte River runs through Torrington to Scottsbluff), and a Japanese family farmed next to where he lived. He had known them all his life and in fact had gone through primary and high school with them.

Well, it so happened that the people he had grown up with now had an eligible son, and he wondered whether I'd be interested in dating this eligible son.

It never failed to surprise me when I was offered a blind date. It didn't happen that often, but it was often enough. At any rate, this man *did* know an eligible Japanese American, and true to form, I was willing to take a chance and meet this man.

The buyer asked me where I was headed, and I said, "Scottsbluff." That was perfect, because that was where Dennis was living. He set me up.

That night, I met Dennis Morimoto, and we went out on the town in Scottsbluff. It was a pretty quiet evening, and we had lots of time to talk.

We got past the "Where do you work?" "Where do you live?" "Isn't it nice of the buyer at Galt to introduce us?" "Where'd you go to college?" When we got to the part about "Where did you grow up?" this Dennis person stopped short.

"Hardin? Montana?" he repeated after I had told him where I had grown up.

"Yeah, Hardin. It's a small town in eastern Montana, just north of here a ways."

"Uh, I think I know some people from Hardin," he said. "My aunt lives there. Lois Mikami."

I looked at him incredulously.

"So," I said carefully, "your cousins are Steve, Tommy, and Kenny?" *Unbelievable*, I thought. *What a small world.*

And how embarrassing! I knew in an instant that word would get back home before I could return to Denver.

The evening progressed rather stilted after that point. Dennis was a nice enough guy, and his cousins and I had grown up together. But our friendship was doomed to remain just that—friends—since both of us felt uncomfortable and somewhat embarrassed that our blind date had turned out to be anything but blind. We both enjoyed the sheer coincidence. It made us both laugh, and at the same time, it made us feel guarded. It felt like our families had suddenly materialized and were sitting in the back seat, whispering behind Japanese dance fans.

I am not sure who may have called family in Hardin first—Dennis's mom or me, but word got around quickly that Emmy's daughter and Lois's nephew had a blind date in Scottsbluff.

I laughed then as I laugh now remembering how awkward it was but also how wonderfully connected it felt in the long arms and comfort of family across the miles.

Merlin the Dog

I had been making the rounds in Colorado and Wyoming for about a year. My business was building, I had seen most of the sights along the way, my record keeping was under control, and my sales territory coverage had fallen into a regular rhythm and pattern. The big push was behind me, and I was cruising.

So what could entertain me on the road, keep me company during the day, and not get in the way of business?

A dog, I thought. Man and, hopefully, woman's best friend.

He had to be a house-type dog; I lived in a town house.

He had to be small enough to travel 60 percent of the time.

He had to be obedient.

And cute.

And smart.

A dog with a pedigree, but not too uppity.

Oh. And cheap.

My search began. I had more requirements for a dog than a husband. Whoever said the pursuit is as much fun as the trophy was right. I followed the ads in the paper faithfully. Dog books and conversations about dogs occupied my spare time.

I had never looked for a purebred dog before. All our farm dogs were mutts, picked up in various and sundry ways or as pups dumped down abandoned roads. This was a new experience.

My first boyfriend, Sven, and his family had an airedale.

An airedale is a large, black-and-tan terrier.

Too big for my purposes.

But there was a mini-version of the airedale that caught my eye: the Welsh terrier. The Welsh terrier is a miniature schnauzer-sized airedale. They are a wire-haired dog, which meant he would not shed like a collie. A book described the breed as flamboyant, happy, and faithful, which sounded perfect to me.

I kept my eye on the classified ads in the paper. I knew my dog would show up sooner or later on the pages of dogs and cats for sale.

Sure enough, a breeder's ad hit the print. I was at their home the same evening.

Welsh terriers seemed perfect in all respects except for the price. A purebred at the time ran from $250 to $500 or more, depending on the sire and dam. That did not qualify under my need for a cheap dog.

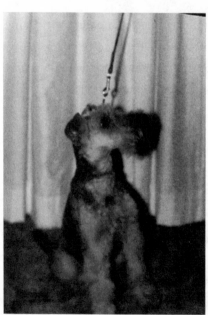

The woman who was selling the puppies had three to choose from—a roly-poly male and two feisty females.

I had known I wanted a male dog for no better reason than I'd thought I'd get along better with a male, but the price for the male was firm. She wasn't about to negotiate.

As I was getting ready to leave, I saw a scruffy little pup come out of a boxed area. He was smaller than the rest and had a soulful look in his eyes.

So we struck a deal on that "defective" dog—fifty dollars—no money-back guarantees. And I drove away with my new dog.

If I knew then what I know now (haven't I said that before?), I would have driven away with the fat, healthy dog. But at the time, all I could see was a warm little scruffball who needed me to feed him and nurse him to grow into a strong, healthy companion.

Mary Stewart had a trilogy on Merlin the magician that I'd just read, and my dog's breed, with its bearded cut, black-and-tan body, and English heritage, was the perfect namesake. So Merlin it was.

Merlin was not really smart, but he did learn a few basic skills. He knew that his basket was where he was supposed to sleep. He had one side of the back seat of my car for traveling. He was not allowed to wander around while I was driving.

This much he could conform to while I was in attendance. As soon as I would leave the car to go in to a call, Merlin would take the driver's seat and drool all over the place. It turned out there was something wrong with his tongue, so drinking and drooling were unresolved issues.

Two sales calls stand out in my mind. One concerned the state legislator from Torrington, Wyoming.

I had gotten to know this gentleman pretty well during my regular calls on him. In addition to the blind date, he referred me to a trucker who distributed salt in the area and who later became one of my best accounts. I had lunch at the legislator's home.

Naturally, I was anxious for him to meet my new best friend, Merlin.

Merlin had been sleeping in his little basket in the back seat for hours. I roused him to go into the legislator's feedstore. The poor puppy was groggy but anxious to get out.

I walked him down the block to get his blood flowing and also to let him relieve himself if need be. He didn't. We entered the feedstore.

The legislator was out (thank goodness, in retrospect), but his office staff was appropriately oohing and aahing over the dog. Merlin sniffed the floor in disdain, probably wondering what all the feed dust and new smells were. He also must have figured any place so dusty and gritty must also be "outdoors." As I was chatting with the office crew, a large puddle began forming around Merlin's feet.

I was mortified. How could so much pee come out of such a little, tiny dog?

Should I grab him and run? And potentially have a trail of pee follow us out the door? Should I ignore it? Impossible. Cry?

Merlin finished, finally, and must have felt infinitely better. He wanted to explore and began padding away, his wet paw prints following him.

I swept him into my arms, asked if they had a mop, and proceeded to the restroom out back where the mop was stored. I could tell I was three shades redder than normal.

The office clerks were kind. They didn't kick me out, nor did they laugh in my face—though looking back, I have often chuckled inwardly at the incident.

How like a child to embarrass a mom in a most public fashion.

By and large, Merlin was a good dog. He traveled well, behaved in hotel rooms, and loved me unequivocally.

He even sold salt.

There are in every territory accounts that, for whatever good or bad reasons, will not buy. I had such an account in Cañon City, Colorado.

This account just didn't have the time of day for me. I would come in friendly or serious, technical or full of fluff. Nothing seemed to light their bulb. Price was not an issue. I knew the market well enough to know that my pricing had to be competitive, and at times, with promotions running, my pricing was probably better than the market.

Still, they would not buy.

They fell from an A prospect to a B prospect. I continued to call on them, figuring that someday I might do something right or the competition would do something wrong and I would get in there.

I was on my regular route through southern Colorado and stopped in to see this account. I parked right in front of their door, figuring this call would be like the past calls—I would stop in, ask how their salt supply was, if I could write up their next order, hear the familiar *no*, and be out of there in less than ten minutes.

The business was run by a husband and wife. The wife was working behind the counter when I came in. She had always been particularly cool toward me, and we began our cautious hellos. I was just beginning to ask her about her salt supply when I noticed her attention was focused outside the door. I glanced over my shoulder to see what she was looking at—Merlin, of course. He had moved from his basket in the back seat and was sitting on the armrest between the two front seats looking at us.

She asked, "Is *that* a dog?"

I carefully and apologetically said, "Yes?"

She asked me, "Is *it* yours?"

"Uh, yes," I replied. "I get lonely on the road sometimes. Merlin keeps me company."

Now I have known people who don't like dogs and cats. I know people who think having a house pet is inhumane, cooping up the animal when it was born to be free.

I hoped that this woman wasn't one of the aforementioned people, but my luck at the account had been so poor, I prepared for the lecture on animal abuse.

The woman was still somewhat transfixed by the cocky little dog looking at us through the windshield. I was at a loss for words, fearing anything I said might be held against me.

The woman who finally turned and focused on me was not the one I had grown to be leery around. She was a new person. Merlin was my Good Housekeeping Stamp of Approval. Suddenly, I was okay.

It turned out that these people made their living running a farm store and elevator, but their avocation was dogs. To them, a dog could do no wrong, and a dog owner (who must also be a dog lover) could do no wrong, either.

We had a long talk about the merits of dogs and the impact that dogs have on our lives. We talked about the dogs we had known and the dogs that were in our lives now. It was a very "doggy" conversation.

It proved to me that persistence pays. All those times I was turned away laid the groundwork for this moment in time.

I left their store with a salt order and a different perspective on their world. Merlin had made the sale without stepping a paw outside the car.

Thanks, Merlin!

Sterling, Colorado

Working the Colorado territory was significantly different from my Iowa sales life. Accounts were businesses, not farmers, and instead of being the next place on the section road, they could be fifty miles apart. Cell phones didn't exist, so a salesperson got to know a couple of things really quickly—locations of pay phones and restrooms.

My territory for Leslie Salt included all of Colorado and Wyoming with fringes of Nebraska, but the concentration of business was in the Colorado Front Range, that corridor from Fort Collins to Colorado Springs. Every so often, I'd loop into Wyoming, and sometimes I'd venture from the Front Range and follow the South Platte River to Sterling, Colorado.

These drives were long, mostly interstate driving, with some two lanes added in. I never had an accident and only one flat tire that I can recall. I was a defensive driver, always looking out for the other guy.

The other precaution I took was napping on the side of the road. Inevitably after lunch, I would get sleepy; sometimes it would pass, and sometimes I would just have to stop and catch ten winks. I was driving my baby-blue Ford Thunderbird on my way to the Cargill molasses plant in Sterling. It was about a two-hour drive, so I planned on staying overnight in Sterling and making a full day of calls the following morning. For a one-nighter, I just packed a change of underwear, a clean shirt, and some jammies and figured that was good enough.

As I was heading east, I was chewing gum and listening to the radio. Traffic in eastern Colorado is never heavy—it was me and the truckers. As I got sleepier, I decided to pull over instead of toughing it out.

Some might think it unsafe for a single woman to pull off at a rest stop and doze, but I always figured it was more unsafe to fall asleep while driving. I came to a stop off by myself in the parking lot, the hot afternoon sun keeping things toasty. I leaned my seat back, closed my eyes, and dozed almost immediately.

Suddenly, I was conscious that I had a wad of gum in my mouth, so, still half sleeping, I plucked the gum out of my mouth, reached forward, put it into the ashtray, and put my hands in my lap to doze a bit more. About ten minutes later, I woke up, refreshed and ready to go.

I started the car back up, readjusted the seat, and pulled out of the rest stop. I reached for the radio knobs to turn on the radio and noticed that the gum wasn't in the ashtray. *Hmm*, I thought. *Where is that wad, anyway?* I was sure I'd put that gum in there. I looked around, my eyes scanning the floor mats to see if I could get a glimpse of the gum, all the while driving. No gum.

I figured I would find it later, so I just drove on to Sterling.

I pulled up to the hotel and swung my legs out of the car to get out, and that's when I found the gum stuck to my butt and the car seat. It had stayed warm from my body heat, so it was stringy as I tried to pull it from my pants.

I checked in at the lobby and asked the young woman behind the counter if she knew how to get gum out of clothes. She barely looked up and had nothing of consequence to say.

I got to my room. These were the days before Google, before a person could just go to the internet, type in "how to get gum out of clothes," and get 19,600,000 results. I was alone and without a clue where to start. And I only had the one pair of pants to wear the next day.

But I had a resource only a phone call away—my mom.

So I called her. Strangely enough, she wasn't sure what to do either, but my sister Bernice was at my mom's house. At the time, Bernice had three little kids all under the age of ten, so she knew quite a lot about clothes care. She and my mom were my Google resources. One phone call, one answer that worked. *Ice.*

The next day, wearing my good-as-new pants, I made all my sales calls, including the one at the Cargill molasses plant.

Robert Pinewood managed the molasses operation for Cargill. He always had a warm welcome for me, gave me his time, and bought my salt. We had a bond because we both worked for Cargill, but he could have bought from my Cargill competitor in Hutchinson, Kansas. I knew some of the guys he knew in the molasses business, so we had a basis for friendship. That and the fact we were both stuck out in the hinterlands as far as Cargill was concerned also bonded us.

I pulled up to his plant office and saw traces of smoke on the outside of the building. The glass was broken. Robert came around the corner of the building and let me in to survey the damage. His office had caught fire earlier in the week. A total loss. It wasn't the charred papers and furniture I remember—although that had to be there—but his telephone, with the keypad and handset melted in a plastic flow like a Salvador Dalí painting.

Years later, when I was in marketing and sales management, Robert became part of the Salt sales team, and we worked together again. That saying about not burning your bridges has always held true for me. People resurfaced all the time, and Robert was one of those. And we continued to have that special bond that was started out on the plains of eastern Colorado, in Sterling.

I was driving back into Denver after having spent a few days out Sterling's way. It was the end of the day and the end of the week of December 8, 1980. John Lennon had been shot and killed only days before. All the radio stations were playing Beatles music, and the talk shows eulogized the man. I was listening to the tributes being played on the radio, thinking how quickly life changes. It was around 5:30 in the evening, the sun sinking behind the Rocky Mountains, golden hues spanning the sky and magnifying the mountain silhouettes, the Platte valley behind me, my face lit up by the lights on the dashboard, darkness in my heart.

Night Fighting

Even though my territory included eastern Colorado and Wyoming, my regional office was Salt Lake City; that was where my product was shipped from and where my boss's office was and where invoicing came from. Once every two or three months, I would be called in for sales meetings either alone or, more often, with the other salespeople.

Brian Jones, my supervisor, was a man in his mid- to late fifties. He had grown up with Leslie Salt and had originally worked out of our office in Newark, California. Brian and his wife, Joanie, took me under their wing right away and made sure I was treated like "one of the boys."

That attitude was just fine for me. I didn't want people to go out of their way for me; I wanted to fit in. Joanie did just that with her warm and friendly ways, her thoughtful birthday cards and Christmas presents. I was not being treated as special; Joanie treated everyone on the sales force the same way. Both salesmen and their wives would receive cards and presents from Joanie, and dinner at Brian and Joanie's home was a given.

I was, of course, the first single woman to work with this group, and Brian made it a point to make sure everyone worked at making me feel included. I felt right at home immediately.

Though I had worked with an all-male sales group in Iowa, midwestern ways are more subdued. The strict, Protestant work ethic of the breadbasket of America colored the Iowa sales force. Now, they were not all angels, but they were definitely midwestern hardworking stock.

The Leslie group was distinctly western. The men were a hard-drinking, card-playing, high-stakes, late-night lot. Whereas the midwestern group played penny-ante poker betting pennies, nickels, dimes, and quarters, the Leslie men were betting bills—ones, fives, tens, and twenties.

My dad had been a rough-and-tumble, poker-playing, Japanese American–Montanan. He smoked Roi-Tan cigars, drank Old Grand-Dad whiskey, and sustained a glancing gunshot wound to his head when he was accused of cheating in a poker game.

I *knew* these men. They were like the ones I grew up around, and though I didn't participate in the smoking, drinking, and poker games, I understood the rules of the games these folks played.

Our sales team consisted of Gene DePena—Brian's boss—a younger guy, California born and bred and of Portuguese descent; Lee Briton, in his fifties, skinny as a stick, ulcer sufferer, Mormon man, married to a large, domineering woman, and a victim of spousal abuse; Gus Canon, who had sustained hearing loss from the gun blasts during the Korean War and who, I found out during a seminar, had only an eighth-grade education; and finally, Bert Spence, a towering giant of a man, yet as gentle and soft-spoken as a lamb, who had been a general manager at a manufacturing plant and wore a ruby pinkie ring on a hand that could easily palm a basketball.

At one time or another, I worked one-on-one with each of these men. I met their wives and their children. We shared stories from our pasts and talked about the future.

Lee told me how hard it was for him to come to terms with a young female selling in a man's world. Gus took me golfing for the first time. We sat together after dinner, stuffed on steaks and whiskey, talking about work and the company. I spent many hours in smoky hotel rooms, watching high-stakes poker games in action.

One evening, we were having dinner in a very elegant Greek Orthodox church turned restaurant in Salt Lake City with the office staff, who did not join us in our evening repasts too often. Gene DePena, the sales manager from the San Francisco office, was there, too. We all had plenty to drink beforehand, and the wine flowed freely during dinner. If these guys were Mormons, they'd missed the sermon on abstaining from alcohol. Bert and I were seated next to each other. George, the office manager, sat across the table in a pointy-collared, flowery polyester shirt. He had a skinny frame and bony ink-stained fingers that nervously fidgeted with the wineglass stem. There were about ten of us at the table.

Bert was one of the best storytellers I had ever met. He was a big guy, silvery hair with buggy blue eyes, who had just a touch of the effeminate in the way he gestured with his hand or held a cigarette and in his sometimes soft and whispering voice. We had a special bond, as we were both the youngest salespeople on the team, even though Bert was likely twenty-five years my senior.

Bert and I worked together on the road making sales calls and filling in the time between calls with wide-ranging topics. He alluded to interesting underwear that Mormon ladies wore, though he never got into how he knew they wore interesting underwear. Once, at the end of the workday, sated on a steak dinner, we sat in his car in front of the dimly lit 1960s-style motel, the doors to our rooms facing us. He turned to me and said, "I feel obligated to ask because guys do this and I'm a guy, but do you want to come to my room?"

I smiled and said, "I appreciate you asking, but no, thanks." And that was that. Like a true salesman, he had to ask, even though he knew the answer was no. He meant no offense, and none was taken. We just had to dispense with old habits in a new world.

He had a wealth of fascinating tales both real and funny and was, on this evening, spewing story after story, egged on by a captured and enraptured and somewhat inebriated audience. We were enjoying one another's company during the dinner and laughing raucously as only people who have had lots to drink can do.

George had imbibed a substantial amount also, but instead of being a funny or happy drunk, George became rather petty and small. He began muttering to no one in particular. He mumbled about the office secretary sleeping around. He slurred, "I wonder if she's a redhead in the basement, too." "No one knows all the crap I do to make the office run smooth." The entire table tried to ignore him, but as it became obvious that we were ignoring him, he became louder. Slumped in his chair, making him look even smaller than he was, he scanned the table to target his comments and locked his eyes not on me (thank goodness) but on Bert, his closest target right across the table. I squirmed, feeling the eyes of the table on George as the tension heightened.

"You're all talk, Bert," he sneered. "No one likes your stupid stories."

Bert tried to ignore him. George wasn't going to be put off. George leered at him, his eyes not focusing together, and said, "You're full of bull, and without me, you guys are nothing. Go piss off."

Suddenly, Bert rose out of his chair, reached across the table, grabbed George's shirt collar, and lifted him out of his chair.

I can still see Bert, with his massive hands grabbing at George's flowered polyester shirt collar, the ruby ring on his pinkie flashing. Bert, well over six feet tall, glared at George, who was slightly taller than I was at five feet five inches and probably not much heavier. Bert was ready to punch George's pie-eyed face out.

I had only been present at a scuffle between two men a few times before in my life. A man I was dating became jealous when I danced with another, and he got in a knockdown scrap in the disco parking lot. One of my brothers got into a shoving-and-punching match with a custom combine crew member who accused us of stealing. That's it.

I could see that this confrontation could easily turn into another dogfight, but a fair fight would not be how it would come down. George was three sheets to the wind, the scrawny agitator poking a stick at anyone who might snap back. It was not going to do anybody any good to have his headlights punched out—deservedly or not.

Quickly, I grabbed Bert's arm and told him to sit down and cool off. Bert, whom I had never seen fly off the handle, must have been thinking the same thing, and he just as quickly backed off.

George, looking a tinge green, excused himself from the table.

He never returned to the dinner, and I learned later that he took a cab home.

Weeks later, George was gone from his job.

I have always enjoyed drinking with the guys after work, after dinner, after hours. Now, more often than not, there are a few women salespeople or managers that are also in the group. But even in the most festive of atmospheres, I have recognized that while we all may jest and boast as equals around the bar, in the morning, we are once again boss-subordinate, manager-salesperson. And through the drink and the talk, underlying it all is a business relationship that may be held against us.

Identity

I loved Colorado. I loved my life there, driving the state making sales calls, skiing, having a circle of friends who were young, active, fun. Colorado was Montana on steroids—bigger business, bigger mountains, bigger cities, professional football . . . more, bigger, faster.

I had a community in Denver, and I had a history there that included my family in Montana. My sister Kathryn had lived in Denver in the early '70s and worked as a beautician. Downtown Denver had a Japantown, with a large grocery, a bookstore, and shopping. One of my 4-H friends from Montana lived in town; a buddy from college was in Lakewood; and Kazuko and Bette Lou Nagashima, childhood friends, lived nearby. An extended family friend who grew up in Broadus, Montana, introduced me to a photography circle. I flourished in Denver.

Being Japanese was always a part of who I was, but I saw the world first through the lens of a Montanan. That was how my dad viewed the world—as a Montanan first. I figured that because I felt Montanan first, it helped me relate to people and helped them to see beyond my Japanese face to the person inside.

One of my responsibilities as a Leslie Salt salesperson was to attend conventions and trade shows to network and represent the company. I have attended hundreds of trade shows over the course of my career and have participated in countless evening receptions, trade show booths, rubber-chicken dinner keynote addresses, and business dinners. While working in Denver, I went to the Colorado Grain and Feed Convention, that year held in Pueblo. Pueblo is about a hundred miles south of Denver as the crow flies. I didn't get down there too often, as business got thin the farther from Denver I worked.

At the Colorado Grain and Feed Convention, there were around ten Cargill people at the show—in addition to me representing Salt, there were about seven guys from the Cargill grain elevators and a couple of other divisions. One of the Cargill family members worked for the grain division, and while he wasn't the highest-ranking guy there, he *was* a family member, which trumped us all. I had called on the Denver Cargill grain elevator, so I knew a few of the guys already.

We had all bumped into one another at the welcome reception. Wine, beer, and hard liquor flowed freely. It was a room of about 250 people, milling about, socializing, networking. Some of my customers were in attendance—managers and owners of feed mills, feedstores, cattle feedlots, some of whom brought their wives. A youngish couple from the Salida area were there laughing and talking it up. They owned a small feed mill, and they were Mexican Americans. (This predates the term *Hispanic*.) I remember them not because they were attractive (they were), lively (they were), or engaging (they were). I remember them because they reminded me of my parents.

When I was growing up, my mom and dad socialized and networked at the Montana Winter Fair, the Montana Wool Growers Association, and 4-H events. My mom would be dressed up in a form-fitting dress, hair in an updo, a string of pearls. My dad would be in a pressed Pendleton western snap shirt and wool gabardine slacks, often with a Roi-Tan cigar gripped between his teeth. They would be working the room together, Daddy jawing with the men, Mom working the women in the room or listening supportively while my dad told a story. They didn't mind being the center of attention and maneuvered the room accordingly.

This couple from Salida was like that. They were outgoing, eye-catching. The husband was short, but not too short, with a broad open face, dark skin, dark eyes, wide tooth-showing smile, dark hair. His wife was petite—light brown hair coiffed in a bubble cut, stylishly dressed. You could tell she was an active part of the business, probably a title like *office manager* but a true business partner to her husband. I relished our meeting because it made me feel close to my youth, close to my family.

Later that night, the guys and I from Cargill's Grain Division went out to dinner. The Cargill family member was sitting at the head of the table and was fielding questions about what he thought the grain markets would do over the summer and what the price of hanging beef might be. I was sitting at his end of the table, and so I heard most of the chatter he was engaged in.

Suddenly, I heard the word *spic* in the conversation at the other end of the table. It was just loud enough for me to hear but didn't reach the far end of the table. The guys were talking about the Salida couple, referring to the wife as being, "not bad for a spic," and how the husband, for such a little guy, was putting on airs at the reception.

I turned my body away from the Cargill family member to face the offending end of the table. The guys, realizing they had been overheard, stopped, looked at me, then looked away. And then I could see the slow recognition in their eyes as they looked at me. Not far from *spic* was *Jap*.

Their conversation went dead.

I thought this could have been a random derogatory act, but not long after this episode, it happened again—this time with Leslie salespeople.

The Leslie Salt team had won an incentive trip to Kauai, Hawaii. In the Nutrena incentive trip, we won as individuals and brought our wives, or in my case, my mom. The Leslie sales incentive was all or nothing; if the entire sales team met a goal, every salesperson and wife went on the trip—if the goal wasn't met, no one went. Like the Nutrena trip, it was all first class; the Leslie Salt group stayed at a luxurious resort in Lihue, enjoying group tours and lavish group dinners.

I loved this Leslie family; the men were welcoming, the wives likewise. The wives treated me like a daughter. I never got the feeling that any of the women felt threatened by me. Why should they have? Their husbands were likely thirty years my senior and not especially attractive to a twenty-six-year-old. I can't say the opposite wasn't true: I was surely attractive to a fifty-year-old man.

One evening, we went to a dinner show put on by local Hawaiians. It was a classic hula show, the nuances of which were lost on us mainland tourists, but it was nicely done and narrated so that we had a vague idea of what was being said through hand, hip, and hula movements. After the show, a subgroup of five couples and I were waiting for the rest of the Leslie group to file out. The men were chatting together, the wives clustered. I was standing between the two, involved in the wives' chatter, but with an ear to what the men were talking about, too.

I caught the drift that the men were talking about monkeys while the women were talking about shopping they had done during the day. Suddenly, Gus's wife turned away from the women and said to the men's group, "Stop that talk right now."

The men stopped, looked at her, and then looked at me. Gus blushed, averted his eyes from me, and mumbled, "Sorry."

I was perplexed. "Sorry for what?" I asked him. "What did you say?"

He didn't reply. They had been talking about monkeys. Was that it? I turned to his wife and asked, "Is it about monkeys? What does that mean?"

She said, "It's not about you."

I turned to the men. "What does *monkey* mean?" I asked, clearly confused.

Finally, one of the men said, "It's just a word we used during the war."

These guys were post–World War II and had fought in the Korean War. Half of them were deaf in their right ears due to sighting and shooting their rifles. *Monkey*, then, meant *Asian person*, as the Hawaiian dancers had all been Asian types. They hadn't been talking about cute little tree monkeys as I had assumed when I had heard them talking. They had been referring to the dancers as monkeys.

We all walked back to the buses. I felt conflicted. These were people I worked with and liked. They weren't calling me a monkey (at least to my knowledge), but they were talking about people who looked like me as monkeys. I hadn't even known what the term meant, which only reflected how sheltered I had been.

I drew on my experience growing up and the adage, "Actions speak louder than words." My dad would have been a bit older than these guys by maybe five or ten years. My dad spoke disparagingly about blacks, but he also said he felt bad for the way they were treated, that life was unfair. And his actions spoke to me how to behave. He hired anyone willing to work—black, white, yellow, brown. I never saw my dad treat any of the men who worked on the farm any differently based on their skin color. He would dole out the work based on seniority and skill level. All of us kids worked side by side with the hired help, doing the same work. That was the world I grew up in.

It cut me to the quick to hear the guys I worked with talk disparagingly about the Mexican American couple and the Hawaiians. I realized that they must not have seen me the same way, or wouldn't they have been more sensitive to the words they used around me? Was I so much "one of the guys" that they no longer saw me as Japanese? Or was I just invisible?

Did the guys call me a Jap when I wasn't around? If the Cargill guys or the Leslie guys called me names when I wasn't there, I couldn't control that, but as long as they treated me fairly and respectfully when I was working side by side with them, I was okay. I had to be. And I hoped that by working with me, they would think twice before calling anyone a *monkey* or a *spic* again.

Abuse in All Sizes

I lived in Denver but worked for the Salt Lake City office for a little over a year and a half. I learned a tremendous amount in that short time. It was different from Iowa or even Kansas City, and I no longer had to learn the mechanics of the job as much as the social and political aspects of business and life. I could turn away from introspection and look out at the world around me.

One of the startling revelations of this looking outward was the condition of some women. *Abuse* was a word that had come out of the closet, but it was still wrapped in ignorance and disbelief.

This was one of the strongest periods in my life. I was in a job I was good at, in a location I loved, with a social life and friends that I enjoyed.

Perhaps that is why I was shocked and saddened by the plight of these women.

Every office that supported the sales teams had a secretary who was dedicated to the manager of the area. This was an era that predated the title *administrative assistant*. Brian's secretary was Diane. Diane had recently remarried and seemed to have finally found a settled situation for herself and her children. Then she discovered she had breast cancer.

She began treatments and suffered the common hair loss. She worked as long as she could and then worked when she could. It was soon apparent that her condition was worsening. I called in to the office one day and asked Brian how she was doing. "That son of a bitch husband of hers left her and her kids. He just picked up and checked out," he said disgustedly.

So in addition to coping with the fact that she was dying, she was abandoned by this man that had enjoyed her during her health. Brian was the man who ended up standing by her. He kept her "employed" until she couldn't pretend anymore.

She took a trip to California to see the ocean, returned to Salt Lake, and died, leaving her children behind.

Another woman who worked in the office had bright red hair and a sunny personality to match. She took salt orders over the phone and was a contact for all of us salespeople in the field. She had been beaten up by her boyfriend and at times came into the office with bruises and black eyes. I remember asking her once about a large bruise on her arm, which she explained away as happening when she "ran into a cupboard."

One weekday when I called in, she told me she was getting married, so she was going to be out of the office for a couple of days. I didn't know her well enough to know whom she had been dating, let alone whom she was now marrying, so I instead asked her where she was going on her honeymoon. She said they weren't going to go anywhere right away.

That didn't seem unusual to me, since I knew several people who either postponed their honeymoon until a more convenient time or when their finances were more flush.

The following Monday, I congratulated her on her wedding and asked her how it all went. "Fine," she said, with very little comment. I did not pursue the issue, probably because I couldn't yet relate to marriage and partly because she seemed reluctant to expand on the topic.

The next week, I was talking to one of the other salesmen, who asked me if I had heard about this woman's marriage. I said I had and said, "Isn't that nice?"

There was a long pause, and then he said, "You don't know who she married, do you?"

As it turned out, she had met a man through a prison "friendship" program. He was still in prison, but they were allowed conjugal visits once a week or some such deal.

I was surprised. She was so ordinary, working at her job, competent, diligent. And then I felt embarrassed. No wonder she didn't go on a honeymoon!

A few months later, she began having trouble at work. She disappeared, absconding with the office petty cash.

I often wondered whether her husband had any influence over her actions.

Then there was my tennis girlfriend I had met through the tennis club in Denver. She divorced shortly after she caught her husband in bed with her best friend.

The abuse was not only inflicted on the women. Lee, the Salt Lake City salesman, also ended up being abused by his wife. Lee was going through a midlife crisis, and word was out on the street that his marriage was on the rocks. The couple seemed out of sync; she was a hearty eater and quite large, and he was skinny and quiet. They had several children, and their youngest son still lived at home.

He and Leslie Salt parted ways. Later I found out through the salespeople's grapevine that he had been beaten by both his wife and son. He shortly thereafter parted ways with his family, also.

About the time I would begin to feel outraged that people would allow themselves to be treated so shabbily, and about the time I would begin to feel that people should quit being wimps and stand up for themselves, I would recall that I had been treated shabbily by Fred and he had taken advantage of me, my family, and our generosity and good faith. I had mourned our separation all the while knowing it was the only solution to a destructive relationship.

Even the strong can be victims—it just depends.

PART 6

Walking

My Promotion

Early in the spring of 1981, I received a phone call from Brian Jones, my boss in Salt Lake. He asked if I could come to town the following day. It was during the National Western Stock Show, and I had friends from Iowa at my home. But of course I left my guests and went to Salt Lake. This was work, wasn't it? And this was my boss calling, after all. So, without really knowing why, I made plans to leave my houseguests and go to a business meeting in Salt Lake.

When I arrived in Salt Lake, I found that it was not a one-person meeting; Gene DePena, Brian's boss from Leslie Salt's main office in California was there, as was Bob Lee, the executive marketing director, from Cargill Salt's main office in Minneapolis.

The four of us met up at the Leslie office in Salt Lake, and two of the men presented job offers to me.

First, Gene explained that there was a sales position opening in California. I would be able to live back near Stanford and all those friends and family that were in California. It would be a much larger territory than the current one, and I would potentially make a lot more money. It was a promotion for me, but the job, while expanded, would be the same as I was currently doing—sales.

Then Bob offered me a job in the division marketing staff as an entry-level product manager. I would move to Minneapolis and manage the marketing (which at that time meant brochures and promotions) for several market segments.

I was taken by surprise. I had gone to Denver with a two-year plan in mind, figuring that I would have at least those two years to figure out where I wanted my life to be before transferring. I was sitting at a little less than a year and a half.

After the offers were made, there was little more the four of us had to talk about. Problems on my current territory suddenly seemed inconsequential, in light of a pending move, so we decided to work out at a game of racquetball before dinner.

Unfortunately, neither Bob nor I had come prepared to play any sports. We considered sitting on the sidelines for about fifteen seconds and then decided all we had to do was go to the store and buy shoes, socks, shorts, and shirts and we would be ready to go.

My potential boss and I hopped into the car and drove to a discount store on the order of Target or Kmart. We walked the aisles, debating the cost of shorts and shirts; tennis shoes were the costly items. In short order, we ended up at the checkout counter with varied apparel for court wear. It was a little weird buying clothes with a man who could be my boss.

The day was one I will never forget. I was a poor racquetball player at best, and so rather than play doubles, which I found a bit dangerous in such close quarters, we played a round robin form of singles, where two people would sit out while two played.

Racquetball is a sport where sweat flows freely. It is a fast and rigorous game, especially for those of us with limited talent. The beauty of the game is that, unlike tennis where a novice spends most of the game chasing balls, the closed racquetball court limits how far an errant ball can roll.

The round robin made for interesting conversation for the two sitting out. At least it was for me, for when I was sitting out, while my physical being was resting, my mental faculties were being taxed.

The first time I sat out, I was with Bob. He began a slow sales job on me, on the merits of the Minneapolis job. He stressed the exposure to management I would get in the headquarters office atmosphere. How badly he needed a person like me. What a fine city Minneapolis was.

I took it all in, wide-eyed, I am sure.

Then, it was Gene's turn. He stressed the great people in the Leslie organization and the potential money I could make in the territory. It was, in fact, about two to three hours from the Bay Area, but it was still within driving distance. He pointed out that I would be a full-fledged territory manager in the company and not a trainee on an inconsequential piece of turf like my current territory. He stressed that I would still be a management candidate, but perhaps a stronger one with the added field experience.

Then, when it was Brian's turn to sit out, it was more like a proud father when his child graduates from medical school. We both knew that my current territory was not big enough or challenging enough for me. I had outgrown the position. I knew it, and Brian knew it. We also knew that I alone could make this life choice.

It was a very flattering episode. I was courted by two big managers in the company. They both wanted me in their organizations. I had the world by the tail at that point in time.

On the other hand, reality struck the next day when I flew back to Colorado. My houseguests were anxious to hear what all the commotion was about. They were duly impressed when I told them. There was still a glow in the air.

That night, when the guests left and I was alone in my town house, the burden of my decision hit me. It was one thing to feel the flush of being wanted in two places at once; it was another to decide where I wanted my life to go in the next few years.

All night, I rolled the choices around in my head. I knew I would take one or the other; staying in Denver—as much as I loved living there—was not an option. I wanted to stay with Cargill, and I knew I had outgrown Denver and the job there. From a professional aspect, I needed to move on.

But where?

California or Minnesota? Sales or marketing?

I had been in an entry-level management job before and I had jumped ship; that was how I'd gotten to Denver in the first place. I didn't quite know for sure what a marketing product manager did, so that choice was definitely more of an unknown. I figured I could sell in the California territory, since I could sell in Colorado.

I asked the company if I could visit the California territory. I wanted to see for myself what the area was like.

The salesman who was retiring met me at the Leslie office. We drove to Fresno and the neighboring towns making sales calls on typical customers. It was clear that I would have to learn the market and an expanded product line, but otherwise, it was basically a larger version of the job I was already doing.

What disappointed me the most was the feeling I got from the area. It reminded me in many ways of Iowa.

The Central Valley in California is one of the most productive farming areas in the world. It has the climate and irrigation that is perfect for truck farming, cotton, olives, dairy, and beef lots. It was like a mega-Iowa, supporting not only the huge California populations of the Bay Area and Los Angeles but much of the rest of the United States, as well.

And no matter how I stretched it, Fresno was not in the Bay Area, nor was it anything like the Bay.

I had transferred enough times, lived in enough locations, to know that I had probably sized the territory up pretty accurately.

As the local salesman was taking me back to the office, he knew I was not overly impressed with the territory. Yet I knew it had served him well for many years and that it was a challenging opportunity. He had raised his family there. I didn't want to offend him by implying it wasn't good enough for me.

I still debated.

Minneapolis was a complete unknown.

At least on territory, I would know what to expect. I had worked with all the Leslie people long enough to know I could get along with them. I knew virtually no one in the Minneapolis Salt office.

Eventually, I drew up a pros and cons list on the two offers. Each list was long and complicated. The lists were written and rewritten.

I agonized.

And finally ended up deciding to go to the unknown. I was ready for something new, and the Minneapolis job was all new.

This whole life-decision process took less than a week; Cargill had wanted my answer yesterday.

Unfortunately, when a company offers two choices to an employee, the employee may win, but the offer that was not taken up becomes the "loser." I was careful to explain my decision to Gene DePena, because I knew we would have to work together in the future. I also liked Gene and regretted that my choice meant that I would not be working for him. He was a good manager, and I felt I could have learned from him.

But the die was cast, and once again, I turned my energies toward Minneapolis.

Sam's Moves

When I moved to Minneapolis, I had to sell my town house in Colorado. I loved that town house—it was new, modern, and in move-in condition.

I soon found the cost of everything in Minneapolis to be substantially higher. I couldn't even touch a comparable town house, so I began to look at what the real estate agent condescendingly referred to as "starter homes."

Starter homes looked somewhat like my Sunset View house in Clear Lake, Iowa. It was depressing to have to revert back to the lifestyle I had two moves ago, but it became apparent that if I wanted to reinvest my money in a house, I would have to do just that. Even more disconcerting to me, the 1980s were inflationary times and the interest rate for a thirty-year home mortgage was 16 percent! This was no typo. Thirty-year mortgages were going at 16 percent. *Creative financing, balloon mortgages, adjustable rates* were the buzzwords.

Saint Louis Park grew up in the post–World War II era, and two-story bungalows dotted the tree-lined streets, some with white picket fences. I ended up buying a three-bedroom ranch with a walkout basement that had been owned by one family since it was built in 1958. It was a quieter shade of red than my Clear Lake house and at least fifteen

years younger than the other homes on the street. It had a mother-in-law apartment in the basement and a tuck-under garage. I knew from an investment angle it was a good buy, but it needed considerable updating and fixing up. The widower who moved out had not made any improvements in the twenty years that had elapsed.

I had a hammer, pliers, and screwdriver, but not much more. I slowly began buying necessary hardware to begin fixing my Edgewood Avenue house—paintbrushes, buckets, tools for leaky faucets and toilets.

As I was getting to know the local managers in the Salt Division, I shared with them my many tasks that waited for me each night after work—a little painting, wallpapering, small repairs. With my previous moves, I was the sole Cargill employee in a community—a field salesperson in a territory. When I had moved to Kansas City, there were fewer than ten people in the office, and the reception from my coworkers was cool. In Minneapolis, the Cargill Salt office housed over sixty-five people, and we were a mere subset of the larger Cargill office of a couple of thousand. The office personality reflected that of the leadership—it was warm, friendly, and inclusive. The Salt Division president played tennis, and right away, I was part of the Saturday morning tennis group. People would meet in the morning at the coffeepot and chitchat. One manager, Sam, offered to loan me a ladder for some of my DIY work. I eagerly accepted, thinking how neighborly he was and how that loaned ladder saved me sixty dollars that a new one would have cost.

He offered to bring the ladder over, but he couldn't make it until later in the evening—like 9:00 or 10:00 p.m. That was fine, since I didn't have any plans. He came over, ladder in hand. I invited him in, and we chatted for half an hour.

I was impressed by his friendliness. Everyone in Minneapolis seemed to go out of his or her way to make me feel welcomed. It was a far cry from my Kansas City move, where in the first week I got a speeding ticket, had to appear in court, was chastised for expensing a meal for my mother, and none of the managers had reached out to welcome me.

A week went by. I finished painting two rooms, the ladder supporting my efforts by moving with me every two feet. We were in perfect harmony. It was infinitely better than the kitchen chair draped in plastic I had been using.

That Friday night, Sam showed up at my door at ten o'clock with a bottle of Cook's champagne. I was surprised. It was a "welcome reception," he explained.

I blurted out the first thing that came to mind. "Cook's?" My eyebrow involuntarily raised. I was familiar with the brand. I have a sister whose last name is Cook, so our family would buy Cook's champagne often. It's a very inexpensive and marginal sparkling wine. "I'll save it for a special occasion," I said lamely, trying to recover and not be too insulting. He looked at me kind of funny. I don't think that was what he had in mind. My stereo was playing soft rock in the background. I stepped back, and he came into the house.

Sam didn't waste any time. He made his move. "Like to dance?"

"Sure."

He put his arm out, and we began to slow dance in my living room. Sam wasn't a tall guy; his chin tucked into my shoulder between my neck and ear.

"I'm glad you moved to town," he whispered, his lips tickling my ear. "You've made work more interesting."

I wasn't totally immune to his charm. Or perhaps I should say the physical response to his warm breath on my neck and his arm around my waist was automatic and undeniable.

"Uh-huh," I murmured, closing my eyes. The Eagles' "Heartache Tonight" started up.

Sam was smooth and calculating. He made it clear what he wanted. He nibbled on my ear. "*It* would make life more interesting at work, you know."

I had to admit, there was a fleeting moment when the temptation made my heart flutter. It *would* make life interesting. And he was so much more experienced in office politics than I was; surely he knew how "interesting" it could get.

But the Agee-Cunningham affair wiggled its way to the top of my consciousness. In the late '70s, William Agee was the CEO of Bendix, and Mary Cunningham was hired as his executive assistant. She rose to power quickly and was accused of having an affair with Agee. Mary Cunningham was a graduate of Harvard Business School, but all the media picked up on was her affair and the insinuation that she had slept her way to the top. Her affair was one of the reasons my mantra was "Never mix business with pleasure."

All these thoughts flashed through my mind in a millisecond. Sam could feel my hesitation. I stayed true to my mantra.

So, like any good salesman, he tightened his grip and tried a new approach. "You remind me of a girlfriend I had in high school; we had a great time. We could, too."

Ooooh! Cold-water shower. *What? Ludicrous*, I thought. *I'm fifteen years your junior.* I, maybe, reminded *him* of a classmate if time had stopped. Unfortunately for Sam, time had not stopped. He had the look of approaching middle age. Balding, salesman's gut, the start of bags under his eyes. And baggage—his divorce papers were probably still in the envelope.

Plus, I thought, *how rude!* I felt my back stiffen and my hair bristle. It was like being told I reminded him a lot of his ex-wife, except better. Uh, no, thanks.

So, as the Eagles finished their song, I maneuvered an arm's distance apart. Sam sensed I had made up my mind to spurn his advances; he was no dummy. He had the good grace to leave the champagne with me. He departed amicably.

The following week, I got two more rooms painted, dancing with Sam's ladder the whole time. At work, he treated me as though nothing had happened. Of course, nothing *had* happened. It was business as usual. There were no references to that Friday night. I figured the case was closed.

Late in the week, Champagne Sam strolled up to me. In an offhand way, he began to chitchat about nothing. He was turning to go when he paused and tossed over his shoulder, "Hey, can I get my ladder back?"

I laughed aloud.

Everything has its price.

Even a ladder.

Being with People

Contrary to popular belief, selling, which had made up the first five years of my working life, is a job of isolation and independence. There is the stereotype that the salesperson is this extroverted people person, and to a degree that's true. But the successful salesperson tends to be resilient, one who can get along with people, actually enjoys them, and yet operates independently and often in isolation, motivated without a boss standing overhead or a whip cracking on the back.

Suddenly, I was in an office again. My only other office experience was the brief and shining episode in Kansas City—hardly a gauge to measure what "normal" might be. Because of Kansas City, I was prepared for the worst—a tyrant for a boss, no support from peers.

My first day of work, my new boss was late. I arrived at 7:45 a.m. sharp. Work officially began at 8:00. I arrived to an empty office. The staff showed up at 7:58.5. Bob arrived at 8:30.

That was okay. I was raring to go.

I received my job description, and then Bob spent about three hours talking to me about my new responsibilities and his love of long-distance running. It was incredibly vague. I marveled at how the man could spend three hours on nonspecifics.

That was okay, too. I had just come from the field. I knew what sales support materials were lacking, and suddenly I realized I was in a position to do something about it. I was going to be responsible for several market segments. I would develop promotions. I would handle sales incentive items. I could design brochures. I could do almost anything I wanted as long as Bob knew what was going on and approved.

Hmm, could this be true?

Well, it was not totally true, but it was very nearly! Bob was a hands-off manager. He was everything Little Napoleon was not—participatory, supportive, willing to praise, personally concerned. I flourished.

Of course, Bob was not perfect, either. I soon found that out. Bob was an endearing guy, but he was a procrastinator and a rambling talker, which I should have figured out at our first three-hour meeting. Bob had scheduled a lunch meeting for me to meet our advertising executive. Bob and the AE were both marathoners—runners and talkers. After two hours of the two men blabbering on about running, we spent a few minutes talking about business. After we got back to the office, I told Bob I *never* wanted to sit through a lunch like that again.

But recognizing this flaw, I was able to compensate for it, and I learned to work around his weaknesses. Besides, I was learning an incredible amount from him, and I felt I was gaining both personally and professionally.

Not only was Bob a friendly guy, so were the others in the office. All the managers would go to coffee and lunch together. This lunch ritual was much more casual and flexible. Many of us traveled for work or had visitors in town, so the lunch crowd changed daily or weekly. They made a point of including me. There were single people working in the office. The division had a softball team, and I joined right in. The only other team I had belonged to was the Clear Lake, Iowa, bakery softball team made up of workers I did not know. The Cargill team would play ball and then go for beer at the local tavern afterward—just a bunch of buddies BS'ing over a few brews. It was just not quite the same in Iowa, where, though friendly and accepting, my bakery teammates and I didn't have work in common and most were married with children.

I was included in the company picnic planning committee. There was a Christmas party. I was overwhelmed by the contact with *people*. I felt like a social butterfly after the isolation of all the transfers and new territories and life on the road. With each of my transfers while in sales, I was alone, establishing myself in a new town/community/territory.

Before I even hit town, I had a friend—my college buddy from Denver told me to contact Larry to play tennis—so I did, and we did. I met Joanne and Sandie at work—neither in my direct work group, both as different as night and day, and both became my best friends. And Carolyn, a childhood friend from Montana, moved to town within weeks of my arrival. This was friend heaven. I had arrived.

Getting It Done

My job definition in the marketing department was nebulous, which allowed me incredible freedom to do whatever needed to be done.

One of the first areas that needed help was in the management of the sales promotional items.

This program, which wasn't a program, consisted of a file drawer filled with pens, pencils, notebooks, thermometers, and paperweights stamped with the Cargill logo. Salespeople would call in, and the secretary would take an order over the phone and send the requested items out.

It was a straightforward process except that no one knew how much of anything we owned, how many we had given away during the year, or how much money was spent.

This went against my controlling and analyzing styles. I found it incredible that no one tracked how much was spent or what we owned. Even though I didn't balance my own checkbook, I always knew in round numbers where I stood each month.

One thing I did learn in Kansas City was about control. On any given day or hour, the plant knew exactly how much of each feed ingredient was inventoried. They had a purchase order system and logbooks on orders, usage, and net remaining. The promotional items in the marketing department were certainly not as valuable as feed ingredients, but not knowing the item position at any given time bothered me. I quickly began to implement an inventory system like the one in Kansas City into the Salt marketing department.

The items in question were too tacky to call sales incentives; they weren't that glorious. But they weren't gimmicks, either. I had sold and knew that pens, pencils, and notepads were all part of the salesperson's repertoire and expected by the customers.

Then one day while grappling with trying to describe these items that we were inventorying, I referred to them as *widgets*. It described them perfectly. They were "things," "sales stuff." *Widgets* defined them to a tee.

So *widgets* it was from that day in 1981 until at least the mid-1990s. The inventory system when it was first implemented identified $5,000 worth of widgets. The program was near $40,000 when I left.

Slowly, insidiously, I made an impact on the organization that was as lasting as some of the decisions the division president had made.

Small or large.

Everyone could contribute.

My title when I first moved to Minneapolis was *division product manager*. The Salt Division didn't really know what that meant, but I did. I had grown up in the Nutrena Feeds Division. They had product managers for each of their major livestock lines—beef, dairy, hog, chicken. They used the classic Procter & Gamble product manager concept—each product manager was responsible for the marketing, sales, promotion, and general management of the product line. The Nutrena product managers would develop the sales promotions and marketing materials for us salespeople in the field. They would teach us how to use the materials and introduce new products.

I took the Nutrena model and applied it to my job. In Salt, I got the second-tier products/markets—in other words, all the product lines except for food production and water conditioning. But that left the industrial, agriculture, deicing segment.

From the first days on the job, it just felt right. I would come into work and I would just *know* what to do. I took the model from Nutrena and how the product managers worked there and applied it to my salt product lines. My boss, Bob, gave me free rein to work with promotion houses, advertising agencies, and PR agencies—within budget. But even without those entities, I had an intuitive sense of what needed to be done and how to get things done in marketing. I began by building tactical support materials that I knew were lacking because I had been in the field and knew the gap. Brochures, presentation materials, packaging. I just knew.

And what a remarkable and refreshing difference from Kansas City. There, I would go into work and be chastised, beaten down. In Minneapolis, I'd go into work and set direction, implement new systems, and receive positive reinforcement from the field I was supporting.

I spread my wings.

Good Dog

I was making great inroads in the marketing shop. I understood basic marketing concepts, but I also knew how to leverage resources—people, money, and time—to get things done.

I had begun to feel somewhat content in my position—several projects of mine had come to a successful and widely acclaimed fruition. I began to have a sense that I was no longer the low man on the totem pole—that I was becoming a force to be reckoned with.

Seth was the Salt Division's vice president and second-in-command. He was a stocky, outgoing man with salt-and-pepper hair and a thick walrus mustache. I personally didn't have daily contact with him, except for coffees and lunches in the group. My boss, Bob, reported to him directly.

It came about that Bob wanted me to gain some exposure and so set up a meeting with Seth where I would present my marketing proposals for the agricultural salt products. I knew in some respects this was a mere formality, since the field managers had already approved and supported my plan, but Seth was the local power.

About this same time, I changed my hairstyle. I had worn my long, black hair in a conservative and tailored ponytail or bun on a day-to-day basis; I had never been one to spend inordinate amounts of time fixing, preening, or coifing. But several years had passed with this square hairstyle, and I needed a change.

Instead of an interim haircut or moderate style change, I opted to go radical (at least radical for me) and got a shoulder-length frizz job—an Afro.

My new hairdo gave me a freer, looser look. The curly hair was easy to care for and couldn't be pulled back in a conservative bun even if I had wanted. But while one's hair can facilitate some personality changes, even hair cannot make a Democrat into a Republican. I was still the same person underneath all the frizz.

This hair change was so obvious, my coworkers could not help but comment. The verdict was split. Like so many people who have trouble growing long hair, one faction could not understand why I would want to cut my long hair shorter. Others thought it was "different, but okay." I enjoyed the controversy that the event caused, and the new do had the desired effect on my life—it was a change.

After the initial furor died down, I once again fell back into the formal, conservative mode of operation that I felt comfortable in. All systems were back to normal—or so I thought.

The day arrived when I was to make my presentation to Seth. I woke early, washed and "picked" my 'fro, and arrived at work in time to review my program before I went into the meeting.

Bob and I walked into Seth's office. Bob took an armchair; Seth got out from behind his desk and took the other armchair. That left the couch for me and my presentation materials.

After some brief chitchat, I jumped right into my program and began to expound on the benefits of my marketing plan. I held Bob and Seth spellbound for twenty minutes. There were few questions. I cruised to my conclusions.

I could feel my heart pumping steadily when I ended; the blood pressure was probably slightly elevated. It had been a good twenty minutes.

Having been schooled in sales, when I quit talking, I looked straight at Seth and waited for his response. Too many salespeople can't stand the silence between when they stop talking and the buyer responds. So they continue to talk to fill in the dead space, giving themselves the reputation of being too talkative.

I worked hard at not talking.

Seth stood up slowly and walked toward me.

I remained seated.

In anticipation of a handshake and the words, "Well done, Koyama. Fine job," I reached out my right hand as he approached.

Well, Seth did shake my outstretched hand, but in one continuous motion he brought his left hand up and patted me on the top of the head. Like I was a poodle that had just finished a whole bowl of Gravy Train.

I looked up at him through my curly bangs.

He said something, but it did not register.

All I could think was that this man hadn't heard or understood a word I had said. He'd patted me on the head like a dog.

Seth supervised our group for another year and then left to work for the competition. We had many other interactions, most positive, some not so. But what I remember about him is not whether he was a good manager, leader, or visionary. It was not whether on whole or on balance he supported women in the organization.

I remember his impulsive patting on my head. The demeaning feeling it gave me and the insight of how Seth perceived me at that moment. I had just presented top-notch work. He saw a twentysomething, fuzzy-haired young pup.

Since then, I have had a myriad of hairstyles—long, short, in between. No matter what style I have had, at any given time, I'm able to style it into a severe, formal hairdo. I also kept a change of clothes at work in the event a client meeting popped up unexpectedly.

It makes a difference.

Perception is reality.

New York City and Our Distributor

In many respects, my first job in marketing was an apprenticeship. Bob's method of teaching was to drag me along on meetings so I could learn firsthand.

One of these lessons was done in New York. Cargill Salt had a plant in Watkins Glen and a mine in Lansing, both in upstate New York. I had substantial experience managing dealers and distributors in the feed business, and I was charged with developing a distributor program for the Salt Division. In order to do so, the purpose of my trip east was to talk to local managers and some of our distributors to begin to learn Salt's current distributor status and find out what our distributors' needs were.

We met first with our own managers at the facilities in Watkins Glen and Lansing. The Lansing underground mine was similar to the rock salt mine I had toured on the training program in Louisiana. Then four of us were going to drive into the city to meet with distributors. The drive was five hours by car. The two host managers drove, leaving Bob and me to anchor the back seat of a salesman's Chevy Citation hatchback for 250 miles.

The first three hours were cramped but bearable. We were full of energy, and there was plenty to talk and laugh about. The last two hours were painfully long.

The shocks on the Chevy were marginal, at best. For the two in the front seat, it was no big deal. For Bob and me, it felt like my old days driving farm trucks.

By the time we arrived in New York City and met up with the distributors, the four of us were travel worn, needing showers, and tired.

The distributor's team consisted of the general manager and two lieutenants. The first lieutenant handled sales, and the other was in charge of transportation and warehousing. They were both young men in their late twenties or early thirties. The distributor had chosen the restaurant, which should have prepared me for the rest of the evening. We ate at a poor replica of a western steak house called the Long Branch Saloon in the middle of Manhattan.

Hey, I grew up in Montana. I'd sold feed to ranches in Colorado. I'd worked in a feed plant near the stockyards in Kansas City. I knew a thing or two about steak houses. Long Branch Saloon in New York City? Really?

But, of course, that was my issue. The restaurant was "incredibly authentic" when the distributor asked for my approval.

We were seated at a round table, Cargill managers and distributors. The first lieutenant sat on my right, and Bob was on my left. The conversation was lively; the four of us Cargill people were beyond weary and getting punchy. This was my first meeting in New York City, and I was high on anticipation.

We covered several business issues, which the local Cargill managers handled quickly with the distributor's general manager. The first lieutenant occupied much of my attention. He was a smallish man with thinning black hair and pointed features, and he was much impressed with himself. He soon found out that this was my first business trip to New York City and was eager to show me the town. He told me all about his job and the big money he was making. I learned that he lived in Connecticut and owned a commuter car and a hot Corvette.

It became obvious to me that this first lieutenant was beginning to reach his limit on drinks; he was, on a social level, a boor. On a business level, he was so full of himself, I was surprised his head fit into the room.

But I was a trooper. I knew this was one of our largest accounts. They controlled a big chunk of the salt business in the metro area. We needed them. Conversely, they needed us, too—as a supplier.

The first lieutenant's arm drifted to the back of my chair, just brushing my shoulder. I shifted, and his arm dropped. I tried to draw others into our conversation. Bob, who was sitting to my left, tried gallantly to jump in, but it was evident that he was the third head in a tête-à-tête.

Suddenly, I felt a hand on my thigh. And it wasn't mine, and it wasn't Bob's. I jumped in surprise, and then I felt my body become extremely still. Like an animal who spots a hunter, I paused just long enough to assess the situation and determine a plan of action.

The first lieutenant kept chatting as though nothing were happening, all the while massaging my leg.

Then, as quickly and smoothly as he had put his hand on my leg, I reached down, grabbed his hand firmly, and surreptitiously moved it back to his own leg. I deposited it there, kept smiling and nodding, and acted as though nothing had happened.

Momentarily, I excused myself to go to the restroom. I really needed to go.

When I came out of the restroom, Bob was waiting for me. He looked worried and asked me if I was all right.

We looked each other in the eye, and I burst out laughing. Bob, not certain whether he should laugh, defend my honor, or escort me away, chuckled uneasily and asked again whether I was all right.

I assured him that I was; I shared with him what had just happened with the hand. A grin spread across his face, and we both laughed at the situation.

He asked me if I wanted to leave or go back to the table. I suddenly realized that Bob had two concerns—one was for me and for my personal comfort and safety. The other was on a professional and business level—could a woman *really* be a manager and contribute without all this sexual interference?

Personally, I felt safe. I knew I could handle this first lieutenant. I also knew that there was safety in numbers, and if I did feel threatened in any way, the Cargill managers would be there. Professionally, I felt challenged, and I knew that how this evening played out would stay with me and other women in Cargill for a long time. This was the test to see if women could handle a business client professionally.

We returned to the table.

The men all looked at me closely, I am sure each with his own private assessment of the situation. There must have been some discussion while I was gone that I was never going to be privy to. The first lieutenant was somewhat subdued. He got the message that I did not want his hands on me, but perhaps he wondered if I'd still liked the come-on?

Suddenly, I realized that I controlled how the rest of the evening might proceed. The others at the table were sensitive to the fact that the first lieutenant had struck out.

Then it dawned on me. The distributors had thought that I was brought along for "entertainment." And I suppose, why not? When I thought of myself in the situation, it was the classic exotic Asian woman in the midst of macho American businessmen. I pictured myself: a young woman, laughing and chatting up these clients, dressed in a conservative blouse and bow tie, suit jacket, and skirt. They may have only seen an exotic Asian woman, charming and being charmed. Their interpretations may have been that I was an available, young Japanese woman playing the stereotypical geisha role of meeting the desires of men.

I was not about to become dessert for anyone, but I also was not ready to put a lid on my first New York City trip. While the first lieutenant was subdued, he was not dead.

He suggested we all go out for a nightcap. We agreed, and he suggested the Playboy Club. We left the restaurant and piled into two cabs.

I had never been to a Playboy Club before. Ten years earlier, in the early 1970s, one of my brothers had gone to one, and I had listened to his stories with morbid curiosity.

We arrived at the club in short order; the doorman greeted us, and we were each handed a Playboy magazine as we entered. It was everything the photos depicted, but shabbier; the bunnies wore fishnet hose and tattered tails.

A disco dance floor was strobing, but alas, Playboy Clubs were in their decline. The place was empty.

We ordered a round of drinks, promptly served by our bunny. We were embarrassed for our distributor; it was obvious the suggestion to come here would have been appropriate fifteen years earlier, but this was definitely not where the action was.

The first lieutenant, seeing the error of his ways, was quick to regroup.

"Regine's," he declared. "That," he said emphatically, "is the hot spot of the city."

We all filed out dutifully. He led us to the curb, and the doorman hailed two cabs for our group.

"Regine's!" the first lieutenant cried to the cabbies.

The cabbies looked at him awkwardly. One asked if we really wanted to take cabs to Regine's.

Four of us from Cargill must have looked like country bumpkins; we had no idea what a "Regine's" was. The first lieutenant boldly repeated to the cabbies, "Regine's!"

I thought, *It must be far, or in a bad neighborhood. The cabbie doesn't want to take us there. Are we going to a drug den or a dive?*

We piled into the two cabs. The cabbies slammed the doors and turned on their meters.

And drove us *half a block* down the street.

To Regine's.

But wait, there's more!

As we lined up to go in, gleeful and high from the ludicrous cab ride, we learned that there was a cover charge to get in. I wasn't surprised; several night spots in Minneapolis had cover charges, and two or three bucks a head was no big deal. My boss, Bob, magnanimously volunteered to pick up the cover charges.

Two hundred dollars later, Bob joined us at the table, looking somewhat shell-shocked. The tab to get in was slightly more than the restaurant tab. And steaks weren't cheap, even in the '80s.

I had often wondered who wore those fancy, fluffy designer evening gowns a person sees in *Vogue*—those with price tags that would support a family of four.

I never knew until that evening.

At the next table sat two women, both decked out in strapless, sequined gowns, drinking Dom Pérignon with a tuxedoed gentleman. They looked not unlike others in Regine's. I thought I had walked into a Harlequin romance novel.

Undaunted in my eighty-five-dollar, navy, calf-length summer business suit, we ordered drinks, and I danced with members of our group.

The first lieutenant, by this time humbled and humiliated by the cabbie episode, nursed his drink while I rocked and rolled on the dance floor, jostled by spiked heels and patent-leather tuxedo shoes.

As happens so often dancing, we heated up quickly. This night spot was definitely where the action was. I was dancing with Bob and decided to take my suit jacket off. He did likewise. We continued to dance when a tuxedoed man walked up to Bob and pulled him aside. I followed and overheard him tell Bob to put his jacket back on. This was "Jackets Required" in action.

That was the tipping point. Laughing, sweaty from five hours in the back of a Citation, a steak dinner, and bizarre night clubbing. I knew it was time to hang it up.

So this was New York!

The distributors, looking as disheveled as I felt, bid us good night at Regine's door. We all jumped into cabs, laughing just at the thought of what had happened a few hours earlier and the half-block cab ride.

We went our separate ways, distributors and Cargill-ites, and later, each of us to our own rooms.

The evening remained part of Cargill Salt legend for many years. The distributor continued doing business with us. The first lieutenant later became one of the co-owners. And laughter bubbled each time the tale was told and retold over cocktails.

This was the stuff that made corporate culture.

Carl Benjamin, Again

Coming out of college into the working world held many shocks, and one of the most surprising to me was the age range of the people I was suddenly working with. In college, peers were all pretty much the same age, save some outliers. The only "older" people were professors. Stepping into the working world, suddenly everyone was older, especially in the sales team I first worked with. I was one of two recent college graduates—the rest of the salesmen ranged from having ten years of working experience to nearing retirement.

My first real boss, Carl Benjamin, was the district manager for Nutrena Feeds. I looked up to him, to the lofty job I thought he had, to his worldly experience. Carl raised dairy cattle, lived on a farm outside Belmond, and was reputed to own another herd of cows in Wisconsin or Illinois. He had his stuff together.

Carl was everything I wanted to be someday—successful, confident, well respected. He was a big manager in the company.

He was an excellent boss. He gave good feedback, he stayed in touch with me, and he always let me know where I stood. He gave me a chance.

Eventually, Carl moved on to other opportunities in Cargill, as did I. We lost touch with each other.

One day, after I had started working at the Cargill corporate head-quarters, I heard that Carl was in town for meetings. I wanted to look him up, since he had been so instrumental in my early career. Before I had a chance to set up an appointment, I ran into him at the cafeteria.

Although I wasn't sure it was him.

The man I ran into was much younger than Carl. He was not as tall. The glasses I always thought looked so serious, intellectual, and firm had a with-it, hip, stylish look. He greeted me in a friendly, relaxed, outgoing fashion. He looked all of thirty-eight years old!

We had a wonderful, warm conversation. Our paths crossed a few times after that run-in, although Carl later left the company.

That incident in the cafeteria reminded me of the first time I returned to my elementary school after I had left home. The chairs were so small, the blackboards so low, the drinking fountain at knee level. This building couldn't possibly house the majestic, ostentatious portals of learning that I had entered as a child. Yet the smell of musty books, the shiny hallways . . . it was all so familiar.

The school hadn't changed, but I had. I had grown up.

Carl hadn't changed, but I had. I had grown up yet again.

Burnout and Discovery

It was 1983. I had been in my marketing job two full years. Its challenges were running thin. I had figured out the toughest time in a new job was the first year—everything was new. The subsequent years weren't as stressful, draining, or challenging.

The social scene in Minneapolis, so invigorating to me when I'd first come to town, was becoming humdrum. I had good friends and an active social life ranging from softball, skiing, and tennis to concerts, plays, and symphonies. But where was I going?

I needed a change. Again.

I had been dating a guy who was on the ski patrol with me, but my best friend in town was a tall, angular man by the name of Larry. Larry was a civil engineer—a shy guy, skier, and tennis player. We hung out together because of our common love for sports. We played tennis against each other and with each other. A woman from my work invited us to play doubles, and afterward we went to her home for a drink. I stepped into her house and had this déjà vu moment that I would live there. It lasted only a moment, and I didn't say anything, particularly because Larry and I were not romantically involved. He and I moved through the entryway to the deck, where we enjoyed a cool beer after play.

One day, Larry mentioned he was thinking of going to business school to get an MBA. It took me by surprise, but then I told him I had considered going to the University of Chicago several years earlier but didn't because of money and time.

He put the bug under my skin again. I looked into the University of Minnesota evening program. My Cargill benefits included tuition reimbursement, so I applied to the University of Minnesota School of Business (later renamed the Carlson School of Management). I was accepted to begin the fall of 1983.

It was an exciting year. I had recently purchased a brand-new silver-gray 1983 Pontiac Firebird. It had taken me eight years of working to buy this fastback four-on-the-floor manual transmission beauty. It was a hot car—sleek and fast. A woman I skied with called it "sex on a stick."

I was in love with my car as only Americans love their cars. It was my statement to the world and my substitution, perhaps, for real love.

And I was breaking up with the man I had dated for two and a half years. He was a gentle soul—a musician by avocation, a draftsman by trade. We were both on the ski patrol. I was still obsessive about my career; he was not. It was an out-of-whack relationship from the start and awkward and unpleasant to end.

But I had things to do, people to see, places yet to go.

Night school filled a void. It gave me a goal to strive for, an occupation to fill my empty evenings, and a new source of contacts.

It was exciting to associate with men and women who were as directed and ambitious in their careers as I was.

And I had reached a point in my career where I felt my learning had slowed; I was frustrated. Cargill's philosophy at the time was to hire undergrads and teach them everything they needed to know. It had worked for decades. But new thought seemed limited, corporate inbreeding rampant. I needed contact with the outside, to learn how the rest of corporate America did things.

I found myself back in the classroom, invigorated with anticipation. I knew the odds were against me finishing a program that might lead to an MBA. History indicated I would be transferred before graduating.

But that thought was tucked away, a low priority compared to the task at hand.

Homework.

The Line Job

Going back to school solved my stagnant social life, but professionally, after two years in the marketing product manager job, I was ready to move on. There had been a couple of false starts: a job offer to Lansing, New York, an opportunity in Cincinnati, Ohio. In both jobs, I would have been a regional product manager, a title which was a misnomer. It was, in fact, an assistant sales manager position, which led to a sales manager job. School was the thread that kept me on track, but I knew I would jump at the right transfer—career was always first.

I had debated long and hard about moving out of my staff marketing job. I enjoyed my work and was good at it, but a line manager was responsible for bottom-line results. It had profit-and-loss responsibility. Line jobs were highly regarded in the organization, and I would have the opportunity to manage a sales force someday. That had been my goal since the day I had begun work.

It was the logical next step in an upwardly mobile corporate career.

I was ready. I had accepted the Cincinnati job. The offer depended on the completion of some work on the salt mine in Louisiana, so my move to Cincinnati was three months away. In order to prepare for the move, I gave notice to a renter I had taken on in my house. I contacted a real estate agent and began the mechanics of transferring.

Then disaster struck. We closed our mine in Louisiana for safety reasons. Although we had contracted salt from alternative sources, the impact on the organization was uncertain. This mine had supplied the majority of products for the Cincinnati region; consequently, my new job was in jeopardy.

They eventually canceled my promotion. They did not want to add a person when they were forcing layoffs because of the mine closure.

I was disappointed, but even more so, I had been put out financially. I had kicked out my renter, put my house on the market, and mentally moved.

I needed to regroup.

This was one of the few times in my career with Cargill I felt I had been dealt with poorly. I put together a spreadsheet outlining the economic loss I had incurred by losing my renter and preparing to move. I asked for some kind of restitution.

Champagne Sam, the same guy who had loaned me the ladder, had the final say on whether I should be paid for my losses.

He did not approve my request. As it was put to me, "It's the risk one takes, and the mine closure was an unforeseen and unpredictable event."

I was angry, and I let people know it. Another job opened up in Hutchinson, Kansas; I really didn't want it, but when another candidate got it, I let the managers around me know I felt slighted for the job.

The clocked ticked on.

Shortly thereafter, a regional product manager position opened in Minneapolis. Golden. I was asked to take the job and gladly accepted.

No boxes, no packing, no relocating.

But a very new job.

At first I was concerned that the job titles—division product manager to regional product manager—implied a demotion, but it definitely was not. The job challenge was greater, the complexity more.

I reported to one of the rising-star sales managers in the company. I looked forward to learning from him. No concise handbook on what my job entailed. It was on-the-job, hands-on training only. I began making the rounds to the various shipping terminals, meeting my counterparts around the country, again riding with the field salespeople to meet clients and learn the business.

Then, as suddenly as the product manager job came up, opportunity knocked again. Champagne Sam and John Walker, the Salt Division president, came to my office and sat across from me, the fine oak desk separating us.

The rising-star manager was being promoted, and they wanted me to take his job. I would be the first female, first minority, and one of the youngest sales managers in the company. I would be responsible for sales in eight states and the seven salespeople in the region.

I would report to Champagne Sam.

Excited, pumped, scared. They all described how I felt. I didn't feel quite ready. Yet the two men offering me the job assured me I would get the support I needed to succeed. It was 1984. I was not quite thirty years old. Eight years since I had graduated from college. Five years in the field, selling. Three years in marketing. Six months in the region.

Personal relationships had blossomed, suffered, and died along the way. In eight years, I had lived in eight different homes and five different cities. I had jumped through hoops, succeeded and failed, and worked my butt off.

I had reached a goal.

It was momentous not only for me but for the Salt Division president, who was making a statement about his faith in me and my abilities. He was plowing new ground, too. No other division had a female or minority sales manager throughout the corporation. It was a statement about Champagne Sam, who, in spite of our "ladder secret," was a huge part of this opportunity.

I looked at each of them silently as they waited for my response.

I looked at Sam. *Does he see a sales manager when he looks at me, or a woman to woo?*

I couldn't tell. I didn't know. At the moment, it didn't matter. I'd take the risk.

I looked at John Walker, shook his hand, and told him, "I'd love to take the job. Thanks!"

The Run-In with the Ladies

Linus, from the *Peanuts* comic strip, once said, "There is no heavier burden than a great potential." I have often thought of that saying in the course of my career. The cartoon shows Linus sucking his thumb and holding

a blanket to his cheek—a little child with all his insecurities and all his unrealized potential. That was me. At no other time did I feel the weight of that burden more than when I took on the regional sales manager's job in the mid-1980s. I was single, focused on work, driven to succeed.

The regional sales manager (RSM) job was the first middle-management job with profit-and-loss (P&L) responsibility. Within the Salt Division, there were maybe six of these positions across the United States, each responsible for the sales and salespeople within those regions. Each region consisted of a sales force of six or seven salespeople; I had the northern region, which encompassed North Dakota, South Dakota, Minnesota, Wisconsin, Iowa, Nebraska, and Missouri. The sales force I managed was older by many years than I was. Five of the six guys I inherited had been recognized by the company as being top salespeople at one time or another. All were men. They worshiped the ground that Scott, my predecessor, walked on. Scott was a guy's guy: he coordinated the fishing trip, had a beautiful wife from a well-to-do family, loved hockey, and was a great networker. He played hard and worked hard. He was a great storyteller and the center of attention at the bar after work. He was a young guy a few years older than I but had proven early that he could make the company (and his salespeople) lots of money. He was the rising star. The senior guys saw him as the next president of the division. He got promoted up and on, and that opened up the opportunity for me.

Four women made up our regional sales office support staff. All had been in the region longer than I. They were referred to as "the girls in the office" by the men in the field. Every office was similar—the men would work in the field as "territory sales managers," and the women were back in the office. There was a clerk who took sales orders and a secretary who worked for me and the operations manager. The transportation clerk and accounting clerk both worked in and for the regional office with indirect responsibility to a staff manager at headquarters. And then there was an office manager, a man. All the ladies reported to the office manager except me. My counterpart was Sven Gustafson, the regional operations manager. He and I had P&L responsibility and reported to the profit center manager, Champagne Sam.

It was an intimidating scenario. The normal career path would have had me as a regional product manager for two years—the position for training sales managers in waiting. As a product manager, I would have shadowed the sales manager, learning the ropes. I may have worked with a particular warehouse, promoting product out of that location and working with the salespeople who pulled from that warehouse. I would have learned about the sales and distribution process and had more time proving myself in a smaller role with a sales manager mentor. But since Scott had gotten promoted quicker than expected, that didn't happen.

I jumped in with both feet, anxious to do a good job, knowing I lacked the two to three years of apprenticeship that everyone (including me) expected. The men I supervised did not veil their skepticism—they would sigh before explaining a business relationship; at meetings with me, they would lean back in their chairs, arms crossed on their chests. They would have conversations designed to exclude me—about fishing trips or meetings they had attended that didn't include me. Some would not call in to report; others called in almost hourly. It was a confusing and uncomfortable first few months. But the most seasoned of them all, Dick Donaldson, took a fatalistic approach—*que sera, sera*—what will be, will be. He would make a point of reminding me how long he had been around but didn't balk at updating me on what was going on in his turf. He was reluctant to have me ride with him making sales calls, but he was the local rep, so I saw and talked to him frequently.

I would travel three out of four weeks a month, riding along with each salesman, meeting key customers, working on sales and pricing strategies. While the men may not have liked having me as a boss, they also understood that if we sold product, they made money, and having me in the RSM position did not hamper sales. Work went on as usual. For most of them, that was enough.

But when I was in the office every fourth week or on a Monday or Friday, even the most mundane tasks seemed to take incredible effort. Desktop computers did not exist. As a manager, I had a desktop ten-key calculator and a telephone. If I wanted information, I had to ask for it. That was why the office staff existed. Getting pricing information from the clerk seemed like an inconvenience that would disrupt the office. Asking for freight costs was like pushing a car uphill. Giving the secretary a written draft to type, which should have been effortless, seemed like asking to borrow money from a bank. I would get exasperated sighs, shoulders slumped in defeat, averted eyes that I could only imagine were rolling behind my back. I just kept plowing forward, not sure if this was normal.

I was not a novice at working in an office; I had been in the division marketing department for several years. I had supervised the one marketing admin there. I helped hire the woman, who was an African American a few years my junior. She was our admin, secretary, coordinator, and gofer. We worked together and set up an inventory and ordering process for promotional products. The field could depend on us to get literature and sales support to them in a timely manner. She and I had made the marketing shop hum. But the sales office I was in now was singing a different tune.

A few months after I assumed my duties as sales manager, my boss, Sam, called me into his office. I reported to Sam, so I didn't think much of it. We'd moved past the ladder episode and had developed a respectful working and personal relationship. He had already formed a romantic involvement with an ex-secretary from the office.

He asked me how I thought things were going. "Fine," I said automatically. *Who in their right mind would respond that things were not going well?* I thought.

It turned out that several days previously, while I had been working on the road, the women marched into his office en masse to complain about me. They jumped rank on the office manager and went straight to my boss. They complained that I asked them for information (pricing and freight rates); they complained that I was demanding and complained that I asked for typing to be done.

Sam said he asked them if they did those same duties for the rising-star sales manager who preceded me. They admitted they had. He asked them if I was asking for more than the rising star had. I was not, they admitted sheepishly. He asked them if I behaved any differently from my predecessor. Um, it did not appear that I did. He pointed out that the only difference between what was asked of them before and what was being asked of them now was who was asking. The rising star was a man. I was a woman. He told them point-blank that things were not going to change. Period.

It was a pivotal moment for all of us. I did not realize that the women were having trouble adjusting to having a woman boss. I had assumed the men would have issues with me, but I had taken the women's support for granted. It didn't dawn on me that they might have mind-set issues to work through. The women in the office did not realize they had their own biases, either. Sam managed the situation based on the facts; he stood up for me and told the women that I was there to stay and they'd better get used to it. He took what could have been an incendiary event, refused to add fuel to the fire, dealt with it, and just shrugged in exasperation.

We all had adjusting to do. Some were not able to adjust totally. We changed secretaries several times, and although it was never cited as one of the reasons, I wondered if having to work for me was part of the problem. The women in the office knew that Sam had talked to me and knew that I knew. I stuffed my worry, sucked it up, and just worked per usual. And soon, they did, too.

Over the course of the next few weeks and months, I noticed that there was more eye contact when I gave my secretary typing and an occasional "Okay" or "Sure" or "No problem" rather than the grunt of acceptance. Sometimes pages would come back to me with suggestions—that were usually right on and made me look smarter. I'd take their edits and give credit when I could. The pricing and transportation clerks would sit with me and discuss unusual scenarios, and we often came up with creative ways to make distribution cheaper and better. We began bouncing ideas off each other to solve issues that came up. The ops manager, Sven, was a prankster, so on my thirtieth birthday, the staff, under Sven's guidance, filled my office with discarded furniture and packing peanuts. I came back from a road trip with birthday balloons and streamers at my office door and no way to my desk. We shared a birthday cake someone had made for me and shared a laugh. After a year and a half, I felt we had one of the hardest-working, most efficient and effective staffs in the division. The women were loyal, energized, and quality conscious. We began to talk about working women and the challenges we faced.

I look back at the mini-mutiny and give Sam credit. As a man and my manager, he could have sided with the ladies and pressured me to change my mode of operation. He could have tried to counsel me to be more sensitive to the women, go easier, be less aggressive—but he saw I was as fair and square as my predecessor. He recognized the root of the issue before any of us women did. His support allowed me to realize my potential as the company's first woman sales manager, and he squelched the undermining backbiting before it became an unwieldy monster. And he managed to move us all one more step forward, together, as a team.

The Sales Meeting

I had been in my sales manager job for about four months when the first sales meeting occurred. This was a first for me in my new role, though I had been involved in many sales meetings during my years in sales and marketing.

Multiple regions were included in this meeting, so the office managers and credit managers were included, as well as my male counterpart sales managers. Many of these office and credit managers were women, and for most, it was their first sales meeting. The meeting was held at a lake resort in northern Minnesota.

From the first day, discontent ran rampant. It was rumored that several of the salesmen's wives had called the division president and were angry that their husbands were at a meeting with *women* in attendance. (Incredible!)

After the first evening, when both men and women were socializing at the bar, the winds of discontent blew harder—how the wives at home knew what was going on when I was right there and didn't see or hear anything out of the ordinary remains a mystery.

That is not to say nothing happened. I cannot say for sure, except that I, personally, did not see or hear of any misbehavior by any consenting adults. Still, the rumors were rumbling.

Cargill Salt gave a sales award to twelve of the outstanding salespeople in the company. The program was called the Knights of the Round Table, and no one knew who the winners were except my old boss and marketing director, Bob, and the meeting planners. They would get the wives of the winners to the meeting in secret. Of the winners announced at this meeting, three were my salesmen. Bob, who had a voice like Bing Crosby and the personality of Bert Parks, played up the Knights of the Round Table theme. While the theme music from *Camelot* played in the background, he would describe each winner without disclosing his name. As the music grew louder and more powerful, Bob would announce the recipient, whose wife would magically appear! The house would erupt in applause, and the spotlight would scan the crowd until it found the winner, who would rise from wherever he was seated and tearfully embrace his wife, who waited for him onstage.

Of the three winners from my region, Dick Donaldson was the opinion leader of the sales troops. In every organization, opinion leaders set the moods and attitudes of the rest.

It was a tension-filled meeting for me not only because of the rumors flying about the women attending but because, again, this was my first meeting in my new role. I was excited for the three men who'd won, because the winners were also a reflection of their boss—in this case, me. And I was nervous about greeting their wives.

The evening of the presentation was the capstone; it was the dinner where everyone dressed up and salespeople who had a good year were hoping against hope that they would soon be recognized by their peers. It was always a tense and highly anticipated event.

After the presentation, champagne flowed freely, and the winners were appropriately recognized and congratulated.

On this evening, after the awards ceremony, there were some awkward silences. Some of the businesswomen in attendance didn't know whether they should congratulate the winners with a warm hug or not. With the winners' wives now in attendance, there was a subdued hush when a female Cargill-ite approached.

Suddenly, Irene Donaldson, the wife of my salesman, went to the microphone. Dick had been a top salesman in the Salt Division for many years, and Irene was one of the leaders of the wives' union. Dick deserved the recognition he received. He could be a dick with the office staff when advocating for his customers, but he was a trusted advisor, true friend to those he chose to befriend, and a top producer year in and year out.

Irene stood before the group, high from the excitement of winning and sensitive to the tension in the air.

She scanned the group as a whole, not looking at me specifically. She may as well have been talking directly to me. She spoke into the microphone in a strong, clear voice.

"It's time for women to be recognized for the work they do," she said. "It's exciting to see the opportunities for women, and I'm proud my husband—as stubborn and old-school as he is—can be part of the change. And I'm fully supportive of what Cargill's done hiring women. Change is going to happen, and it is for the good. Let's get over it!"

I was stunned and humbled. I knew how important her support was to my success. She could have just as easily taken the other stand and made my life a living hell. But here was this woman, who more than anyone could have felt threatened by me and my new position, supporting and welcoming me.

The next day when the winners and their wives met with upper management, some wives (I am sure with encouragement from their husbands) voiced concern that the men might be working on the road with female employees. As the story got back to me, management listened, then told the wives that there would be more women managers. Everyone would have to get used to it and, paraphrasing Irene, get over it.

The meeting ended on schedule, and like a hundred other meetings, each participant went home with memories and impressions uniquely theirs.

I look back and remember a wife who took a vocal stand to support change and many who did not.

Scott—From A to Z

Though I may never admit it, I was likely a victim of the biological clock pressure to get married. Marriage was an institution always nagging at me through relationships where I would, in the recesses of my mind, play what-if games. *What if I married this man? Would he be a good father? Be faithful to me? Be threatened by my success? Be fun and exciting and steady and stable?* Certainly, the list of what-ifs was endless and unanswerable in most cases. In fact, I had met many marriageable men in the years of dating from college on, but there was always something wrong with the

relationship—the overriding issue in most of the cases was whether or not I was willing to give up my career.

My mother had a very Japanese relationship with my father. She took a back seat to him on most issues. His decisions drove the family. She never argued with him. He was always right. And although they had a loving relationship, there was never a question over who was boss. My mother had always warned me that my life would no longer be mine should I get married. It was an ominous warning for a young woman in a liberated career.

Because of her perspective, I perceived marriage as giving in or giving up. And as a fast-tracker in a corporation, I also perceived that I had accumulated status in the organization that I would lose by marrying.

What I did not anticipate were the social and political changes that would occur as I moved up the organization. This was evident when I became a regional sales manager.

While I had been on the road selling feed and salt, I felt that my position in the organization was low. I was expected to pay my dues and transfer at the drop of a hat; loyalty was tested by what I would do to get the job done: Would I exceed the call of duty on the job? Was I sincere about my career? Was I willing to fight in the trenches to get into management?

My first entry-level management jobs were much the same—low man on the totem pole, being tested for stamina, loyalty, and how I rose to the challenges. Even at these entry-level positions, most of the men were married, but many were not—yet.

When I became the regional sales manager, suddenly the questions posed while I was a salesperson and rookie were not an issue. I got the job *because* I had proven myself. The sales manager job was the reward for my past performance and willingness to jump through any hoop.

The men who had been assessing my performance before suddenly became my peers. I had proven I would transfer at a moment's notice, would work sixty-hour weeks, and could do the job. Now the norms were different. Sales managers, profit center managers, and marketing managers were married. They had wives that would transfer at the drop of a hat. And if they were single, it was because they were divorced. At thirty, I was the youngest middle manager on the team and the only one never married. None of the men had waited that long to get hitched.

But now the standard was different. It was okay to be married, with a family, dog, cat, station wagon. It was an anomaly not to be married.

The rules had changed on me.

So it was under these conditions that I began the University of Minnesota's evening MBA program. I had considered the men at work off-limits, and since work was where I had spent the preponderance of my time, the opportunity to meet eligible men was low. By going to graduate school, I was thrust into a group of men and women whose goals, ambitions, and ages were very similar to my own.

I was planted in fertile ground, rich with potential relationships based on common interests, goals, and ambitions.

Eureka!

I saw him sitting across the classroom from me. It was the first evening of Management and Organizational Behavior class. Fred Fox was the professor. I was scoping the classroom out, checking to see if I knew anyone.

He was sitting in the second row, intent on the professor—his tie loosened, pen poised in his left hand.

I could tell he was available. He had sun-bleached blond hair (strange, we were in Minnesota). Intense blue eyes. Broad shoulders, oxford cloth button-down shirt with just a bit of chest hair peeking out. He just *looked* single.

I made a mental note of it and didn't pay much attention to him after that.

By the next class, I had come down with a massive head cold. We ran into each other at the cafeteria, where I was buying several orange juices to get me through the evening. We started talking, and he sat next to me in class.

When I caught head colds, which was quite frequently, they were severe and obnoxious. My nose would be raw and run profusely. I had trouble talking without having to dab my nose. I would have used and new Kleenex littered around me. It wasn't a pretty sight.

We set up a date anyway.

On the way to our first date, I stopped behind a Honda Prelude at a red light. Preludes were relatively new on the car scene—they were just shy of a sports car but had a sporty two-door look. I suddenly had a premonition—that he drove a Prelude. *How strange*, I thought at the time. It was such an insignificant flash and yet one I could not ignore. Indeed, he *did* drive a Prelude. It was unnerving.

My new romance was novel for my coworkers. My evenings and weekends suddenly had a plus-one. We studied together and took classes together at the U's evening program.

At one point, my boss's name was Scott Sage. I spent more time with coworkers than I did with any other group, so Scott Sage and I were together at work, on the road, and after work at dinner or happy hours frequently. Our advertising agency's account executive was Scott Abrahams. Scott Abrahams and I worked together on communications plans for the product lines I managed in marketing. He and I would play tennis and go out for fun. And now my boyfriend's name was Scot Zimmerman.

Incoming phone call messages were often confused and funny. Voice mail was in its infancy, so we still had a live person answer our phones and take messages. I'd get a message that Scott called, and I'd have to guess which one. Office staff had many a chuckle at my expense. As did I.

As many night school students who are also employed by a company full-time could attest, maintaining a relationship outside of those two venues is difficult at best. Most students must spend twenty-five to thirty-five hours in class or studying and another fifty hours at work. It leaves very little time for anything else. Our relationship flourished during those school hours. It could not have survived otherwise.

Scot grew up in Redwood Falls, a small town in Minnesota, and went to college at the University of Minnesota. His friends were all in town. He had a totally different social group than I. My friends came from work or skiing, and most in my social circle were older. Scot's friends were college buddies and their wives. Suddenly, in this setting, I became one of the *oldest* in the group.

My social skills as a plus-one were rusty. I had moved away from Stanford immediately after graduation. The skills I had cultivated in the last ten years had been business skills. That is not to say I didn't have a social set of friends, but my friendships were based on common activities—skiing, tennis, or work—not as a romantic add-on.

Moving into Scot's world was a rude awakening to how I had been oblivious to women my own age in more traditional women's roles. His buddies were all the fraternity boys. The women in the social circle were wives or girlfriends. Business? Business wasn't a part of this gathering, nor were women's issues. In my work world, I was one of the guys, but not here. I felt out of sync. Alienated. I wasn't sure how to fit in. And it surprised me that there were young women who had graduated from college who did not aspire to be on a career fast track. Wasn't that everybody's goal? We all have our blind spots, and this was mine. I made allowances for my sisters and sisters-in-law to take traditional roles, but I couldn't wrap my head around the choices these women had made. Yet it was the same; it was their choice, different from mine, but no less right or wrong.

One of the girlfriends was finishing a degree in psychology and planned on getting a master's and PhD. We gravitated to each other probably because of our girlfriend statuses, but also likely because we were both career women. We became fast friends.

The evening Scot and I told my mother we had decided to marry, she looked straight at Scot and said, "Are you sure you want to marry *her*?"

I laughed at the time, but in looking back, it is clearer that she doubted whether her daughter, who had been so career focused, so driven, so corporate, could become the wife she herself had been forced to be—obedient, subservient, second.

And surely, we, like every other couple on the verge of union, were different, special, committed to each other enough to overcome the obstacles ahead.

We married a year and eight months after we met.

August 31, 1985.

My little house in Saint Louis Park had served me well, but with marriage to Scot came the desire for the larger, quintessential house in the suburbs. A woman at Cargill was going through a divorce, and she told me to take a look at her home—they were "motivated" to sell. This was the same home that I had the premonition about years before with my tennis buddy, Larry. It was a fixer-upper, but I was compelled to buy—and we did: 6608 Nordic Drive.

The Fishing Trips

Some institutions die harder than others. Being the first woman sales manager opened opportunities that had never been available to women before. In the formal organization, I was an equal, involved in the decision-making and management of my region.

But the informal organization proved more difficult to access. Drinking after work was not a big problem. In most cases, I was invited along as one of the guys. My tennis skills were good enough to be part of the Saturday-morning foursome—another one of the guys. I didn't play golf, but neither did our division president at the time (he was a tennis player), so the greens were not where the business chatter was happening.

The president was a born-and-bred Minnesotan, and one of his loves was going to a cabin in northern Minnesota to fish. Each year, sales managers, upper managers, and some long-serving territory managers— all men, of course—would spend a week at a cabin in the far north.

It was the Outward Bound of the Salt Division.

It was not a business meeting, but it was the equivalent of business golf for a week. The northern region sales manager who'd preceded me had been the point guard of this fishing trip. When I took over the region, there was a ripple of debate that traveled through the core cabin group.

Should I be included, as any male manager would have been, or should I be excluded because I was a woman?

There was concern about where I would sleep if I went. Since it had been an all-male dominion, sleeping arrangements were never an issue. The beds went to the old-timers; the floor went to the new inductees. There was talk that I could take the one bedroom. It would have displaced a couple of men, but it was doable.

I never personally became involved in the debate. Frankly, going to a cabin with a bunch of men was not really my idea of the best way to spend my own vacation time, but a part of me wanted to be invited, even to be able to say, "No, thanks."

As it turned out, the decision to go / not go wasn't mine to make.

I was never invited to attend. It remained a male bastion.

It never felt right, not being invited, yet I had many battles to fight, more balls in the air that needed attention. I had to pick my battles.

The women in the office, after our initial working through of job responsibilities, became my staunch supporters. The second year in my job, as the men planned their fishing trip, the women in my office rallied. We decided to have our own "fishing trip."

Carol, our order clerk, had a coupon for a free weekend night at a resort in northern Minnesota. We got a condo that slept fourteen, and the women's weekend was on.

It wasn't a week, like the men's. Most could not afford or did not want to spend that many vacation days. And fishing was not on the agenda.

When we arrived at the condo, bottles of champagne waited for us, compliments of Sven Gustafson and the men's fishing group. While they wouldn't invite me along, they were supportive of the women's weekend.

Instead of fishing, we shopped, boated, golfed, played tennis, read books and magazines, ate wonderful volumes of food, and talked. We talked a lot about work, but we also got to know one another in a different context. Some of the leaders at work took a back seat to the leaders who helped organize the weekend. Roles changed, and personalities did, too. It was a fun, relaxing, and positive experience for all of us.

We bonded in ways that would have been impossible in a work environment.

And every year we talked about doing it again.

But we never did.

PART 7

Falling Down

Derailing, Again

When I inherited the northern region, the all-male sales force was one of the oldest and staunchest in the company. Three of the men had been with the company for over twenty-five years. Another had over fourteen years, one was a black male with seven years, and one was a management throwback—he had failed in an entry-level management job, and instead of letting him go, they gave him a large territory in a prime market.

Whether it was timing, circumstances, or my management style, I'll never know, only that when I left the region two and a half years later, the sales force looked considerably different from when I had arrived. Two of the original team remained in their territories; one was promoted to a sales management position. Three were let go—fired. Four new salesmen worked for me—a white male who was a direct hire from a regional company, an admin manager turned salesman, and a Japanese American man and a young white woman both recruited out of college.

The changes were not without tribulation.

The first to be cut had virtually quit working several months before I arrived. He was the African American man working out of Saint Louis. He was supposed to be covering two-thirds of southern Illinois and half of Missouri, but he was working the Saint Louis metro area almost exclusively, rarely venturing beyond. He and I had many frank conversations about his work and life. He didn't feel safe outside of metro Saint Louis. He wanted a change, knew he wasn't doing his full job, but just couldn't initiate the break. I just nudged him toward the rest of his life.

I have always believed that we spend too much time at work not to be enjoying what we are doing. There are slumps in our level of enjoyment, and there are times when *enjoy* may not be the correct word to describe how we feel about our work, but on balance, I still believe we should be positive overall.

The second man left the company after he was "demoted" to a territory after trying his hand at management. In fact, the company did him a disservice when they put him back on territory. His goals were lofty; since Cargill Salt could not meet his goals, it was constant conflict for him to be on territory and not in a dream job. It was also a no-win situation for me. At one of his reviews, I was handing him a "does *not* meet expectations" while my boss, the profit center manager, was handing him a raise. I also represented what he did not have in the company—the sales manager job. The day I terminated him, he handed me his resignation letter.

In the third case, the man admitted to me that his conservative German upbringing made it difficult to accept me, a woman and a minority, as a boss. Gordie's style was very different from mine. He chose to take the car allowance of $250 per month instead of the company-issued four-door Chevy or Ford. Instead, he drove a used, late-model Mercedes-Benz sedan. A Mercedes-Benz in the 1980s was *the* prestige car—very few on the road, very hard to come by, especially in Iowa, where he worked. He was a promoting, flashy, appearances kind of guy. I tended to be more analytical, controlled, and formal. He flirted with waitresses and hotel clerks. He sold on personality and favors.

Gordie was using what I considered outdated techniques to sell in a rapidly changing marketplace. The sales buzzwords were *value-based sales* and *solution selling*. There were more women in purchasing positions, and they were not impressed by flirtation. He was the Willy Loman of the sales force. His results were flat. Accounts that needed attention were not getting it. Total number of calls were low.

He was in a downward spiral.

We would have conversations that, if they remained light, were fine. If we had to talk about working the territory, improving results, the conversations would be confrontational, emotional, and irrational.

It was all the more difficult for Gordie because I tended to be too calm, unemotional. Our defense mechanisms were totally and diametrically opposed. As he became more excited and volatile, I became more tightly wrapped.

Gordie had his fiftieth birthday while I was his boss—that was tough. He talked about retirement, taking it easier, how old he felt. His best friend on the sales force had just turned sixty, but Gordie considered them both contemporaries. He began drinking. Sales is a tough business for drinkers, because the temptation is everywhere and there are plenty of people to drink with. Evenings on the road were an invitation to imbibe one, two, three, or more drinks with dinner. No one was watching or chastising if a person had a drink at lunch. After all, compared to the generation of businessmen preceding us who made the three-martini lunches infamous, we were nearly teetotalers.

On one occasion when I was riding with him, he began yelling at me, swerving in the road, pounding on the steering wheel. I was alone in the car with him when he flipped out, triggered by who knows what—frustration, jealousy, resentment, fear of growing old, a sense of entitlement. It was after that episode that I set the gears in motion in earnest to have him terminated from employment. I agonized long and hard over the decision. I knew that the corporation seldom fired people who had been longtime employees. I felt that part of the problem was Cargill's fault and that he should have been fired long ago.

But the problem was now, immediate, and my responsibility.

And then Gordie entered the Hazelden treatment center for alcoholism. Cargill had a great program for substance abuse, and the company supported those willing to go to treatment for help. Part of the program required that I go for one of the sessions so that Gordie could vent his anger toward me and then admit that his drinking was impacting his judgment toward me. I think back and wonder how the treatment center allowed the patient to berate the boss (in this case, me). What about my fragile ego? What about all that I was dealing with? But that wasn't considered, and on my visit, Gordie harangued me and verbalized what he considered my faults. These treatment centers were pretty new—Betty Ford's disclosure that she was dependent on alcohol and painkillers came in 1978, and the Betty Ford Center was inaugurated in 1982. Gordie went into rehab around 1985 or 1986.

Cargill kept Gordie on the payroll during this treatment, and we held his job for him. His termination proceedings were put on hold during this time. After his release from the center, he resumed his territory responsibilities, and we continued to work together.

Going to Hazelden was a big step, but the tough part came later, when Gordie was back on the job, the everyday stressors back in his life. I continued to be an irritant to him, and at one point, he referred to himself as a "dry drunk." He had quit drinking, but getting back on track at work, making even the minimum number of sales calls and meeting sales goals continued to be a problem for him. During his twenty-fifth year with Cargill, I was forced to terminate him.

It was an ugly episode. My boss and I flew to meet Gordie in a hotel room. We terminated him and told him the terms of the termination.

When we were finished, he shook my boss's hand, and I offered mine. He looked at me, his face white with anger, his fists clenched, and refused to shake my hand.

I was stressed out from the work. I came down with a horrendous head cold, which confined me to bed for several days. I felt I had done the right thing in the long run not only for Cargill but for Gordie. We had allowed Gordie to hide behind his job and his friends at work. He could do that when his boss was one of his buddies and the managers were his fishing partners. He could not work with me in the same way. I didn't fish. I had been measured by performance. I wasn't a part of the old-boys' network, so I didn't function under the same guise. It was clear he did not like the stand that Cargill was taking by promoting people like me.

When he left, he took with him one large account. There may have been more, but I was not around to count the fatalities. I hired his replacement and prepared to pull my new team together.

Spinning Plates Under Duress

In the 1960s, *The Ed Sullivan Show* would feature singing, comedy, magic, and talent in a variety-show format. One talent that always intrigued me was the guy who would spin plates on the end of long, skinny sticks. He would get multiple plates spinning, moving from one end of the stage to the other, keeping them going by giving the sticks a periodic booster shake. He would do this until at some point, a plate would go spinning out of control or drop from lack of momentum. That's how I felt entering this stage of my life. I had more plates spinning than I knew how to handle.

The final quarter of night school, in the spring of 1987, I became pregnant. Spring quarter, I spent most of my weekends lying in bed with my Macintosh computer, writing papers for my final classes. Unlike the laptops of today, the Apple Macintosh was portable, but about the size of a carry-on bag with a nine-inch black-and-white screen. Unlike many pregnant women, I did not glow. I felt slightly lime green most of the first five months.

I was also in the process of working out my differences with Gordie, training two new salespeople, and trying to maintain a handle on the rest of the region. I was traveling weekly.

The gears were in motion to terminate Gordie in April, so until then, it was business as usual, and I was beginning my second trimester. I thought I would have some breathing space to get my troops together and begin more team building, since the past few years had been more on the order of team reorganizing than building.

One day during that spring, my boss met with a competing salt company on an issue that was unrelated to my region. After he got out of the meeting, he took me aside and told me to call the sales force and begin raising prices in the region. He said that the men he had met from the competition had told him they were going to raise prices and we should, too.

Now I had gone through numerous antitrust seminars at Cargill. We were a company extremely sensitive to the antitrust issues. Why a red flag did not rise on this occasion, I shall never know. I do know that, anxious to please my boss, I hurried and let the word out what my boss had instructed me to do—raise prices. Even one of my new sales reps questioned me on the instructions. I rationalized it away for her. I figured that if my boss wanted it done, it couldn't be illegal, could it?

Several weeks passed, and the instruction was forgotten. I had already gone on to other fires that needed to be extinguished, other plates that needed a booster shake.

I was asked by the Cargill Women's Council to be one of three or four women on a panel to discuss career and advancement in the organization. I had been a founding member of the group, originally formed because of a class-action suit against Cargill for discriminating against women. I was more than willing to talk about my fast track in the company. It was to be a noon luncheon and panel.

On the morning of the panel, the division president, John Walker, called me into his office. I entered his room and saw the corporate attorney in attendance, too. I had no idea what was going on.

It was the pricing incident. And it was brought to their attention by Gordie, the man I had terminated just weeks before. He had still been in his territory, had taken down my instructions, and had them typed up. He sent them to the division president and wanted him to know that this was the kind of manager he had running his northern region.

I looked at the instruction and could not deny that I had given it. I explained how my boss had told me to send the word out. They told me that the incident would have to be investigated and I would have to compile pricing activity that had occurred after I had given the instruction. They said they would be investigating the matter, that it was very serious for me, and that they would get back to me.

I left the room stunned. I knew that the organization did not take kindly to infractions of this type. Several of my peers had sent wires out that were deemed violations of antitrust, and they were strictly warned.

My visibility in the corporation and the fact that an angry ex-employee was waving the flag were not in my favor. I knew that the situation was grave.

From that meeting, I had to go into the Women's Council panel. John Walker and the corporate attorney stood in the back of the room full of young women. I felt as though I were holding back the trump card in my talk. I made sure to tell my story about Kansas City. That one can fail and rebound. I hoped that the same would hold true for me in this latest fiasco.

A week later, I was stripped of my regional sales manager job. I was offered a job in staff marketing, working with my previous boss, Bob. It was obviously a severe demotion. I consulted with an attorney. He felt we should fight, since I was not the one who had met with the competition, nor was I the one who had gathered information illegally. The attorney said it was really my boss, who had told me to raise prices, who was the real culprit. I was just a pawn in the much larger game.

I debated long. I was crushed. Quitting was a viable option, but only long enough to realize that I was four months pregnant and dependent on the insurance with the company. I knew it would be difficult to find another job while I was with child. I was also in the final quarter in school, with graduation only weeks away.

I decided to stay, figuring I would do so just long enough to finish school, have a baby, and enjoy some paid maternity. I knew also that I could do the marketing job and that it would be a breather compared to the past several months.

I negotiated that the job title would not be the same as the marketing job I had left two and a half years ago, but a more elevated title. I was scrambling to save face.

Within days, I was gone from the northern region. I had been training my regional product manager, and though he was not ready for the job, I knew he would be a good replacement. After all, hadn't I been put into the same predicament just a few years before?

Emotionally, physically, mentally, I was drained. I gave the company my heart, my best. They did not stand behind me but made me the fall guy. They allowed a vengeful ex-employee to have the final blow. The boss who had given me the order was Champagne Sam. He was never chastised and actually got promoted.

If ever there was a lowest point in my career, this was it.

PART 8

Running

Zeroing In

My return to the marketing shop was with tail between legs. I was the disgraced child returning home. Bob became my boss once again. He was sympathetic, but he also needed help. The marketing shop had developed a reputation for not getting things done, and I had, if nothing else, a reputation for getting things done. He was eager for me to become a productive member of his team.

And frankly, I was anxious to get some distance between me and the episodes that had just occurred. Since I'd made the decision to stay at Cargill until my baby was born, I also made the decision to make the time productive. I had seen too many people leave the company, their contributions to the organization forgotten because their last months or years were spent coasting.

The first time through marketing, I was the Widget Queen. I had made small changes and implemented some programs that were still in effect. They were major accomplishments based on what I had to work with.

This time, I came in with accomplished management skills and an MBA. I never really thought about what I was learning in business school while I was going through it. It happened at a time of life when I was learning an incredible amount anyway, with managing people and a part of the business. But there were elements that I picked up on in business school that had nothing to do with sales management, but much broader in scope and range. Suddenly, I found myself in a job as marketing manager, where other business disciplines played a part. No longer was I solely concerned with the tactics of sales and sales management, but I began strategically setting the direction of future product lines and market segments.

My geographic responsibility was the entire country—not seven or eight states. I worked with all levels of management with more confidence, since shortly before I had been one of the key managers. I could say I had walked in their shoes, because I had.

I felt more powerful in marketing, because I was.

I had begun to formulate a total quality process (TQP) while I was sales manager, so I got involved in the corporation's search for a TQP consultant. Business school had exposed me to several leaders in TQP, so I had the jump on other managers. I was sold on the process. Unfortunately, it was outside the domain of the marketing shop, and the ultimate operations and management of the TQP did not end up with us.

I ran into problems when I wanted to purchase a desktop computer. At this time in history, individuals did not have computers—laptop, desktop, or otherwise. It was before e-mail. I wanted an Apple Macintosh to do my day-to-day work. The corporation was totally IBM. The IBM personal computer was too cumbersome and unfriendly for my purposes, as it was using DOS, which wasn't intuitive for the average user. I didn't need to link into the mainframe; I only needed some word processing and spreadsheets.

I had been using my personal Apple Macintosh computer to develop budgets. As a sales manager, I would have to budget and forecast sales dollars and products for six salespeople and six to eight production plants or terminals. The other sales managers were using huge ledger-lined paper, a pencil, and an eraser. I put my budget on my Mac. I remember changing a number for one of the salesmen and having to wait five minutes for the recalculation to flow throughout the spreadsheet. On the ledger sheet, it was a twenty-minute mathematics exercise.

My new boss, who had been my old boss, Bob, did not approve the expenditure. Computers were perceived as glorified typewriters, and he did not believe that managers should type.

My tolerance for bureaucracy was at an all-time low. I was recovering from a major setback. I was trying to get my feet back on the ground in a new job. The last thing I wanted to do was begin a fight over a computer. I had bigger battles to wage.

I ended up buying my own Macintosh computer for work. I figured that the $1,800 I spent out of my own pocket was money well spent in reduced stress and increased productivity. And just because the company wouldn't buy one for me didn't mean I shouldn't have it. The computer made me better, faster, and, some would say, smarter. I was an early adopter and the first manager with a desktop computer.

I became involved in the development of several new products. I realized from my MBA classes that we were sorely lacking in any type of new products or product life cycle management. My strengths were in organizing and getting people to act, two critical skills in getting new products off the ground.

I buried the hurt and the disappointment of my demotion with work.

And, of course, I was due to have a baby in November.

Vision-Ship and Champion-Ship

A basic tenet of the total quality process is to serve both the internal and external customer. That meant at any given time, my boss was my customer or the field managers were my customers, just as the people who bought our products were customers. It seems like a no-brainer now, but back in the day, this was a novel concept.

This sensitivity to customer needs eventually translated into a vision for the product, market, or division. By having a sense for what was needed, one could translate those needs into a vision that led toward the fulfillment of those and other unanswered needs.

In order to produce results on projects, I became a champion of sorts. Not "champion" in the sense of *best* but of *advocate*. I became, in effect, a champion for several products very quickly. I took them under my wing and fostered their good health. We began developing anticorrosive deicers for highways and sidewalks. These products were innovative, needing considerable nurturing and advocacy within the organization and also needing management support to continue funneling funds to them.

Another new product was a mentor program.

I had long felt there was a need for a formalized mentoring program. The time of knowing all the employees on a first-name basis or golfing to get ahead was passing. Just on the Salt sales side alone, where we used to hire two college recruits a year in the early '80s, I had been involved in over ten college recruit and direct hires in 1988. I saw the same thing happening in other disciplines within the Salt Division. So, in less than ten years, sheer numbers of new employees were making the "family" company too large to adequately nurture new people.

I was also in the position to make a mentor program happen. Unlike the quest for total quality, where I had been involved in the search but had not been included in the implementation, in my current position, I wore the hat of sales trainer in addition to my marketing hat. Therefore, under the guise of trainer of new employees, I was able to develop my mentor program.

The mentor program, Professional Advice Liaisons (PALs, for short), was named late one night when I was ruminating in my office. It became one of my "children," as did the other products I had been championing. I took great pride in the developmental process—taking concepts and turning them into physical entities. That was compensation that the corporation could not dole out but was as important as the money.

I found that I was very good at the developmental process, just as there are those who are good maintainers of business and those who are good closers of business. As a manager, one is called upon to do all three tasks, but the three modes—development, maintenance, and closing—require skills significantly different. Knowing this makes the accomplishment of each task less of a mystery and more methodical and therefore more predictable in outcome.

Mom-Ship

It was 1987. One would think that the world of men and women would have progressed further than it had. I was living a liberated life, yet my own sense of the new age rules was vague at best.

I took my last out-of-town business trip before giving birth in early October 1987. I was going down to interview candidates for a sales opening in Dallas, Texas. It was memorable because I was huge, lumbering down the aisle of the airplane, sweating in the Texas heat. I wore a light gray oxford cloth maternity dress with a matching bow and spent every break in the ladies' room, relieving my smashed bladder. We interviewed several people and ended up hiring Roberta Darcy for the open sales job.

On November 11, 1987, I gave birth to Tom. The agonizing details are fruits for another book, but for these purposes, it is enough to know he arrived, I survived, and I planned on taking the six weeks of maternity leave and four weeks of unpaid leave. With Thanksgiving and Christmas thrown in, I had effectively twelve weeks off.

Frankly, the first few weeks after he was born, I was in no condition to go back to work, nor did I feel motivated to do so. All my energies focused on healing and coping with this new family member. I also wanted to take some time to step back from work and assess my goals. We had arranged for a new college hire to act as my liaison while I was gone, tending to tasks she could attend to and filtering my mail so I would not be deluged with correspondence while on leave.

I had set out to find suitable day care just as I set out to accomplish projects at work. I had must/want lists and a questionnaire that I filled out on prospective candidates. I first looked for someone who would come into my home and care for Tom. It was soon evident that the dependability of this form of day care was not as high as I needed. I was one of the first female managers in Cargill to have a baby, so the spotlight on how it would impact my job was intense. One of my fears was to get a phone call at 7:00 a.m., telling me my caregiver could not show. It was a dilemma I did not even want to confront in a what-if scenario.

Since that was one of my prime concerns, I began looking at institutional day cares that had regular working hours and holidays similar to my work. I visited virtually every day care in a five-mile radius, talking to the directors, sitting in their infant rooms, rocking my baby in their rocking chairs.

I finally found a day care that scored high on my questionnaire and also had the kind of quality people working there so that I felt my baby would be well cared for during my absence. It was closer to Scot's work, but that was okay, too. As long as it was close to one of us, I did not feel compelled to have it closer to me than to my husband.

The weeks went by. Slowly, I was able to get around easier as the stitches healed. The college hire and I would talk several times a week, and I thought I was keeping in touch.

What I didn't realize is that while I was talking to the college hire frequently, she was filtering information before I was getting it. Consequently, I was only getting her version of what was going on. I didn't maintain close contact with the field managers I was working with, nor did I stay in frequent contact with my boss. Bob was more concerned about keeping my maternity leave "pure" and uninterrupted.

My first day back at work felt as though I had never had an extended leave. The work was waiting, and I was anxious to get back into the swing of things. The hours flew by. Before I realized, it was 4:30 p.m.

Now Scot and I had agreed that he would drop Tommy off and I would pick him up. Scot's normal work hours were 7:30 to 5:40 four days a week. My work hours were 8:00 to 4:30 five days a week. We figured he would have more time in the morning to drop off, since it was on his way to work, and since my working hours ended an hour and ten minutes before his, the pickup would be easier for me.

What we didn't anticipate was my modus operandi. I was not a morning person, and I liked working late. I liked having the office clear out so the phones were not ringing and the constant interruptions of the day ceased.

Our designated roles lasted less than a week. We quickly changed our responsibilities so that I was the dropper-offer and Scot was the picker-upper. It worked better immediately and ever since.

After I got back into my work, twelve weeks after the birth, I found that information had slipped through the cracks. While the college recruit had appeared to have done a good job overall, she did not have the experience, nor did she know the company structure and culture well enough to make decisions on projects that she tried to control. And it became more evident to me that she had rather reveled in my absence. My boss, who I knew was a hands-off kind of manager anyway, had not become involved in the activities of the college recruit. And since I was not watching too closely during my leave, she had pushed beyond her limits.

We had not managed my maternity or my stand-in as well as either needed to be managed. But in all fairness, we had no framework to guide us. Many of my coworking managers asked me why I wanted to come back to work after having a baby. One man outright told me he thought it would be better if I stayed home. I felt as though he said that just to prove a woman's place was not in a challenging corporate job.

And, unfortunately, maternity leave back then was a highly visible and suspect absence in the corporation. To have projects completed less than perfectly during that time was dangerous.

Even after I returned from leave, managers were suspicious of my intentions. Was I going to stay, or was I going to quit and become a "full-time mom"? Should they invest time and energy in me—a new mom who might at any moment defect? Again, we were plowing new ground here. The overriding belief was that a mom couldn't be as focused or committed since a mom also had a baby. No one who had come up the ranks of the management trainee path in Salt had ever been pregnant or given birth. The only female manager at the time besides me was Coco Summers, the HR manager, who was married but had no kids.

By falling out of touch during my maternity leave, the silence allowed the managers who harbored the above suspicions the time and reason to support their concerns. I returned to work somewhat behind the eight ball, scrambling to adjust to a new baby and a new attitude confronting me at work.

Long-Distance Relationships

One of the products that needed some guidance and management was called Dust-Off—a dust suppressant produced at our San Francisco Bay facility in Fremont. Dust-Off was liquid magnesium chloride that was sprayed onto dirt roads to control the dust. I had been involved in the branding and marketing of Dust-Off in the marketing department the first time around. At that time, we created a brochure and sales literature for the product. We had begun to sell it as a dirt- and gravel-road stabilizer, so the sales channel was very similar to selling highway deicers. That had been about four years previously, and nothing new had happened since then. Mag chloride was a by-product of our salt operations. For every ton of salt produced, a ton of mag chloride would result. It threatened to overwhelm our solar evaporation plants if not sold. For years, it had just been piled up and out of the way, but we were running out of room.

When I returned to marketing, they needed help to pump some life into Dust-Off sales. It had, in MBA terms, plateaued in the marketplace, and sales were flat.

A distributor of the product had found that when used in a particular application, it hurried the cure rate of a surface, which could mean considerable dollar savings for the contractor using the product. I began investigating this usage.

Dust-Off was produced and marketed on the West Coast. I was living in Minneapolis and commuting to California to work with the managers on the product. Several of the men working on the product were cronies from my old Leslie Salt days. Our relationship started out fine because of that old tie.

The West Coast manager who controlled the Dust-Off product needed help and guidance, but his boss, the general manager, viewed me with suspicion and didn't want me involved. My boss told me to manage as much of the project as possible, so I tried to reach out from Minneapolis.

I had made it clear that I would be interested in leading the Dust-Off product and would be willing to transfer to do it. I was told very early on that I was not going to get the position—they were not going to transfer anyone to manage it.

I continued to work on the project, but I soon found that I was having trouble gaining access to information. I would call to check the status of a project and would get enough information to placate me, but not the full story. If I did not call or initiate contact, no one would keep me abreast of activities. I was in a dotted line management matrix and didn't have the position to demand compliance.

I fell out of grace with the general manager on the West Coast, who supported his own managers first. Suddenly, I could do nothing right on this product. Bob Lee felt I should be managing the product from Minneapolis, but it was obvious to me that the West Coast managers were not in agreement with that.

And then I realized he who controls the information controls the project. And he who has the ear of the senior-most manager wields more power. I could not manage Dust-Off from Minneapolis because I was not privy to all the necessary information that was being generated on location, and my backer was lower in the pecking order than the West Coast managers.

It was much the same situation as what happened during my maternity leave: information is power. And I was not getting it.

Once this dawned on me, I went to my manager and explained how I could not do what he wanted (manage the product) if the local managers refused to share information and continued to wrestle for control. They would always win, since they had the firsthand access and they could block my involvement. The only way I could be successful was to move out to the location or have upper-management support. I was getting neither.

Since this was one of several products and markets that I monitored, my boss did not push the matter, and the field managers regained complete control of the product.

Before derailing, I may have fought harder for control. I may have made it an issue that I could and would succeed at managing the West Coast product from Minneapolis. But I now began choosing my battles more carefully, and I began to recognize that there were plenty of battles to pick.

PART 9

Gymnastics

Scot

People have said that my husband, Scot, likely has a story more interesting than mine. I agree, but it's not my story to tell. What I can say is how Scot's actions and behaviors in our early marriage made my continued quest possible and how his involvement in raising our babies was instrumental to my success and the success of our relationship.

Scot was a high-powered, ambitious college graduate in his own right. Out of high school, he took the entrance exam for the Air Force and scored the highest that the local branch had ever seen. He was on track to gain admittance to the US Air Force Academy. On his first day of active duty, they discovered he had a healed fracture in a neck vertebra. Scot figured it was the result of an old football injury, but regardless, he was honorably discharged the same day, and his dream of the academy evaporated.

Instead, he attended the University of Minnesota–Morris for a quarter, where he was on the tennis team, and later enrolled at the University of Minnesota–Twin Cities campus. His interests ranged from meteorology to mathematics and finally settled on the challenging field of electrical engineering. Before graduating from the University of Minnesota, he had already received a multitude of recruitment letters from companies across the country. He could pick and choose. When I graduated from Stanford, I remember exactly how many recruitment letters I received. Zero. Nada. None.

Hughes Aircraft hired him out of school into their rotation program for almost twice the salary I had received. It was somewhat similar to the Cargill College Program. After transferring to Los Angeles, California, he spent months rotating throughout Hughes, working in different departments. He became a California beach boy, sun-bleached blond hair, sky-blue eyes, and sunburned skin. After a couple of years, the thrill of Southern California wore off, and Scot returned to Minnesota to join Honeywell's undersea division, where he worked on the Mark 50 torpedo system and began the University of Minnesota evening MBA program. That's where he was when I met him.

We both graduated from the MBA program. I was a solid B student. Scot was recognized by the professors and *Twin Cities Business* magazine as one of the top students in the graduating class. I had me a pretty smart guy.

But when I began thinking about settling down, smart wasn't one of the criteria on my spouse must/want list. In one of my conversations with my oldest sister, Carol, I told her there were only two criteria on my must list: must play tennis and must ski. She added another: must be gainfully employed.

Today, I have heard it said, "The most important business decision a woman makes is choosing the person she marries." I never heard that back in the 1980s. When I began to think about marriage, I thought more about a playmate than a business mate. I had lots of business mates at work. Smart was important to me, particularly smart in ways different from me. I had always been attracted to geeky, slide-rule/HP-calculator-carrying guys. They were the exotic animals roaming fields I could only imagine but not comprehend. And like any good animal husbandry 4-H'er, I figured with my people skills and Scot's technical aptitude, our children would be the perfect balance of the two.

In retrospect, maybe I should have had more criteria: must have good work ethic; must be trustworthy, loyal, helpful, friendly, courteous, kind, clean, brave, reverent. Wants could have included rich, famous, body like a professional athlete, Boy Scout type. But those wants weren't important to me, and I can't say any of the traits above would have made me the perfect spouse or partner.

Scot only knew me as one of many women in the evening MBA program. We were all motivated, driven to achieve, and successful individuals. When we married, he had no qualms about me keeping my maiden name—I had more concerns than he, and several in my family raised an eyebrow. He dove into parenting much more enthusiastically than I. He was at every doctor's appointment. He gained almost as much weight as I did. He was at each delivery and was the first to hold the babies. He changed the first diapers. He was up in the middle of the night bottle feeding.

He was also the first on the business front: first man to be a "wife" at company management meetings. He joined the wives at events scheduled for them while managers were in meetings or workshops. He welcomed my male coworkers into our home for business socials and parties. He never questioned my need to travel with male coworkers. And because of our roles and how we embraced them, more women employees were invited to participate in business social activities. Most importantly, he was a single dad many evenings, days, and weeks while I traveled on business. I was envious when he took the kids to the mall and the female salesclerks would ooh and aah over him and the baby in the stroller. They never did that to me! And he did all this while maintaining a challenging career for himself, first at Honeywell and then at MTS Systems.

He relished his role as one of the first men. He viewed my work as important. Our incomes over time were comparable. We made financial decisions together as partners. And even now, I generally refer to and introduce him not as my husband but as my partner in this fifty-fifty deal we're in.

But ours was not an unending honeymoon. My sister Carol imparted wisdom to me that she had to struggle through. She had been married for over twenty years by the time I married. She knew for a fact: couples fight. It's normal. Our mom vowed she would not fight with our dad because she grew up in a home full of strife, possibly fueled by alcohol. Consequently, we never experienced parents arguing, never experienced how compromise, negotiation, or give-and-take worked in a marriage. We only saw that my mom took it all the time and gave in to our dad to keep the peace.

My girlfriend Richelle has a PhD in psychology. She gave me the book *The High-Conflict Couple* at one point in my marriage. I could be described as "independent," "ambitious," or "self-centered." Scot likely fits the same descriptions. While our intellectual strengths may be in very different areas, we were driven in much the same ways.

So in saying that the most important business decision a woman makes in her career is deciding whom to marry, I don't agree. Making a business decision at thirty years old and expecting that decision to last a lifetime is virtually impossible. A business grows, changes, and morphs many, many times in twenty, thirty, forty years. The business environment changes as much or more. Decisions made at the inception of that business need to flex and change over the course of the years to meet the needs of the organization or it will die. Marriage is a business, too. Sometimes Scot flexed, and sometimes I did. But for sure, the business of our marriage changed over time.

Pride and Prejudice

When I was pregnant with Tommy, we had an ultrasound performed. The doctor, in his very clinical way, said he liked to have ultrasounds done to detect any deformities that may exist. It was not exactly what I wanted to hear, but we were anxious, and in my typical controlling style, I wanted to reduce the number of surprises by reducing the number of unknowns. This meant that knowing the sex of the baby before it popped out was very desirable.

With Tom, the lady running the ultrasound found his genitals right away and asked us if we wanted to know. In unison, both Scot and I said, "Yes!" We were both excited when she announced, "It's a boy!" In my family, there were fewer boys than girls, and so I was especially happy to hear the news.

During my second pregnancy, even though the need to know the sex was not as pressing, we decided early on that we would have an ultrasound and try to find out. I really didn't care as much as the first time, because I had been through the process before and I knew what to expect (let's not get into why, knowing the pain of childbirth, I would do this again). I also had a "mother's intuition" kind of feeling that this baby was also a boy. I was so sure of this feeling, we always referred to "it" as "him."

Scot and I met at the doctor's office, and the same woman did our ultrasound. We were asking her what "he" looked like, if everything looked okay and oohed and aahed over his fingers and toes. Again, she asked if we wanted to know what sex the baby was. We said yes, albeit less enthusiastically than before. Without hesitation, she said, "You had better start calling him a her!"

Then she proceeded to show us chubby little mounds with no male appendages.

Both Scot and I were silent for a moment. I laughed nervously and sheepishly said I had been *so sure* she was a he. We finished the ultrasound and left the doctor's office. Inside my mind, I was disappointed, but I didn't want to say anything. Gosh, I loved this baby, and I couldn't possibly be disappointed because it was a girl instead of a boy. How sexist was I? Hey, I was an enlightened, liberated woman—*wasn't I?*

Neither of us said anything about the sex of the baby. We discussed the wonders of modern technology on how they could do the procedure. We talked about how the pictures had compared to when we had viewed Tommy in the uterus.

Only late that night did we begin to talk—about being so surprised. Thinking about the clothes and toys we thought we could hand down if it had been a boy, but now that it was a girl, why some of those clothes and toys would be inappropriate.

What? Inappropriate? What happened to gender neutrality? Who were these people?

But more threatening than the thought of buying new clothes or toys was my own realization how sexist and stereotypical my own thinking was. I was so afraid to think I may have wanted a boy more. I was afraid to think I may have considered a girl as "not as important." Pink! Blue! Who had taken over my brain?

I shared my fears and realizations with few people. It just seemed so out of character and 1950-ish.

And now as I look back, those days seem pale. My second child was special from the day she was born. She was different from Tommy, not only because she was a girl but because her personality was so totally her own. Where Tom was the oldest and the caregiver, Maiya had the second child's defiant spirit.

She was fiercely competitive, played soccer and hockey, and played tennis on the side. She was strong physically. A girl in looks and style, she indeed primped in the mirror in ways I never did. She was tough but charmed you with her eyes and smiles. We talked, half jesting, half serious, about when she would become a rocket scientist.

It was easy to fall into a "Dad and Tom, Mom and Maiya" routine, where the boys would hang out and the girls were left out. The community education night school offered a class called Fathering Successful Daughters. I made sure we attended, and the information was enlightening. The premise of the class was that for a girl to grow into a successful young woman, she needed the father to include her in his life and interests; that the actions of the father had a much greater impact on a girl than the mother's.

But the impact Maiya had on my life was significant in a special way. She was the mirror reflecting my innermost hidden self.

We chose Maiya's name because we were looking for a Japanese name, and when we couldn't find one we both liked, I recalled the territory manager in Saint Louis had named his daughter Maya, after Maya Angelou, the well-known black author.

We changed the spelling, because I thought the *i* in there was more Japanese-looking.

I hoped that my Maiya had the strength and intelligence of Maya Angelou, who overcame incredible social and economic barriers to rise to the top of her field.

I hoped that my Maiya could someday do the same.

Whatever her field of wonder might be.

Canadian Public Works

In the spring of 1990, I went to Winnipeg, Manitoba, to the Canadian Public Works Association trade show. We were promoting one of my championed products, an anticorrosive highway deicer. There were four of us from Cargill who attended the show: Harry, who worked for me as an outside public relations consultant; Roberta, the Dallas woman I'd hired in 1987; Sven, the operations manager I had worked with in my sales manager role and who now headed up the anticorrosive product; and me. I was the marketing expert for the anticorrosive product.

Two men and two women working a trade show. It did not seem that unusual, except for the fact that only a few years earlier, the only women a person would see at a trade show were the sequined beauties that adorned booths but did not, in the business sense, "work" the booth.

Roberta and Harry were new on the project. This was one of the first trade shows for both of them on this particular product.

Harry, who (like my older brother) had been named after Harry Truman, was a supportive fellow, mild mannered, and not one to take charge and lead the troops over the hill. His style was steady and constant, and, like the tortoise, you could place money that he would finish the marathon but wouldn't win the 100-meter dash.

Roberta and I were roommates during the trade show. She and I had lots of time to talk and share, I would guess much like the men on their fishing trips talked and shared. It was gratifying and warming to have a woman with whom to share fears, hopes, and concerns, to be able to advise, question, and listen to another woman as involved in the business as I.

More importantly, neither Roberta nor I were threatening to each other. Neither was a queen bee, trying to squelch the other. When we went to the casino at the top of the Winnipeg Hotel, Roberta was the one who walked away from the blackjack table with the winnings. Whereas I had always wanted to play blackjack but had been too shy or afraid to take the risk, she stepped right up and had the time of her life. I admired her.

Sven and I had been working together since I had been regional sales manager and he the operations manager—a time span of over five years. He was one of my favorite coworkers—worked hard, played hard, and had a great sense of humor.

When I first became involved in the CG-90 anticorrosive product a year and a half earlier, I was working full-time in a pivotal position, coordinating research, legal, and negotiations with the inventor, in addition to responsibilities for other product lines. As the anticorrosive product developed, it was clear to me that we needed more resources and a full-time product manager assigned to the project.

I wrote the job description, made the projections, and helped with the hiring for the job that I would have loved to have taken on. But with another baby on the way, I stepped back, and Sven took the position. It was a tremendous move for him, and I knew that because of him, I would be able to continue to contribute marketing expertise without threatening him or his position.

The show was a great success. We introduced our product into Canada and began developing contacts in that country. We worked with one of our distributor's employees in the booth and solidified our relationship with the distributor. We adopted a potential customer into our small family.

I look back on that week in Canada as an example of how far we had come and how good things could be. We were four individuals, brought together by a common goal for a new product. We worked together as a team, leveraging one another's strengths. We worked together, drank together, played together.

Without fear. Without threat. Without worrying. No one was looking for a roll in the hay. That was a nonissue. We were managers, working and having fun at the same time.

And it was great fun! It was fun to talk about our product and the problems and opportunities we would confront trying to sell it in Canada. It was fun trying to play out marketing scenarios. It was fun working the booth, trying to qualify the "deadbeats" from the true prospects.

And I thought, *This is how I know it can be.* Men and women working together as people and not as objects or challenges. Being recognized as a person and a professional, in the most positive sense.

I have a dream.

The Curse of Part-Time

I started working in 1976. The mommy track had not yet been identified or defined. We were creating the working woman's world, but we were also defining marriage in the modern world. When Scot and I first began having kids, MTS Systems had a four-day workweek. It was fabulous and really made our homelife more balanced and equal. I had a demanding job and really didn't want to give up my dream of being a senior manager at Cargill.

But things change, and one day, the opportunity came for Scot to work on a team that was developing a new sales channel for MTS—a catalog business—that required working five days a week. It is breathtaking the difference turning a three-day weekend into a two-day weekend. Suddenly, Scot's available weekend was 33 percent shorter. We adjusted to the schedule and increased day care hours. It was still manageable, and the workload was still relatively equal between us.

But the real change in our relationship happened when I reduced my hours to part-time. That happened with kid number three. When Lee was born, it was a game changer. Two kids are easy: one kid for each parent. With number three, suddenly there isn't a person to hang on to a baby, while the parents chase two toddlers. Day care was dependable, but it was 50 percent more work to get that third kid packed up. I decided I would begin working part-time. Back in the day, working from home was unheard of—face time at the office was everything. We had desktop computers but just barely, and laptops were rare and just beginning to come into vogue. I negotiated a part-time salaried position, basically keeping my marketing job at reduced hours.

Since I was the pregnant one, I was the "logical" candidate to investigate the part-time route. But even greater than the "logical" choice issue were my own personal needs. I had always been a solitary individual. As a youth, I spent hours in my room or on my horse or in the machine shed, dreaming. I was the youngest of eight children, and although only eleven years spanned the oldest to me, there were three years between me and my nearest sibling. At times, I was like an only child.

Having one child cut into my personal time significantly. With two children and working full-time, my self was totally marginalized. I figured with three, I'd implode.

But when I went to my boss three months pregnant with my third child and requested an alternative work arrangement, I didn't try to explain my concern for myself. It sounded too much like Maslow's hierarchy for a bunch of men who called the shots to understand. I explained it in words that I thought corporations would understand. "More time with my children." "Struggle with the superwoman syndrome." "Early childhood developmental needs." "Motherhood as my first priority." All these things were true, too. But to be successful with my children, I needed to take care of me first. That meant time for me.

In a way, I felt as though I'd sold out by using the mother/child excuse when I asked for special consideration from Cargill. I felt backed into a corner with the job responsibilities and the kid responsibilities, knowing there was going to be another baby coming soon. I put my head down and plowed forward. What happened for me would impact woman managers following behind me.

The corporation was uneasy about working out special arrangements. I was an exempt manager. I was a fast-tracker and had proven that even after two children, I could do overnight travel and manage exempt-quality work. There was a fear that if special arrangements were made, "everyone" would want special arrangements. My boss even suggested that I take on less-challenging work and do telemarketing on a part-time basis rather than try to maintain my exempt, managerial position.

I was overqualified to do telemarketing. I did not want *less*-challenging work but just *less volume* of challenging work.

I had worked for Cargill for over thirteen years. The timing was right for me to be requesting special dispensation, because the company was tight on good, strong, and solid middle managers. The company was also tight on good, strong, and solid women and minorities.

I like to believe we were at a time when they needed me more than I needed them.

The division president (a new one by this time) assured me there would be a job for me when I came back from my third maternity leave. I stayed in close contact with the office during my leave. (I had learned a considerable amount since the first time.) I came back mid-leave to complete some work that needed attention. I had a second phone line and a facsimile machine installed in my home. I stayed plugged in.

We finally ironed out an agreement. I would continue to be a class 12 manager, but my salary and workload would be 60 percent of full time. When we finally pared down my workload, I figured it was about a thirty-five-hour-a-week job. That *was* down 60 percent. The ground rules were simple. I could spend as little or as much time at work as I needed— just so the job got done. That was the same as I had been doing before. It was just that the job to be done back then was considerably larger.

The part-time arrangement was a positive change for me, and the company got a large volume of work out of me. At times, I felt guilty, not working full-time and not being a full-time mother, either. As a fast-tracker, it hurt me deeply to see less-qualified men pass me by.

As a woman raised in a very traditional Japanese / June Cleaver household, letting a day care spend forty hours a week with my children was foreign. Yet I was comfortable with the arrangement, knowing that the day care providers were experts at their job, just as I was expert in mine. I never felt like I would have been a better caregiver than the professionals.

Motherhood and approaching forty humbled me and made manifest that choices were limited and "having it all" was not my reality. I was on the mommy track. Life happened whether as originally intended or not.

My kids went to day care; I still worked. It was the ratio of both that changed. I also had time to be alone—without coworkers, children, or husband. It was a luxury, too rich to last forever, but so wonderful at the moment.

What I'd neglected to negotiate were the working rules at home. With Scot's hours increasing and my hours at Cargill decreasing, the shift in housework and childcare fell directly on me. We never analyzed whose career had the most potential, who needed support when, or what the demands would be to achieve our goals, professionally and personally. There was never a question in my mind that the welfare of the kids came first, but at what cost?

In the early years of our marriage and having kids, Scot and I were able to have it all—work, family, house in the burbs, friends, vacations. Scot's job changed from a four-day to a five-day workweek. My work-week got shorter. As time passed and Lee got older, I had the day care / work / home processes down pat. I figured I could begin working full-time again. I could get my career back on track, rocking and rolling.

I ramped back up to working full-time, adding more product marketing responsibilities onto my plate. What I didn't anticipate was the reluctance on the part of my partner to reassume home chores that we had shared before my part-time stint. Now that I was going back full-time, I didn't get to off-load those chores as I'd thought I would. It was a battle that was never won by either of us.

The Trip to Target

The summer of 1993, I asked my niece Kam to come and nanny for me. Tom was five, Maiya four, and Lee two. Kam was a natural caregiver—she was just starting college, elementary education—and the second oldest of my brother's four kids. Tall, beautifully exotic, long dark brown hair, oversized Asian/Caucasian eyes artfully made up. We were all excited for her to come and stay with us for the summer. I had worked hard to stay connected to my roots in Montana, and Kam was part of that legacy. She arrived with a suitcase full of games and activities for the kids. I was thirty-seven years old, back working full-time in the marketing shop at Cargill Salt, mother of three, juggling life. Having Kam arrive seemed like help was on the way! Three months of extra hands!

The first Saturday of her stay, we planned a trip to Target to round out her activities supplies. We woke early; I made a big breakfast of pancakes, eggs, and sausage. Scot had gone into work to get a jump on a project. It felt like a holiday, the two older kids chattering away, trying to impress Kam and garner her focused attention. Lee was almost two, strapped in his high chair, wide-eyed and wondering.

After we ate, I started Kam on the cleanup process and ran upstairs to get dressed. What a luxury to have her there, ready and eager to lend a hand.

I showered and lay down for just a second. I had a feeling of indigestion, probably from the pancakes and eggs. The feeling passed. I finished getting ready, and we loaded up the family van for the Target run.

When we parked the car and loaded the stroller with Lee, I had the beginnings of a side ache, but nothing to write home about. We were in a festive mood, ready to spend money on art supplies and paper and who knows what for the kids' summer. Life was brimming with anticipation.

As we strolled up and down the aisles, the side ache became progressively worse. By the time we were at the checkout, I was doubled over in pain. I made it to the car, had Kam drive us home, and once there, I made a beeline to the family room couch to lie down.

I was perplexed. I had felt fine except for that indigestion after breakfast. I called the local pharmacist and asked if there was an over-the-counter drug I might take, but he said the symptoms didn't point to anything a drug would alleviate.

I called Scot. "Scot, I have a terrible pain in my side. I don't know what it is."

Scot said irritably, "Well, what do you want me to do about it? I'm not coming home unless you have to go to the doctor." Clearly, he was head-down working on his project.

I pondered his statement. The burning in my left side continued to grow. I didn't want to go to the doctor—we had so many fun things planned for the day! Kam had just arrived; I wanted to show her the parks, the pool, the school, and welcome her to the family.

But I could do none of those things with the pain I was in. I could barely stand. I finally said, "Scot, you'd better come home and take me in."

We went to the hospital's urgent care center, and because I was a ten on the sad face end of the pain scale, they took me in promptly. The first thing they did was draw blood. I asked for painkillers, but they wanted to wait for the results. It was a long twenty minutes.

The doc swung into the room with a folder and said my white blood cell count was extremely high. What did that mean? I had an infection that needed treatment with IV antibiotics. How long would that take? I was thinking minutes, hours maybe. I had things to do, places to go, people to see. The doc eyed me thoughtfully and said, "I'm recommending that you stay at least overnight in the hospital for the IV and painkillers. Then we want to run some tests to try to figure what this infection is about."

I looked at this urgent care doc as if he were speaking Greek. Stay at the hospital? Never in my wildest dreams had I thought this could happen. But the pain reminded me that it could happen and I didn't have a choice. It was a pain I could not ignore, so I nodded weakly, on the verge of tears, and checked in to Methodist Hospital in Saint Louis Park.

The good news was that the kids had Kam, and so I didn't even have to think twice about their well-being. The other good news was that they gave me painkillers. They dulled the pain enough that I could start thinking straight.

The bad news was I was lying in bed with the tie-in-the-back faded-green hospital gown, on a *no food* order, and no idea what was wrong.

For *five days* they kept me on IV antibiotics and bags of IV food. *No* oral food, period. I started to feel better each day, and by Thursday, I was feeling good enough to go home. The doc said I could eat a meal at the hospital, and then he would release me. I had a gleeful smile on my face.

So the Thursday after the Target fiasco, I had my first meal: toast and white-looking stuff—probably pork and potatoes with gravy—and something pale green, like lima beans. I ate with relish, the first food passing my lips in a week! Next, I would go home!

I was happy for about twenty minutes, and then the food hit the wall. All of a sudden, my gut constricted, and the crazy pain recommenced. I was back to square one. They hadn't even had time to unhook the IVs.

They ordered a barium X-ray for that afternoon. I had to drink a chalky concoction that I playfully called a milk shake. Less than ten minutes later when that chalk hit my guts, I thought I was going to die. Really! The painkillers weren't packing it! Oh God, take this pain away!

They rolled me to the X-ray room. I said through clenched teeth, "I am going to die."

The tech looked at me impassively, eyebrow raised, and said, "Lie still. We can't get a good X-ray if you're moving."

Lie still? A person could die, and I guess at that point, lying still would have been a given. I lay there as still as possible and squeezed my eyes shut. Tears ran down the corners of my eyes.

They ran the X-ray over me, then told me to drink *more* of the chalk. I was at their mercy. This was what torture must be like. I drank more chalk.

Finally, it was over, and they rolled me onto a gurney. I looked at the one in the lab coat who had told me to drink more and said, "I thought I was going to die." He just pushed my gurney toward the door, and someone rolled me toward my room while I lay there inert, exhausted, with the barium slowly moving through my system.

The doc arrived with the results, and they were not good. There was a mass in my gut, irregularly shaped. The irregularity of the mass was problematic, and they wanted to test more. They thought it could be a tumor or diverticulitis, a pocket of rotting gunk in the large intestine. With the pain I had experienced and the shape of the mass, they wanted to take me to the next level—the colonoscopy.

By this time, it was late afternoon on Saturday, a week since being admitted. They scheduled the colonoscopy for Monday, as I would need a day of prep. Scot was coming in daily, juggling kids, Kam, work, and hospital. I had kept my mom and family in Montana informed of the progress, in a lighthearted fashion, chatting on the phone. I was coincidentally continuing to take IV antibiotics to help fight whatever it was that was infected.

I never knew anyone who'd had a colonoscopy, and so the experience was new. On Sunday, the nurse walked in with this gallon jug of GoLYTELY, and told me I had to drink it all by the end of the day. I looked at the jug suspiciously.

Scot poured me a plastic cup full of the GoLYTELY, and I began to sip. It was five in the afternoon; I had plenty of time. I watched TV and sipped on the drink, chatting with Scot. It tasted like bad lemonade, a little thicker than water. The nurse came in to check on me.

"How is the GoLYTELY going?" she asked.

I said, "Fine." She left.

Two hours later, she came back. "How's the GoLYTELY going?" she asked again.

I said, "Fine."

She looked at my glass, half-empty. She squinted at the gallon jug, which was still 95 percent full. She stood up tall, looked me in the eye, and said, "This is *not* a cocktail party. Drink this GoLYTELY. Drink it fast. I expect the jug to be empty in the next four hours."

I called my mom. My mom had been at every birth and many holidays. I was on the verge of tears. I asked her if she would come out and just sit with me. She and I had always been close, and I needed my mom. She said she would come. Then I began guzzling GoLYTELY.

Having a colonoscopy is not the same as going to a cocktail party, I will attest to that. And they don't get better. I am, by now, an expert on colonoscopies. The prep is the worst, and the best part is that they drug you when they do the actual procedure. Back then, the drug didn't totally knock a person out, so that first colonoscopy was like watching an interesting TV documentary—interesting and intellectually stimulating, and drugged up, it was fascinating, even if it was a bit strange looking at the inside of one's colon.

I wish they had skipped the barium X-ray and fast-forwarded to the colonoscopy. Neither are fun procedures, but the colonoscopy told the story immediately and visually: I had a gross, irritated, ulcerated mass in my large colon, high on the left side, where the large intestine goes laterally cross-body south to the rectum. These are not the medical terms, rather how I describe what I saw. I'm sure the doctor's description would have been more colorful. The colonoscopy doc took a snippet of the mass to test, but he said it didn't look good.

By then, my head was reeling. And I really could have used a cocktail. Or two. And my mom.

The next few days were a blur. I had a stage II colon cancer tumor. It had likely been there for a few years. It was unclear whether it had metastasized beyond the colon, and the recommended procedure was a resection of the colon. They would open me up, cut out the bad part of the colon, and stitch the ends together, all without the need for a colostomy bag.

In the meantime, my tongue had turned black! All the antibiotics were killing every bacterium in sight, good and bad alike. My mouth lacked the good bacteria that kept it healthy and fresh (and pink). A black mouth does not go well with our standard of pretty, but it was what it was. Minor in the scope of things.

I signed the release to get the surgery. My mom arrived. My kids were having the time of their lives with their nanny/cousin Kam. They were not really aware of what was happening. Mommy was sick. Work was on hold, my coworkers and boss more than understanding. I racked my brain, trying to think of any symptoms that might have warned me something was wrong. Nothing jumped out. The week before, I had been at business meetings in Baltimore, eating, drinking, and working with the guys on the team. We were planning a customer event during the MLB All-Star break at Baltimore's new stadium. I was helping coordinate the event and promoting it to customers.

On a Tuesday morning, I was being wheeled into the operating room. Scot and Mom were at the hospital. Right before the double doors to surgery, my primary care doc, whom I'd known for years, came up to my gurney. He grabbed my hand and told me how surprised he was when he saw my name on the chart. He looked at me, still holding my hand in both of his. I am sure he sensed my fear. He said, "This is not your fault. Sometimes bad things happen." He stopped walking. I kept rolling. A wave of relief flowed over me. And then the doors closed.

I remember being groggy, Scot by my side. He said, "Everything's okay. They got the whole thing. They cut out a foot of your gut. But everything looks good." Then I went back to sleep.

I went in and out of consciousness. They told me to push this button when the pain got bad and it would shoot me with morphine. I remember being scared of too much morphine, but the pain was worse.

Mom was reading *The Bridges of Madison County*. I'd open my eyes, and she would be reading, tears running down her cheeks. She was at the good parts. Scot was going into work, Kam taking the kids, Mom watching over me. I had great care.

They made me walk right away. The doc said it was important to keep moving. My guts, inside and out, hurt. They had cut out about twelve inches of my large intestine. The tumor had almost broken through the intestinal wall but hadn't. It had been growing from the inside of the tumor out, so the center of the tumor was necrotic and infected. None of the lymph nodes were involved. A fact that, given the size of the tumor and the time it had been incubating, was just plain dumb luck.

Day three after surgery, I was beginning to feel human. I was sitting up but hadn't eaten yet. Every day, they'd get me walking; that day, I walked twice. Mom had been there the whole time—I'm not even sure she went home to sleep.

In the afternoon, I was sitting up. Mom was at the side of the bed. I was feeling better.

Mom said, "Do you have a will?"

"No," I said, looking away. I couldn't believe she was asking me this! I almost died, I know, but cut me some slack!

She forged forward. "What are you going to do if you die?"

I knew she was thinking about the kids. "I don't know. We haven't really talked about it. I guess it's time we do."

And so we sat for a while, not making eye contact but talking to each other about possible scenarios if I died, or if Scot died, or if we both died.

They said they didn't bring the kids in right after surgery because I looked so scary—tubes up my nose, down my throat, into the veins of my hands, oxygen mask, black tongue, catheter. I wish we had taken a picture of me at my worst so that I could say how good I looked later (!), but we didn't, so I can't.

On day four after surgery, day fourteen in the hospital, I ate real food! And it didn't hurt! So later that day, I was released from the hospital—weak, shaken, but alive.

Recovery—Back in the Game

I spent the next couple of weeks back in Montana, at home. My mom and I flew back, and Scot, Kam, and the kids drove. I was weak as a kitten and mentally worn out. I couldn't believe what I had just gone through. I was a woman, under forty, and had just gone through a colon resection to take out a cancerous growth. At that time, colon cancer was something old men got, not young women. Yet here I was with a scar from sternum to just above the pubic bone as a testament to what had just happened. I spent two weeks at home recuperating.

We drove back to Minnesota in the family van, three kids under the age of six, Kam the nanny, Scot, and me. We stopped at Devils Tower and the Black Hills. It is amazing how quickly the body works to recover. I could walk but not carry heavy objects. I slept a lot, but my sleep was disrupted and disjointed. I began communicating with the office. This had all taken place in the midst of the Baltimore Salt terminal's customer outing to the All-Star Game. I still don't know who was so lucky to score my ticket to the game. My other major project was a package redesign of the Salt Division's water conditioning product line. This was a huge project, involving focus groups, design agencies, marketing communications, bag production plants, and our own salt processing and packaging plants. A big rollout at the sales meetings was scheduled in August. I began reengaging as the lead project marketing manager.

At the same time, I began chemotherapy. I was amazed when I was leaving the hospital that the oncology doctor presented postsurgery chemotherapy as optional.

Optional? I thought. I could *choose* chemotherapy? I couldn't imagine not choosing to do chemo. I wanted to increase my chances of survival any way I could. To me, it was a no-brainer. I was doing chemotherapy, any flavor that the docs thought would be helpful.

Six weeks out of surgery, I began treatment. It was mid-July.

I was put on a regimen of 5-FU and Leucovorin and was part of a test group undergoing a condensed version of the standard treatment. I would undergo six months of treatment—one week of IV, three weeks off. I'd feel sick for a week, fair for a week, and okay for a week. Then it would start over. The week of IV infusion was the worst mentally. I began to dread the needles. I tried to watch movies—I remember renting a VHS cassette of Daniel Day-Lewis in *The Last of the Mohicans*—but I couldn't concentrate for the few hours it took to get drugged. Chemo sessions for me were totally wasted hours. That was tough for a person used to making the most of every minute—multitasking, managing.

My work schedule was flexible. Cargill was more than accommodating. I never thought of not working. The schedule, routine, and pace were comforting and healing. At times, I could almost forget the month of June.

The reaction of my coworkers was interesting. My boss, Bob Lee, was great. We talked about the cancer, about work, about how I thought I could do the design rollout, and then he more or less got out of my way. Carol Hines was the marketing administrative assistant, and she would be my arms and legs when I was out. On several occasions, Carol came to the hospital to fill me in on what was happening in the office and to get approvals and direction. The rest of the marketing team offered their support and proceeded with their projects. The rookie of the group and recent hire helped watch my projects. The larger group was the one where reactions varied. Some brave souls broached the subject like a hot potato—they'd toss around the C word and then drop it cold. Others ignored the topic like it didn't exist. Still others, like the guys who wondered why I would go back to work after having babies, wondered why I would go back to work after a cancer diagnosis, surgery, and chemo. By now, they only raised their eyebrows but didn't bother to offer advice as they had when I was pregnant.

The external vendors stepped up. We had a design firm, market research firm, and PR firm. Meetings that would normally be held at their sites were moved to accommodate me. They had their marching orders, decisions had been made, and they just needed to execute. And they did.

Bob Lee was a showman when it came to sales meetings, and he was going to be presenting the Knights of the Round Table program. We had a professional meeting planner tend to the meeting minutiae like menus, venues, and activities. An audiovisual firm worked with each presenter on the sales meeting content. It was their job, along with Bob's, to orchestrate the sales meeting with draping, lights, music, and AV. These affairs were long before digital cameras or videos, and Bob's meetings were some of the first that showed pictures taken during the event at the finale. The AV company would put together an elaborate slideshow with visuals of us in meetings, at dinners, golfing, or lounging, taken during the event. We thought it was magic to get photo slides done that quickly. Today, a fifth-grader could do the same thing—only faster—with an iPhone.

Bob had the voice of a radio talent—low, mellow, resonant. He knew how to work the crowd. The first woman to be named a Knight had her husband magically appear just like the wives before him. The Knights show continued to be an institution.

Each of us in the marketing shop had a role at the meeting, either to recap the past year or present what was planned for the future. The division president also took to the podium for his state of the union address. I was presenting on the water conditioning segment, one of the largest and most profitable for the division. I had my obligatory PowerPoint presentation, and at the last minute, the AV firm put together a prelude to my kickoff, a video highlighting the hoops we'd jumped through to get the package redesign work done while I was coping with cancer. The video included shots from the hospital, meetings with the design team, and getting the final approvals from the president. I presented near the end of the meeting, as it was a highlight that impacted virtually every salesperson in the company. It was a presentation, but it was also a sales pitch to gain buy-in from the field.

As the summer sales meetings approached, all systems were go. We were going to present at four meetings—San Francisco, California; Hot Springs, Arkansas; Minneapolis, Minnesota; and in the Poconos of Pennsylvania.

Sales Meetings, Round Two

The California meetings coincided with my week of chemotherapy, so my teammates presented for me. This would have been the toughest crowd to face, since the West Coast—even though my former team—still thought they had the corner on understanding the retail market. As the Leslie Salt Company, they had been firmly ensconced in selling salt rounds in grocery, packets in food service, and water conditioning salt direct to consumers. Cargill, even though the acquirer of Leslie, didn't have the background in grocery or food service. Cargill was just beginning to recognize marketing as an area of expertise, and selling as a career was still not widespread; the company roots were still firmly planted in grain trading and merchandising. The concept of selling to consumers was still pretty foreign to the corporation as a whole.

I got the easier meetings—Minneapolis, Hot Springs, and the Poconos.

Minneapolis was a cakewalk. This was my old stomping ground, and the field sales teams were already on board. By now at the sales meetings, there were a handful of women in sales attending and also women on inside sales support teams. I presented the new designs, the background on how the choices were made, and the justifications and projections on the new designs. There was a Q&A period, cheers and whoops went up, and the show moved on.

Midweek, we flew to Little Rock, Arkansas. This was about five days out from the end of my second chemo session. I felt punk right after the IVs, and the Minneapolis meeting was nice because I was near home and could retreat when I needed. My energy level was high during the Minneapolis meetings, as it took a few days for the chemicals to hit me.

Hot Springs was a different story. Flight to Little Rock, bus to Hot Springs, hotel check-in, meetings in the convention center. The good news was that Hot Springs in 1993 was a small tourist town, population around thirty-five thousand. It was easy to walk around. The mild nausea that I experienced with the chemotherapy was passing, the nerves of the first presentation in Minneapolis behind me. I was hungry after the long flight and hour-long bus ride. A group of us went to a local restaurant on the main street. I loved trying new foods in new areas, and I had never been to Arkansas before. They had a muffuletta sandwich.

"A what?" I asked. I had never heard of it before.

"Muffuletta," they said. "Try it. You'll like it."

And I did. This sandwich had a thin focaccia-type bread split with layers of salami, mozzarella, ham, some other kind of white cheese like Gouda or Havarti, provolone and this fabulous olive spread. I worked for the Cargill Salt Division, I loved salty, so olives were mouthwatering. This olive spread had chopped black and green olives, maybe celery, cauliflower, carrots, pickled peppers, tons of garlic and oregano, all soaked in olive oil. It was all generously layered and presented with a side of salty potato chips and an ice-cold beer. My mouth waters as I write this.

Some people talk about chemotherapy killing their taste buds. Some say their smell is altered. People lose their hair. I think everyone loses weight.

This muffuletta sandwich remains in my memory as the best sandwich I have *ever* eaten. It was spicy in all the right ways. But there was a price to pay.

I relished each bite. The savory goodness! The combination of cheeses and meats, the olive tapenade, the beer. The chips were the extra-crispy type that I love—almost burned, but not quite, thick and loud when you bit down. This was a large sandwich, and I ate the whole thing! And the chips. And the beer.

About two hours later, I had this burning in my gut. Not the "I'm going to die" burning that I had experienced earlier in June, but the "If I don't get to a bathroom, I am going to die of embarrassment" kind of burning. We were still walking and shopping in downtown Hot Springs when I turned to the shopkeeper and asked for the restroom.

Thirty minutes later, I emerged a new woman. The muffuletta was flushed down, as was, I am sure, the chips and the beer. I also think the entire lining of my large intestine accompanied the sandwich and chips. One way the 5-FU and Leucovorin work is that they kill off the cells of the intestine. The dead cells are flushed out with undigested matter, so that cancerous cells can't hang on and grow. If my poop was any indication, the drugs were working.

It was the best sandwich, it was the worst sandwich. I never again ate spicy after chemo, and I have never had a sandwich as good as that muffuletta in Hot Springs, Arkansas.

The presentation in Hot Springs went off without a hitch. We had gotten the routine down, and we were on a roll. One more meeting would culminate our summer's work. Our last meeting was in the Poconos of Pennsylvania.

Pass the Creamer, Please

If you have ever been to upstate New York, you know it's one of the most beautiful places in the world. Our salt mine was on the shores of Cayuga Lake, in Lansing, outside the city of Ithaca. The salt evaporation production plant was in Watkins Glen, on Seneca Lake. All are part of the Finger Lakes region. It is nothing like New York City, and like nothing I had imagined in New York: pristine lakes, pines, hardwoods, and mountains; wood stoves heating households, curls of smoke the only indication of a house hidden in the trees. This area was the headquarters for Cargill's eastern region salt operations, which extended down through Pennsylvania, Maryland, to the Carolinas, and covered basically the Eastern Seaboard.

The New York sales meeting was the last one of the four-stop tour. It was being held southeast of Ithaca, New York, in the Poconos of Pennsylvania. Bob Lee, marketing manager Tim Krone, and I flew into New York, then drove together to the site. As the last meeting and one of the larger ones, senior Salt management was all there, from the president of the division on down.

A company president shapes the company's personality. Before I began working in the Salt Division, Tom Clayton was the president. He was a University of Minnesota football star, hard-drinking, skirt-chasing, big, handsome hunk of a guy. Sales meetings were legendary—womanizing, parties, rooms trashed, furniture tossed out windows. Even during work hours at the office, stories of "afternoon delight" were outed over drinks. Tom moved on, and John Walker took charge. John was the

president when I transferred to Salt. He and his wife were graduates of Carleton College, a prestigious liberal arts private school in Northfield, Minnesota. His wife was an artist and tennis player, and they would include me in weekend tennis gatherings. John managed by consensus, obviously loved and respected his wife, and was the perfect guy to work for as a woman. John was quiet but connected. The word *gentleman* would describe him. The Knights program likely started under his leadership, and meetings were fun but discreet. There was always time for a tennis match or two.

Following John and the president at the time of these sales meetings was Cy Thompson. He came in from the grain business; his roots were in Iowa. He was a high-strung, intense, competitive guy. Cy had a ruddy complexion, like a heart attack waiting to happen. He was a scratch golfer, so tennis was out and golf was in. I took up golf during his reign just so I wouldn't be excluded from the field. We connected on a personal level for a couple of reasons—I had worked farm to farm in Iowa; he had good friends that I knew in Montana; his second wife and her twin sister were career women running a home-decorating business. I had, by this time, finished the MBA program and was implementing value pricing for an anticorrosive deicer, which was a novel strategy for the historically cost-plus mentality of the traders. The old thinking was to calculate the cost of producing product, add $20/ton, and that would be the price. Value pricing didn't consider the cost of production, but the dollar benefit of the product—how much corrosion could we control or eliminate? He supported the changes. I felt that as long as I performed, Cy was okay and had my back. But Cy was struggling with a few of his own demons. He was currently on an alcohol-free diet.

The New York meeting was during the third week after my chemo regime, which meant I was feeling pretty good. The next week, I would be getting the 5-FU and Leucovorin drip again. But for the time being, I was high on a successful package launch so far and feeling good about presenting our dog and pony show to a friendly audience. Half this group was the region that I had been working with on the All-Star break customer outing—they knew and loved me. Wally Claeys—who had taken on the regional sales manager role when I was demoted—was the area general manager. This was safe ground.

The first evening of the event was a group dinner at tables of ten. There were probably one hundred people there. Paul Bono, the Baltimore sales manager, was seated at my table, as were some other sales and operations guys. Seated at the table directly behind me was the division president, Cy Thompson; my boss, Bob Lee; and the operations manager, Sven Gustafson.

Drinks were flowing freely, but a few folks were drinking alcohol-free O'Doul's to keep Cy company. Our table was lively and loud, not drinking O'Doul's but stronger stuff. Bono had just come off a successful baseball outing that cemented some key relationships; I felt strong and healthy going into my last design presentation. Those of us in sales had a reputation for telling good stories, and we all knew each other well. The person to my left asked Bono for some coffee creamer. The little bowl of single-serve creamers was right in front of Paul. He grabbed one of the 0.4-ounce plastic cups and tossed it across the table to the guy on my left.

I'd played a little softball in my early years at Cargill and played catch with my brothers growing up. I just instinctively reached out with my left hand and caught the creamer like it was an easy pop fly. But unlike a softball, it didn't smack my palm when I closed my fingers over it but exploded like a water balloon!

It sprayed me a bit, and the table burst out laughing. I was laughing, too.

The next thing I know, there's something pouring over my head and down my back. I figured Sven, the prankster, was horsing around behind me, so without looking and just as quickly, I flipped my glass of water back over my shoulder to get him back.

I was laughing, thinking I had gotten him good, when I realized my table mates were not laughing but looking horrified. One guy had his hand over his mouth, eyes transfixed. Forks skewered with food were paused mid-mouth. My brow furrowed. I looked at Paul Bono. Paul's jaw was hanging and his eyes were focused just behind me.

I turned slowly and then realized what everyone else already knew. It wasn't my ops buddy Sven but the division president, Cy Thompson, who'd been sitting behind me. He'd emptied his glass of fake beer on my head.

"What the hell's going on?" I remember hearing.

"Cy got hit with creamer," someone else whispered.

"He just poured his beer over Elaine," another amazed voice uttered. Then the entire room went mute. I still didn't realize how angry he was or why. We were just having some fun. I looked at Cy, stricken, confused. And then I realized—I had dumped my glass of water on him! Sven was sitting nearby, but he wasn't the culprit. I said a quick "Sorry" and turned around and looked at my table mates. I shrugged and picked up my fork and pushed the food around my plate. The rest of the table mirrored my actions, and the room conversation picked back up.

As the feeling returned to my extremities and the racing of my brain calmed, I realized I was wet—nothing like being dumped in a swimming pool (which I have been), but beer was over my head and shoulders. I got up to go to the restroom.

Looking back, in the early 1990s, having cancer was still like getting a death sentence. There were the survivors, but not near like it is today. Every person in that room knew I had colon cancer, that I had been through surgery, that I was getting chemotherapy treatment. They all knew I had worked through much of it and had finished the package redesign during the peak of the life crisis. I think they all thought I was going to die, though no one, not even myself, would speak to that scary ending. It wasn't that I didn't want to talk about it—if anyone asked, I would tell them anything they wanted to know. But I was very good at putting the big C in a box and keeping it contained. I was too busy during working hours to open that box and poke at its contents. Fear. Worry. Anxiety. All contained. I was working with it, not working through it. I treated having cancer like having a wart—ugly, unsightly, annoying—but not something that was going to kill me.

The first person who stopped me on my way back to my table from the hotel restroom was Roger Johnson, one of the Salt VPs. Roger had a reputation for being a tough but fair manager. He was well over six feet tall, a big guy, Vietnam marine vet. He had worked his way to VP via the Cargill Salt career path: sales, product manager, sales manager, regional manager, profit center manager, and up. I had never worked directly for Roger, but I always thought I would have benefited greatly from the experience, as he was known for challenging his staff and pushing them to succeed. He asked me if I was okay. I said yes. He castigated Cy for targeting me of all people—the one "struggling" with cancer. I didn't think my cancer had anything to do with the situation. I was horsing around and caught a creamer, and some of the spray hit Cy. Bad luck, I'd say. It got out of hand. For sure. I assured Roger I was fine. And I was.

The meeting went off without a hitch. Our design kickoff presentation was flawless. Except for that little 0.4-ounce creamer, this would have been the end of a very successful run.

Two weeks after the eastern region meeting, I got a call from a woman, a secretary from the Cargill "mansion." Senior management officed in a home converted to executive suites. The mansion was built by a World War I veteran for his French wife. It was a replica of a French château, replete with its own man-made lake in the backyard. There were many employees who had never been to the mansion. This was auspicious, indeed.

William Wooters, one of the Cargill corporate vice presidents, wanted to see me in his office. I wasn't sure what he wanted, but I thought perhaps he had heard of our successful package launch. Wooters was the Salt Division president's boss. In other words, he was my boss's boss's boss. A big fish. He was originally from Belgium and may have come from the chocolate business or perhaps the malt business. He had risen at Cargill by being tough and dispassionate. I thought at the time that his style was a trait of being Belgian, but years later, a Belgian French teacher assured me people from Belgium were not like him at all. On the designated day, I dutifully marched through the underground tunnel that connected the mansion to the Lake Office where my office was. I wore a conservative navy suit with white buttons and a few pleats in the skirt. I was ready for my gold star.

When I got to his office, the receptionist ushered me in. It was an impressive space, dark mahogany bookcases, French provincial curved desk and chair, comfortable cushioned armchairs with a round table a little off to the side for a tête-à-tête.

It's funny what your mind does to bury unpleasant experiences. This was a big deal in my career. I was sitting in front of one of the senior-most managers in the company. I thought I was going to be lauded for the package redesign. But the events as they transpired are fuzzy to me, and the order in which things happened is unclear.

The gist of the matter was that the creamer incident had come to Wooters's attention. Individuals within the Salt Division who had been at the eastern regional meeting and who had witnessed the event or had been in the room brought the issue to him. He told me that the company took this situation seriously and that actions were being taken. Cy was to issue a formal apology to me.

I sat there, taking it all in, not saying too much, but of course answering his questions. Wooters did not apologize, nor did he apologize on behalf of the company. He was acting as a messenger, doing his duty. I had thought I was going to be rewarded for a job well done, and instead, I was being spotlighted as a victim. To this day, I don't hold Cy responsible for his actions toward me. It wasn't about me. Cy overreacted, not at me but at the situation. It could have been anyone. I was guilty of being in the wrong place at the wrong time. It was Cy's bad luck that the target of his snap was the Japanese/woman/chemo/cancer victim. That doesn't excuse Cy. He overreacted, and while I am not a counselor, it was likely caused by his drinking, or lack thereof.

What's clear to me now is that I was a pawn in a political game. There were people who did not like Cy, didn't like his headstrong management style, his playing favorites. This incident was a catalyst to get Cy out of the job and put a black mark in his column.

What I missed and what a more astute and politically savvy person would have leveraged is that as a victim, I got nothing but a hollow apology. My successful package redesign and product repositioning, all a marketer's dream of success, were overshadowed by political posturing and never acknowledged by senior management. I wish now that I had been quicker to see and say what I wanted out of the deal—that I was in that auspicious office not for a political maneuver but for recognition and reward for a stellar job repackaging and repositioning the entire division's water conditioning line.

I wish I would have been smart enough to have said, "Yeah, that beer over my head is going to cost you. I want to be compensated in promotions, money, and recognition, not for the beer but for the performance."

But I didn't. Ask or get.

PART 10

Value Management for Non-Marketing Professionals

Overheads

A two day seminar to introduce terms, processes and models of value management

Elaine Koyama
6608 Nordic Drive
Edina, MN 55439
612.829.0911
Management
Protemps
Copyright 1999

Home Stretch

Changing of the Guard

Shortly after the marketing meetings, Bob Lee, my boss and mentor, retired. He may have been asked to retire, but either way, he got a great package to move on. Bob had spent his career at Cargill, the son of the past president of the Feed Division. His strength was not as a doer but in recognizing talent, pulling a team together, and having them get the job done. Bob was a master at getting out of the way so others could do their jobs. This was not only for us employees that worked for Bob but for advertising and PR agencies and promotion houses. Bob masterminded several fabulous sales incentive programs that were great successes—the Knights of the Round Table being his most memorable.

I thought that this might be my chance at his job, but looking back, I see now that no one was talking to me about my next promotion. About the same time, Coco Summers, who had long been the Salt Division human resources manager, discovered she had lung cancer that had metastasized to her bones. Coco and I were for years the only women in management. I had been in a meeting with her and other middle to senior managers with a document she'd dubbed "The Dead Sea Scrolls." This was literally a rolled-up piece of white butcher's paper that had the division org chart and names of successors for each position "in case the plane went down." At the time, my name was there as a sales manager. But this had taken place a few years earlier. Now as part of the marketing team, I was no longer part of the group deciding whose names were on the scrolls.

No sooner was Bob's retirement announced than the next announcement was made. John O'Roarke, who had been part of an oil-processing acquisition and was currently a profit-and-loss line manager, was to be the new director of marketing. The department was in an uproar. So many announcements, all hitting me blind! I went back to my office and picked up the phone. I called John O'Roarke to welcome him and pledge my allegiance. When he answered, his first words were, "Tim Krone already called. We just got done talking." Tim was one of my marketing cohorts. He was several years younger than I, a bold and brash guy who came across confident and knowing. I had significantly more experience than he, but I didn't have the in-your-face style.

Tim had beaten me to the punch. The jockeying for position had begun, and I was in second place.

Bob moved out, and John moved in.

The Transition

I had known John briefly as a line manager since I was marketing staff but hadn't yet worked with him. He was fast-tracked to our group, and I knew I had to prove myself again. I didn't get any warm, fuzzy feelings from John. He came from Greenville, North Carolina, a fact I only knew because I had called on our plastic packaging company there to make sure the designs I had been working on would print on their systems. John's family was prominent in Greenville; his wife was from a well-established family, too. The guys who ran the packaging business knew him well and had grown up down the road from him.

Tim Krone and I were the two most senior managers in the marketing department, and even though I was senior to Tim, with the cancer, chemo, and beer incident, it felt like I was scratching my way back up to par. Suddenly, I noticed Tim never left before John left and was getting to work abnormally early. Bob had been a hands-off manager—we came and went as needed. I had three kids, the oldest just in kindergarten, the youngest just out of diapers. I had day care drop-off duty in the morning, so I struggled to get to work by 8:15 a.m. I preferred working late, but

I still had family responsibilities, so I'd leave by 6:30. Tim beat me in and outlasted me most nights. John never acknowledged that I had kid responsibility or talked to me about what he expected. I was stressed not knowing where he was coming from—did he know I had to get one kid on a bus, two others to day care? Did he understand that I worked harder and smarter to get my projects done? Our conversations were always work related and specific to what he wanted to talk about—I wanted to bring up the family responsibility topic, but my skin crawled whenever I was ready to broach the subject. I began to deny my homelife existed. I was afraid that bringing it up would be a career showstopper. Unlike previous bosses, John never stopped in my office at the end of the day to catch up on the day's activities or chat about an upcoming weekend. He never once asked me about my family.

Tim didn't have these issues. He and his wife were newly married and hadn't started having children yet. We all traveled frequently in our jobs, meeting with our internal business clients and working with them to develop brochures, sales plans, strategies, and promotional events. We worked to streamline work processes and met with customers to stay on top of changing needs. One of these customers was Pillsbury. We supplied salt to a refrigerated bread dough plant. They used a truckload (twenty tons) of salt a week. At a teaspoon of salt per tube of bread dough, that was one big loaf of bread. Their biggest concern was running out of salt, a situation that would shut down their plant.

John, Roberta Darcy, and I were sitting together discussing the Pillsbury account. The contract was coming up for bid, and we were concerned about losing it. Running out of salt was a recurring issue. We had no warehouse close by their plant and didn't want to establish a warehouse just for a few tons of salt. Our production plant was at least a two-day drive away. We all were throwing ideas around the table. I suggested using an old, out-of-service van, keeping it full and on the Pillsbury site—a warehouse on wheels. Salt has a very long shelf life—it could just sit there for insurance. Roberta, the regional sales manager at the time, thought that could work. John pooh-poohed the idea and moved on.

Not ten minutes later, John suggested using an old, out-of-service van to warehouse a load of salt on their site. I looked at him askance (*Dude! I just said that!*), but he avoided my eye. Roberta said, "Yeah, good idea." And he ran with it.

Tim's star was rising. He was selected to participate in a young manager's networking group, hand-selected by the company to enhance the careers of the up-and-comers. It was the first time I had ever been passed up for this kind of opportunity. I was in year eighteen of my career. Tim was in year ten maybe.

I kept fighting, pushing to be recognized for my work. In a meeting with John, I was presenting him with a proposal for approval. As I sat before him, with financial justifications and rationale on spreadsheets, I struggled to maintain eye contact with him. But inevitably his eyes would drift from looking at me to *looking at me*—at my chest. I got the approval (on my proposal), but I left uncomfortable and a bit creeped out. I never felt threatened; I never felt as though there was quid pro quo expected, but it was still creepy.

I had helped hire Roberta back when I was pregnant with my first kid. Roberta had a soft Southern drawl that she worked to her advantage. And Roberta was well endowed, whereas I was definitely lacking in that area. She was a hoot to be around—bold, funny, ready for adventure. We had a running joke every time we had lunch together that we had to lose ten pounds. Then we would order a burger with fries and a beer. I took her aside one day and asked her if she noticed John looking at her chest. She regarded me wisely, eyebrows raised, and said, "Of course."

Passover—This Ain't Easter

John was quickly moved up to become the Salt Division president, and it wasn't long before Tim got his chance—he moved from the staff marketing job to a position in the field that had profit-and-loss responsibility. I was a bystander in all the activity, pulling the plow, unnoticed.

John's position as director of marketing was a job I wanted and was eminently qualified for. I had done fieldwork with P&L responsibility; I had worked in staff marketing; I had completed my MBA almost ten years earlier. I was the only MBA in the sales-and-marketing functional areas and one of the few in the entire Salt Division. I had contributed through thick and thin, through sickness and in health, literally. And yet, with John moving up and out, opening up the coveted position, they announced Geoff Nameth to be the new director of marketing and my new boss.

Geoff came in with no marketing background, but neither had John. Geoff had been a general manager for the eastern region, his roots being in Pennsylvania. With John, I felt as though he brought in the oil business background, a different twist. But Geoff? Geoff was a nice enough guy, another good-looking man. But clearly, to me, aside from having ten years on me, he was not more qualified to be the director of marketing.

Part of my job was to get Geoff up to speed—after all, I had the most tenure in the marketing shop at that point. He and I took a road trip to the mid-east region, flying in and out of Cincinnati. We spent three days together in a car, making the rounds, calling on customers, and visiting salt terminals. After the first day and a half, I was struggling to keep a conversation going. He was my new boss, and we had chitchatted about work and personal issues. I was building up the courage to tell him that I wanted to be considered for promotions and advancements. That I wasn't a dead horse. That cancer hadn't killed me.

But the weirdest thing happened. Geoff just kind of quit talking. As I was driving him to the airport after a day and a half of pretty much no verbal conversation, I was at wit's end. My window of opportunity to spew my guts and tell him my ambitions was closing. And yet it was so awkward. He was in the car, present, I think aware, at least not comatose, but just out of touch. I had always prided myself on being able to connect with people, able to draw them out, find mutual ground.

And then he spoke, about an hour before I was to drop him at the airport. He said, "I'm so glad we've been able to have these great conversations. We'll do this again sometime."

I mean, really? Had he been in another car with someone else? Because I certainly didn't remember "great conversations." And if riding in silence for a day and a half is what he considered "great conversations," we were definitely on different planets. And so I gave up. I was not going to put my career into this man's hands.

As I look back now, it all seems so clear, the handwriting on the wall. But at the time, I didn't realize I had become a nonentity, that I was no longer a player. I see now that no one was asking me what my career goals were. Did they think because I had three kids and had survived cancer, I didn't want upward advancement in my career? What would they have thought if I had been a man?

The flip side of the coin was that I had not told anyone—not Geoff Nameth or John O'Roarke or William Wooters—that I wanted more, I wanted to grow, I wanted recognition, money, and the title. I made some assumptions. One, I assumed senior managers knew that I was still ambitious and wanted to rise in the organization. I also didn't recognize that I wasn't the only odd man out—Geoff Nameth likely got the job I coveted because they didn't know where else to put him. Ultimately, I had no mentor high enough in the organization pulling me along. The guys I knew back when I was the rising star were retired or gone.

Then I made a fatal error. (Probably not the only one.) One evening, the marketing group was going to dinner with Wooters's successor, who was my new boss's boss's boss. We were all walking down a hallway to the dining room, and he asked me what I did. I thought he was kidding— like, doesn't he know what his people do? I laughed and said flippantly, "Everyone wonders what I do." I had been in Salt for so long, around Cargill for so long, had been a poster child for women and minorities, it didn't dawn on me this corporate vice president only one level away from the Cargill president and CEO wouldn't know who I was. I thought perhaps at dinner the question would arise again, but it didn't. I never got the opportunity to clarify and blow my own horn.

But I certainly blew it.

Elaine Who?

In the spring of 1996, I was forty-two years old. I had been working at Cargill since graduating from Stanford in 1976. Cargill Salt needed a sales manager, so I made the lateral move back into the field as the mid-east sales manager, again having salespeople reporting to me and working the Ohio and Illinois Rivers area. I didn't have the same resistance as the first time I became a sales manager—this group included women (!) and was younger and less entitled than the first group. And Roberta managed the northern region after I had. Women in middle management were no longer as novel as even a few years earlier. The job was a piece of cake. My new team consisted of two women and four men, one of whom was African American. They recognized and appreciated my competencies. I took great pride and satisfaction seeing my team prosper and grow individually and as employees of the company.

Some would say I had a successful career—highly visible, cushy corporate jobs, jetting around the United States working with branch offices, managing sales budgets and dollars that included spending with a major advertising agency in the Minneapolis market. Negotiating contracts with customers and attorneys. Three kids, ages nine, eight, and five. A husband of eleven years. A house in the burbs.

Women were beginning to make inroads not only in Cargill Salt but at Cargill corporate. The highest-ranking woman served as corporate vice president of human resources for the corporation. There were a few others in staff positions rising quickly. Things were still slower on the P&L side of the business, but even in the Salt Division, at one point women ruled Saint Louis—Janet was the territory sales manager, Betsy managed the East Saint Louis salt terminal operation, and I was the regional sales manager. East Saint Louis was a tough part of town, and we tended to call on customers in the not-so-desirable parts of the city—railroad and river industrial areas, grain elevators, factories. Janet had been in a shooting cross fire leaving a feed dealer in East Saint Louis. It would have been scary for anyone.

We had a young woman selling salt in Peoria. We called on Janine, who managed a grain elevator in northern Illinois. The Peoria saleswoman's key customer was Gateway Milling, and we referred to the owner as Jabba the Hutt. He was a tough and scary guy, big and burly. But after working with us women over a period of time, he became less scary and more respectful of our abilities, and he recognized he made money working with us. Jessica worked for me out of Chicago. She was one of the top salespeople in the Salt Division and won numerous sales awards. Women were being hired and succeeding in the entry-level management jobs, which meant they could have the opportunity to rise through the ranks.

At one point, I officed at the Cargill Research Center, located across the road from the Lake Office. I met Polly Caruthers there—she was hired for a technical research job—and I met Milo, who was the head of research and a Cargill family member. Milo's office was just down the hall from mine, so our paths crossed frequently. We had some hilarious interactions. I was a relatively new mom, and we shared parenting stories. His wife was a stay-at-home mom. I confessed to Milo one day that I loved going on the road because I got a breather from kid duty. I didn't feel particularly guilty saying this, since I had heard several of the guys say the same thing. Milo and I ended up teaming up to do food safety training throughout the Cargill Salt organization. At one training, I was presenting, and John O'Roarke interrupted my presentation to correct some detail. I didn't want to directly contradict him, but Milo and I had gone through the materials thoroughly together. John kept jumping in while I was up. It was apparent to me he was working to undermine my credibility. At the break, I saw Milo take John aside. They were in an intense conversation. When we resumed, John sat quietly at the back of the room, lips zipped. Only a family member had the clout to put a lid on him.

Clearly, women were making inroads in ways that were unimagined when I had started twenty years earlier. Another change taking place during the mid-1990s was the evolution of the independent consultant and the onset of job-hopping for advancement. When I had begun work twenty years earlier, Cargill boasted "lifetime" employment and claimed the company could teach us everything we needed to know to succeed. As I looked around Cargill, it was evident that high-potential employees—men and women—weren't sticking around for life. They were jumping for better pay and better opportunities. Other companies offered their employees stock options in addition to pay—as a privately held company, Cargill didn't have that carrot. And bringing in 1099 contract workers was more prevalent not only in the Salt Division but throughout the organization.

I had a successful, limelighted career at Cargill, but at twenty years in, I had no career track in front of me. I had created a mentor program for new hires, but I hadn't created mentors for myself. I felt invisible as younger recruits kept coming in. One day, I bumped into a Montana acquaintance, Nate Kolbe, who had spent his career at Cargill. He was heading up the Cargill human resources department. His wife's family had raised sheep in Belgrade, Montana, and we competed at the Montana Winter Fair in Bozeman every year. I asked Nate if he would have time for coffee. We set a date.

I knew Nate was involved in the hiring of new recruits for every division, and he interfaced with managers across Cargill because of that job. He had also spent his entire career at Cargill, so his network was vast. Nate was a trim man, about my height, intense blue eyes, his blond hair graying. I had never had much interaction with him, but he was well placed and knew the lay of the land.

At coffee, after we dispensed with the social chitchat, I said bluntly, "Nate, I've had a great career so far. I work really hard, but I don't seem to be getting ahead. Can you help me out?"

I didn't expect him to help me out literally, like promote me or throw my hat in the ring the next time an opening came up, although that would have been nice. I expected some words of encouragement, maybe some strategic or tactical tips. I thought he might ask me questions about jobs I had held, key successes. I was ready to spew about bag designs and sales management, people I'd hired and fired, my MBA, deals I'd fostered. Instead, he looked me dead in the eye and said, "When we're sitting at the table talking about high performers, your name doesn't come up."

Ouch! I was caught off guard, and that left hook leveled me. When had the world shifted? When had I fallen off the edge of the earth?

I asked him to clarify. He said, "When senior managers are talking about filling jobs, you aren't mentioned." And then he softened the blow. "I'm just telling you like it is."

I limped back to my office and licked my bloodied ego. I was hurt but also thankful. I needed to hear the harsh words, the cold truth. Nate did me an enormous favor. I'd been in enough meetings and performance reviews where managers sang praises in front of a guy and dissed him behind his back. I'd seen guys get raises when they should have been fired. As much as it hurt to hear, I knew it was better to hear it than to be led down a dead-end path. On the other hand, Nate could have offered some advice on how to get back into the discussions, but he didn't.

What surprises me now, as I look back, is that I *was* so surprised. I was so deep in the forest, I didn't see that I was not being considered. I thought I was being passed up, but I wasn't even on the road.

I was at that proverbial fork. I figured if I lived long enough and worked at Cargill for another ten or twenty years, there would be bones thrown to me to satisfy a lifer. I would rise higher, but would it be at the level I wanted with the responsibility I yearned for? And how long would it take? Another twenty?

For most of us, this crossroads happens at some point in our careers. For me, it was the spring of 1996. My sister said, "Stay another ten years and you'll be eligible to retire." I thought at the time she was crazy. I had seen too many people, all men, who had done just that. They started at Cargill and stayed at Cargill, and at fifty-five years old, they were treading water, coasting to the finish line.

I'd had a twenty-year run. I'd had highs, and I'd had lows. But coasting wasn't part of the game plan I had for my future. I spent time thinking about my life goals, what I had been happiest doing, what I wanted the end game to be. Frankly, I wasn't sure. But I knew what I didn't want.

I didn't want my headstone to say, "Lived and Died at Cargill."

Speech to the Rookies

In 1990, Cargill still hired college graduates much the same way they had when I'd started with the company fourteen years earlier: they recruited high-potential candidates from across the country but with a focus on the Midwest. The training after the hire had changed considerably. When I had been hired out of Stanford in 1976, I began a three-month training program, each week jumping on a jet plane with my clothes bag over my shoulder and a briefcase in hand, meeting with a different business each week and picking the brains of the managers at their desk.

Over the course of my twenty years, all that changed. As Cargill began to hire "nontraditional" management trainees, another cultural phenomenon was happening. Young people didn't have the fear of losing their jobs like their baby boomer counterparts. Cradle-to-grave employment was a thing of the past. Besides, no one wanted to be with one company forever—job-hopping for advancement was the norm. So while some at Cargill thought it was a problem with hiring women, minorities, or non-midwesterners, the fact of the matter was that times were changing and the management hiring program had to change, too.

No longer did management recruits have the option to look at divisions and choose a field. Now they were hired for a specific division and a position. There were no "general trainees"; all were assigned a track before they were hired. The three-month training program I had participated in was now squeezed down to ten days in a classroom where the new hires were indoctrinated by sitting in a cavernous, wood-paneled, curtained, noise-muted auditorium, listening to droning business presentations driven by PowerPoint.

I became one of a list of speakers whose task was to convey what our business was about and to describe my career track—in twenty minutes. I never spoke of the lonely nights spent in nondescript motels in nameless small towns. I never told young women about the stolen kisses, the misplaced hand on my thigh. I was professional. My career followed the path others before me had taken. The unspoken challenges stayed in a box I rarely opened. The classes fluctuated during the ten years I represented the Salt Division from as few as twenty to as high as ninety recruits per class. The program evolved through the years to fit the needs of the corporation. The caliber of recruit also evolved from Iowa and Minnesota ag degrees to include prestigious MBAs from Chicago, Wharton, Stanford, Yale.

The faces changed; the hopes, dreams, and aspirations remained the same.

On the last day of the ten-day orientation, the new recruits had the opportunity to rub shoulders with upper management. One of those managers was Howard Carsons, a senior group vice president. Howard was a tall, balding, distinguished man, raised in Virginia with a gentle Southern twang. He had over twenty-five years of service with the company. Howard gave the recruits their send-off speech at the end of their last day. Each of the recruits was seated with a senior manager from his or her division. On several occasions, I attended as that senior manager.

Howard gave a well-rehearsed speech. He always delivered it with elegance and aplomb, with his graceful stature, dark suit, crisp white shirt, dark red tie, reading glasses perched on the end of his nose. He spoke about his son's graduation from Yale and the commencement speaker at that graduation. The speaker said, to paraphrase, "For some of you, graduating from Yale will be your life's greatest achievement. It is an accomplishment of which to be proud. But for some, probably most of you, the best is yet to come."

The first time I heard that statement and every subsequent time, the truth and depth of its meaning touched me. It seems like a million years ago that I left the protection of my home in Montana and traveled to the sheltered walkways of Stanford University in the Bay Area. Four years at Stanford was a blink of an eye, and the diploma I received on April (Fools' Day) 1, 1976, no more than just a piece of paper.

I arrived at Cargill full of hopes, dreams, and aspirations. I sat in a company orientation program, fully expecting to rise to greatness.

Naïve, innocent, I came to the table armed with energy and enthusiasm.

My weapons had served me well. A twenty-year career at Cargill. A good salary, good management positions. Respect. Responsibility. Great reputation. Three little kids, a house in the suburbs. An MBA. I had cut a wide swath in the doing. I had met many of my goals but had not reached the pinnacles of Cargill management. But I was no longer willing to invest more into this company that had been my home for twenty years.

My style had never been that of an expert. I thrived at being a generalist, having many interests, focused on breadth of experience rather than depth. It was time to spread my wings and broaden my experiences.

I walked into the Salt Division president's office wearing a dark conservative suit and skirt, a white silk blouse tucked in. My hair pulled back in a professional chignon. The president had a corner office with windows on two sides, the afternoon sun glowing off the trees on the cusp of autumn. I sat across the desk from John O'Roarke, the man who had been my boss in marketing. There was no love lost between us. I handed in my resignation. I wanted to keep the door open, as I didn't have a clear vision of the future. I told him that I had learned a tremendous amount at Cargill. The company had taught me the ins and outs, ups and downs of business. But getting the MBA had challenged me to do more, and I needed to explore the outside world. Someday, I said, I might come back smarter and contribute in different ways to this company I loved. My work, in the capacity I was in, was done.

He accepted my resignation. He wished me well. He never said he was sorry to see me go.

There are many accomplished women and minorities in business today. Many have risen higher and have achieved far more than I could. There are women in business who are leading great companies, achieving their dreams.

Others may see my Stanford degree as a great achievement—and it was. But when I look back and picture myself, I see a strong American girl with a Japanese face. I see a field of open prairie with an endless horizon. I'm leaning into the yoke around my shoulders, pulling a plow behind me, turning the earth upside down so that others behind me can flourish and grow.

Good-Bye/Hello

On a cool fall day in 1996, I gathered my suit jacket from the back of my office door. I took a final look out the windows that spanned my office, one of fifteen managers' offices along the perimeter of our corner of the Cargill Lake Office building, and said a silent good-bye to the pine trees I had enjoyed for the past few years. I picked up my Scully leather briefcase for the last time in that office and walked out around 5:00 p.m.—unusually early for me. As I turned the corner and climbed the one flight of stairs to the exit level, I ran into more and more people, many I knew or had worked with or had casual familiarity. Polly Caruthers was one of the people I bumped into on that final walk out the door.

I was ending twenty years and five months' work at Cargill, still the largest privately held company in the country. I had risen from a college programs trainee to a feed salesperson to a merchandising manager to a salt territory manager to a product manager to a sales manager to a marketing manager. I had worked in line management and staff positions. But the end had come, my head bumping that proverbial ceiling, and I was headed out the door.

Polly was a new VP, a manager of a small team of people who were in corporate quality, working on the total quality process, Cargill's version of the Baldrige National Quality Award for business excellence. As we walked out together, she asked me how things were going. I said, "This is my last day at Cargill. I'm moving on."

Surprised but undaunted, she queried, "What are your plans?"

I said, "I don't know. I can flip burgers at McDonald's. I'll start job hunting."

She said, "I need some training done. Would you be interested?"

She offered me my first job after quitting my twenty-year career at Cargill. A consulting gig back at Cargill. Go figure.

The Great Unknown

So, I never flipped burgers at McDonald's. As soon as I walked out of Cargill, I began setting up a consultancy. Management Protemps was born. I positioned myself as an interim middle manager to span a resource gap. A new dream was formulating—that of an independent consultant and entrepreneur.

I left the security of a big corporate job, competitive salary with benefits, more vacation than I could take, and status. I walked out into the great unknown.

But I had the security of a husband who supported me and who had a company job with benefits. I had the Cargill job that Polly Caruthers offered. I had vast experience facilitating, selling, and putting together marketing plans and promotional collateral. I knew selling would be key to the success of the venture.

I remembered when I first moved from field sales to the office job in Kansas City. I had wondered where the mail went after I put it into the out-box. Where did it go? Who took it? Who handled it next? What did the secretaries do with what we gave them? Now I began to realize how much I took for granted at the fancy corporate job I was leaving. Suddenly, I was the president, general manager, secretary, mail clerk, receptionist, and janitor.

We had a spare bedroom in the house, and that space became Management Protemps world headquarters. It was the fall of 1996, and I began shaping my future at the oversized walnut office desk that I had acquired from the Cresco Nutrena plant twenty years earlier. The job with Polly Caruthers and the Cargill Quality Process group grew from employee training to quality process management consulting throughout Cargill. I picked up a subcontracting job with a firm that was beginning to train Wells Fargo employees how to cross-sell products. And I joined forces with the newly formed Cognis Consulting Group, a strategy consulting firm, to develop a business plan for a Twin Cities construction mortgage company. Demand for Elaine Koyama and Management Protemps was booming!

I started checking things off my bucket list. I loved snow skiing, and before kids, I had volunteered as a ski patroller at Hyland Hills, a small downhill ski area only three miles from my home/office. The kids and the Cargill job travel had made it impossible to continue. Now, as an independent consultant, I reengaged in the ski industry that I so loved. In the fall of 1996, I got a part-time job as a ski instructor. Teaching was always in my blood, so in addition to becoming a ski instructor, I auditioned for an adjunct professorship at the University of St. Thomas Opus College of Business and was hired to teach the upper-level Introduction to Marketing for MBA students.

Suddenly, my stage expanded. I began engaging and networking in the greater metro area. I never realized how small my circle of influence was until I left the comfort of Cargill. I felt energized, jazzed, eager to start each day in my new frontier.

The last years at Cargill, I had been sick continuously, not including the traumatic cancer episode. It was common for me to go down with a head cold once a month with sore throats and sinus congestions and to just tough it out. Many times, my ears would scream as the planes landed, a head cold plugging my eustachian tubes. This occurred off and on for at least five of the last ten years of work. After I quit, I went *six months* without even a sniffle. I had no idea.

My weekly out-of-town travel regime ended—and fortuitously so, as Scot's travel increased. I began to engage at the Edina French immersion school, where all three of our kids attended. Never one to jump in halfway, I ended up cochairing the parent organization and eventually chaperoning our little French-speaking fifth graders to France.

The learning curve of life accelerated. Around every corner was a new opportunity, a new skill to add to my already burgeoning bag of tricks.

It wasn't easy. It didn't happen overnight, but eventually, I became physically stronger, mentally more confident in my new business, and I adapted to the isolation of being a sole proprietor. The Venn diagram circles of my life began to equalize. Whereas before the work circle was overwhelmingly large, now I felt the intersecting circles that were always overshadowed by work grow larger and more prominent. Work, volunteering, networking, teaching, and family created my Olympic rings.

I left Cargill but was still engaged there. When I had first started at Cargill Salt, they had a saying: "You quit, you're dead." Pretty grim, but that was the philosophy back then. I was one of the first "quitters" to find life in other forms at the company.

I started my solo consulting firm, Management Protemps. It later became Interlinx Associates, the IT consulting partnership I ran with my husband, Scot. The new millennium arrived, and computers didn't crash. September 11, 2001, changed reality forever. The Great Recession came and went. My children morphed into adults. All the while, I continued knocking on doors, strong and steady, continuously expanding my horizons, discovering delights that made me smile and try-fail-try-succeed again.

Lately it occurs to me what a long, strange trip it's been.
— "Truckin'" by the Grateful Dead

Epilogue

Carol Seymour published a book, *Wisdom Warriors* (Atlanta: Signature Leaders Publishing, 2017), about successful women and their words of wisdom. Cargill backed a special edition featuring some of their own successful women.

Ruth Kimmelshue, who graduated from Stanford about ten years after I did and grew up on a farm in California, was the second woman president of Cargill Salt and is now a member of the Cargill executive team, the highest level of Cargill management. And she isn't alone—LeighAnne Baker, also a Stanford grad, is the human resources executive. Cargill remains one of the largest privately held corporations in the world. At the time of Seymour's publication, Sarena Lin, an Asian American woman, was the president of the animal nutrition business, my old Nutrena Feeds division.

After leaving Cargill and selling our IT consulting business in 2016, I began my next career: that of writer, speaker, facilitator. This book is the first step on that journey.

Acknowledgements

To Scot Zimmerman, who was my partner and alter ego. Finishing this book was on his bucket list. My dream was his dream. Though he died before he saw the printed words, his high expectations and work ethic continue to push me onward.

To Tom and Paige, Maiya and Tony, and Lee. The kids have been my constant cheerleaders and encouraged me to continue the journey.

To my grandchildren Silas, Everett, Wesley, and all those who may come. They are the reason I started writing this book.

To my parents, siblings, and extended family who shaped the childhood that shaped my life.

To all my friends and critics who read early versions and gave me sound feedback and input.

To my nephew Andy, who told me it was okay to be attractive, sexy, and a hero. He shared what he learned at USC to help a Stanford grad.

To the cast of characters that populate the pages of this book. I couldn't have done it without them.

And to the team at Beaver's Pond Press, whose advice and counsel have been the equivalent of an MFA and MBA rolled into one.

Discussion questions for *Let Me In*
can be found on Elaine's website:

www.elainekoyama.com

To schedule interviews, events, and
other press opportunities, visit

www.elainekoyama.com/contact